The Mavericks

Rob Steen

The Mavericks

English Football When Flair Wore Flares

MAINSTREAM
PUBLISHING

EDINBURGH AND LONDON

First published in Great Britain in 1994 by
MAINSTREAM PUBLISHING COMPANY (EDINBURGH) LTD
7 Albany Street
Edinburgh EH1 3UG

ISBN 1 85158 740 3

A catalogue record for this book is available from the British Library

Typeset in Janson by Litho Link Ltd, Welshpool
Printed and bound in Great Britain by Caledonian International Book
Manufacturing Ltd, Glasgow

To Laura, a London Tendaberry

Contents

Acknowledgments

Thanks to the following kind souls for their assistance, advice, information and general prodding: Malcolm Allison, BBC Video, Diane Bowles, Ken Furphy, Brian Glanville, Bobby Grossmark, Paul Hince, Ian Hutchinson, Chris Lightbown, Joe Lovejoy, Paul McCormack, Roy McFarland, Frank McLintock, Lawrie McMenemy, Neil Morton, Jeremy Novick, Steve Pinder, Huw Richards, Phil Shaw, Alec Stock, Dave Webb. Special thanks to Radio 5, Patrick Murphy and Mary Shatila.

Thanks, too, to the following for availing me of their research facilities: David Barber at the Football Association, the Colindale Newspaper Library and everyone at Hayter's Sports Agency. I would also like to take this opportunity to thank the late Reg Hayter, a good sport in every possible sense.

I am grateful to David Ashdown and the Independent Picture Desk for granting permission to reproduce the photo of Charlie George, and to Colorsport for providing images of a vivid era. Love and kisses to those whose generosity and visual splendours brought memories into the present, namely Anthony Crolla and Graham Goldwater.

To Bill Campbell and all the patient folk at Mainstream and, above all, my agent, John Pawsey, thanks for all your encouragement and support.

THE MAVERICKS

To the men whose philosophy shaped this book, thank you for your time, your company and your inspiration – and for making me feel 14 again. Stan Bowles, Tony Currie, Charlie George, Alan Hudson, Rodney Marsh, Peter Osgood and Frank Worthington – may your whistles always be wet.

Last but foremost, I am indebted to Anne, who I suspect is bucking for sainthood.

Rob Steen
Alexandra Palace
August 1994

Preface

19 June 1994: 12.30 a.m.

Dear Mr God (excuse the informality but you forgot to leave your surname on the ansaphone),

Yellow submarines remain elusive, but I think I've finally located the sea of green: Holloway Road at midnight. Two days into the World Cup and 'Jack Charlton's Ireland' have just defeated Silvio Berlusconi's squillionaires. For a few sweet hours, even the kebabs are getting well and truly Guinless. Green shirts, green caps, green scarves, green neon. Oversized leprechauns raise glasses to passing motorists, toasting the crack, blissfully unaware that some of their spiritual brethren have just been blown away by a gale of Loyalist bullets in Lochinisland. My, what withering irony. You *must* be an Englishman.

Yet doubts persist. Forgive the bare-faced effrontery, but there are a few bones in urgent need of picking. What on earth possessed you to invent religion, or, for that matter, Toast Toppers? Furthermore, if you truly are an Englishman, why have the backhanders dried up? (While you ponder that last teaser, may I humbly suggest that you must be a Him. 'For Goddess's sake' simply doesn't emit the requisite spite. Besides, only the male instinct for the absurd could dream up a game in which John Burridge and Albert Camus could both excel in the same position.)

Time's up. For what it's worth, as an undeniably middle-class North London Semite, I prefer to think of you as the Bernd Schuster of Elysian Fields FC, a nomadic midfield creator who lost his bearings when he turned away from his kith and kin, in your case we Chosen Ones. You, an Englishman? Pah. How could someone with any regard for his country's well-being be capable of even contemplating the stunt you pulled off shortly after 8 a.m. on 17 October 1973. There I was, one-third wondering how long Tony Currie lingered under the covers on the morning of a big game, one-third mid-canoodle with Olivia Newton-John, one-third glued to the end of Tony Blackburn's faa-aan-tabulous Top Thirty rundown. Would it be the transvestite majesty of 'Ballroom Blitz', or the stonking honky-tonking of 'All the Way from Memphis', or the raunch 'n' roll of 'Nutbush City Limits'? No chance. There it was, number bloody one for the fourth week running, toot-toot-fucking-tootling its way to Shopping Centre Hell: 'Eye Level' by the Simon Park Orchestra.

Three stops down the Bakerloo Line in less than 12 hours' time Currie and his compatriots would be kicking off Wembley Stadium's most important match since 1966. West Germany and the World Cup would be at stake, not to mention a nation's self-esteem. So what do you do? Take the theme to a worse than useless ITV show about a poncy-looking Dutch cop by the name of Van Der Valk, chuck in a slice of prime middle-of-the-road sub-Mantovani rib oozing with ten times the nausea content of the 'Theme to Owen MD', then ensure it's still sizzling away on the nation's collective stove come the moment for rousing chords and rolling drums. I suppose awarding England 26 corners to the opposition's two was part of the wheeze too, eh? No wonder the Poles thought nothing of putting a clown between the sticks.

You may recall that 1973 was the year you urged me to sue football for divorce on grounds of mental cruelty and dereliction of duty. Subsequently, there have been periods when we have barely been on nodding terms, usually when Wimbledon are on a roll or Argentina are playing for penalties. Yet that umbilical tug persists, the affection too entrenched to permit prolonged indifference. Indeed, thanks to that walking, talking, galling Gaul, Eric Cantona, the 1993–94 season wooed me anew. In 1973, though, I found new lovers, reliable lovers, lovers who gave more than they took. *American Graffiti* came to the Edgware ABC, *A Clockwork Orange* to the Harrow Granada, Steely Dan and Todd Rundgren to my shamelessly mono record player, 'Summer of '42' to my bedside, snogging to my sexless existence. Half a decade after its release, I fell for *Astral Weeks*, Van Morrison's unique, timeless fusion of jazzy bel canto and bittersweet Belfast, rebirth and revelation.

You signed the decree nisi on Wednesday, 17 October. That was the night 'Spiny' Norman Hunter let Lato escape his clutches and Peter Shilton let Domarski's dribble of a drive seep through his legs, when England's sole route past Tomaszweski came via the penalty spot; the night when Alf Ramsey so lost track of time that he brought on Kevin Hector for Martin Chivers with, ooh, a minute or so remaining; when, in the dying seconds, the selfsame Hector botched a point-blank header your mum would have put away with her curlers in. What a silly old Hector.

What stuck in the craw was not so much that 'we' (okay, so I'm a schizophrenic) failed to win as the sickening sense of waste. Having helped whup an inept bunch of Heidis 7–0 a month earlier, Currie was there, true, but where were all the other Merlins? Peter Osgood was on the bench, Rodney Marsh on the shelf, Alan Hudson and Frank Worthington in the queue. Stan Bowles had the decided disadvantage of turning out for Queen's Park Rangers, a club awarded one full England cap (to Marsh) in the 65 years since Evelyn Lintott and his mischievously upturned handlebar moustache were summoned to face the Irish in 1908. Charlie George was either injured or having a tiff with Bertie Mee. It was usually one or the other. To spectators, these were the Mavericks, heroes blessed with x-ray vision capable of ridding the world of dastardly man-markers. To managers and coaches they were drinkers, womanisers and, worst of all, non-conformists. They didn't know their place. At international level, accordingly, they were thrown scraps. The Poles knew full well they hadn't nicked a point off the best 11 players in England.

You signed the decree absolute at Stamford Bridge on New Year's Eve, the day Hudson and Osgood took the field together in Chelsea blue for the last time. Dropped for the next game, battle of wills with the manager lost, Hudson ultimately went to Stoke, Osgood to Southampton, yours truly into a major funk. It wasn't so much the discovery that every man had his price – though neither, it soon transpired, had done it for the money – as the realisation that talent was not enough. Craven images whose onfield extravaganzas and off-field excesses went some way toward blanking out the robotic/psychotic tendencies of the supporting cast, Hudson and Osgood were the personification of everything I cherished about football, the soul of my team: a chunk of my heart went with them. Within weeks I was monitoring the teleprinter in as ardent a quest for a Stoke or

Southampton victory as one for my King's Road knaves. Blind, even one-eyed allegiance to a football club, to anything, was now utterly beyond me.

My main grievance with you, Your Loftiness, is your less than generous timing. You dropped me into a void. Not only was I too young to wear beads and kaftan with conviction, I was also too old – in spirit if not in flesh – to stick safety pins up my nose without feeling like a prize pranny. Offering as it did excitement and creativity plus a better track record for dispensing justice than any court, sport became my sect, the maverick breed apostles of free will. Best, Botham, Nastase, McEnroe, Higgins: actors without lines, highwire acts *sans* safety net. No editor to cut out the cock-ups; no art director to decorate the humdrum; no make-up artist to concoct a fresh image. Their mission, even more forbiddingly, was twofold: do your job *and* brighten people's lives. Men of this ilk stood out during the Seventies because that was the decade when sport, thanks in no small measure to the media, became a fully-fledged, megabuck business concern, generating greed and its alter-ego, fear. Given the comparative shortage of decent wars on the market, international sport swapped communication for one-upmanship. My question is a simple one: where did you hide the laughter?

I remain your devoted, ever so 'umble servant.

PS. Thanks ever so for the motorised stretcher, the three-point win and all those other new-fangled devices devised to sell football to the Yanks, but don't imagine for a second that that makes us quits.

Sucking in the Seventies

'Can you tell me where my country lies?'
said the unifaun to his true love's eyes.
'It lies with me!' cried the Queen of Maybe—
for her merchandise, he traded in his prize.

'Paper late!' cried a voice in the crowd.
'Old man dies!' The note he left was signed 'Old Father Thames' —
it seems he's drowned;
selling England by the pound.

Genesis, *Dancing with the Moonlit Knight*, 1973

Dennis Potter wisely recommended looking back on the past 'with a sort of tender contempt'. Hip though it may once more be to totter down the high street in a pair of grotesquely reinforced soles, shake one's booty to Abba under a multicoloured strobe or chuckle along with *Only When I Laugh*, celebrating the Me Decade in its entirety is best left to those thirtysomething ad directors busy reliving their youth by dusting off every three-minute vinyl wonder from 'Two Little Boys' to 'Another Brick in the Wall'. Asked how he achieved the ravishingly eerie landscapes that rendered two hours of Richard Gere at his woodiest worth enduring in *Days of Heaven*, Nestor Almendros explained that filming always took place during what cinematographers call the 'Golden Hour', that ethereal sliver of the day when sun has set and daylight lingers. In actual fact, Almendros explained, this 'hour' lasted between 20 and 25 minutes. It is hard to conceive of a more apt metaphor for the Seventies.

By the time I got to Woodstock, everyone else had gone home. I did know one of the half-a-million strong: my group leader on kibbutz, an American lass who appeared to have swallowed Arkansas and who, at one point in the movie, fills a third of the screen for 3.7 seconds. And I did once conduct a phone interview with Carlos Santana. Some consolation. Having missed the bonding event of the century, I strove to prolong the Sixties, chewing on the gum of civil rights and student demos and All-You-Need-Is-Luvvies long after the sugar had evaporated. John Lennon claimed the dream was over in 1970; for me, it had just started.

Having been hatched in 1957, I was too young to fully appreciate, let alone understand the Sixties. I can remember hearing 'Please Please Me' on the loo the week it came out (and being convinced it was by the Everly Brothers). I can remember the opening lines to just about every Motown hit from 'My Guy' to 'Heard it Through the Grapevine'. I can remember being utterly convinced that every chorus of every single Bacharach & David coffee breakdown opus from 'Walk on By' to 'You'll Never Get to Heaven if You Break My Heart' was written specifically with my parents in mind. I can remember the last day of Radio London and the first day of Radio 1. I can remember Neil Armstrong jitterbugging on the lunar surface. I can remember my first date with sport: Cup final day 1966, cheering on Sheffield Wednesday against Everton (my maternal grandfather had informed me the latter were financed by some fat cat pools promoter), then watching that fuzzy Ferguson screen in dismay as Mike Trebilcock converted a 2–0 waltz into a 2–3 slink. In terms of clarity of memory, however, goals and choruses and parental rows are pretty much the sum total of my Sixties, save, that is, for the assassination of Bobby Kennedy, and the only reason that stuck was because England were playing Yugoslavia in a Nations' Cup semi-final the day his dying moments were splashed so chillingly across the front page of *The Evening Standard*.

Having missed out on the Sixties in any meaningful sense, and thus probably idealising it out of all proportion, the Seventies assumed an inordinate burden. Popular culture-wise – music, movies, TV, sport – it was a pretty golden 25 minutes, even if I did enjoy too much of it after the fact. 1970 donated *Abbey Road* and *Moondance*, 'Tears of a Clown' and 'Ball of Confusion', *Five Easy Pieces* and *Performance*, *Monty Python* and *The Female Eunuch*. Astride them all were the coolest, sharpest, streetwisest dealers in the known history of the people's opiate: Pele, Tostão, Jairzinho and Rivelino, the Modern Jazz Quartet of forward lines. Brazil's World Cup victory was a triumph of self-expression and enterprise, Carlos Alberto's celebratory rocket against Italy the culmination of a move that was pure stream of consciousness, a fantasia for feet. Pele's halfway-line biff against the Czechs, that outrageous dummy against Uruguay: never has a man been so loved for the audacity of his failures.

For one surreal Sunday evening, it was just about possible to forget that, 48 hours earlier, Harold Wilson's fatally diluted socialism had dissuaded so many lifelong Labour voters from turning out on polling day that the Tories had sneaked back in. During the four-minute spell that saw Gerson's drive and Jairzinho's tap-in transform an unsteady 1–1 into a swaggering 3–1, it didn't even matter that John, Paul, George and Ringo had split up. The names of two Nineties pop groups testify to the enduring reverence: Pele and Mexico '70. Mind you, the former did issue a word to the wise with their 1993 flopperoonie, 'Don't Worship Me'.

1971 ladled on 'Won't Get Fooled Again' and 'Get it On' and 'Maggie May', French Connections and Clockwork Oranges, George Harrison staging an all-star gig in aid of Bangladeshi refugees, thus taking over as everybody's Fave Ex-Beatle. Evonne Goolagong on Centre Court song, micro skirts and hot pants. John Jonah Steen and Shirley Ruth Simpson finally did the decent thing and split up. When my father came for his records and movie books, the trannie, somewhat cerily, was filling the house with Carole King's 'It's Too Late'. I lay on the now ex-conjugal bed and sobbed until every duct was dehydrated.

By 1972, quality control was becoming increasingly wayward. An Irish maverick by the name of Alex Higgins became the youngest potter to win the world professional snooker title. A Romanian maverick, Ilie Nastase, took on Stan Smith and the rest of the US Army at Wimbledon and went down on points. The Cold War invaded chess in Reykjavik as Boris 'The Spider' Spassky sat toe-to-toe with Bobby 'The Nutter' Fischer. *The Godfather* went head-to-head with *The Poseidon Adventure*, the first wave in a deluge of Hollywooden disaster epics. At the Olympics, Black September guerillas overshadowed the astonishing Lasse Viren. Cleese, Palin and the rest of Monty's pythons produced a special episode for German viewers. Fortunately, the language of the semi-intellectual nutter is universal.

Musical trends collided like swinging clackers. Alice Cooper and Slade slugged it out with Lieutenant Pigeon and the Royal Scots Dragoon Guards Band. Bowie claimed he was glad to be gay and glam held sway. Then David Cassidy and Donny Osmond got to work on 14-year-old schoolgirls from Paisley to Plaistow. Combining ancient ditties and fresh cheekbones, the teenyboppers had a good innings, but even they had no answer to pure, uncut nostalgia. Instead of peddling all those laughable Music For Pleasure cover versions, canny firms with daft handles like K-Tel, Arcade and Ronco came up with the bright conceit of buying the rights to a batch of hits of varying vintage, assembling them under some thematic umbrella or snappy-but-meaningless title, then touting the result on primetime TV alongside the latest dustbuster or multi-purpose kitchen knife. In 27 of the 29 weeks from 18 June to 31 December, the best-selling LPs in the UK were compilations of this ilk: *20 Dynamite Hits*, *20 Fantastic Hits*, *20 All-Time Hits of the '50s* and *25 Rockin' and Rollin' Greats*. Retro ruled, OK.

The following year, 1973, was a similar fusion of the good, the trad and the unmitigatedly ugly. The best, typically, went largely unnoticed. That maverick of the English cinema, Lindsay Anderson, unveiled his magnum opus, *O Lucky Man*, the second part of a trenchant trilogy on contemporary England and the most potent stretch of celluloid to emerge from these shores in the Seventies. A modern *Pilgrim's Progress* enacted by a luminous cast (Malcolm McDowell and Ralph Richardson, Arthur Lowe and Dandy Nicholls, Rachel Roberts and Helen Mirren, plus the godlike Graham Crowden) and a gem of a soundtrack (Alan Price), it threw in the lot, kitchen sink included. Nuclear plant explosions, an arms deal with a repressive foreign régime, experimental scientists welding sheep to humans, murderous tramps, a judge with a yen for S&M: a howl of despair for Albion. The Odeon queues, needless to say, were a sight bulkier for *Bequest to the Nation* (Glenda Jackson goes for a degree in tempestuousness as Lady Hamilton, Peter Finch opts for a horny half-Nelson).

In Noo Yawk, Scorsese and De Niro kicked down the door to Hollywood in *Mean Streets*, paving the way for Rotten and Vicious and Dee Generate. In Newcastle, Bob and Terry returned as *The Likely Lads*: kipper-tied, flounder-lapelled Bob doing the Bourgeois Boogie around the Elm Lodge Housing Estate, Terry, fresh out of marriage and army, imploding at the prospect of having his hair blow-dried. Terry wouldn't have had much time for that guitarist from Mud with the ball gown and hooped earrings. *Serpico* converted Al Pacino into the hottest pin-up in bedsitter land. *Tubular Bells* began financing Richard Branson's dream of being Biggles. White America swarmed over my turntable – Steely Dan, Todd Rundgren, Little Feat, Tim Buckley, the Allman Brothers. My hero, Pete Townshend, shifted from the Messianic message of *Tommy* to the identity crisis of *Quadrophenia*, one of the last and most creditable examples of the oft-ridiculed 'concept album'. The movement effectively expired a few weeks later with the advent of *Tales from Topographic Oceans* by Yes. Its four 'songs' – 'The Revealing Science of God', 'The Remembering', 'The Ancient', 'Ritual' – the last word in fourth-form masturbation.

Retro still ruled, as it generally does when people lose their sense of adventure. Admittedly, *American Graffiti*'s rites-of-passage charm was irresistible. I'd never seen the Sixties in colour before, never heard the Beach Boys or Del Shannon in context, and certainly never fallen for a White T-Bird. 'Where Were You in '62?' is still up there with 'Be Afraid – Be Very Afraid' in the Movie Poster Catchline Hall of Fame. *That'll Be The Day*, the Anglicised version, was grittier but far too sour, all soggy Butlins and boggy fairgrounds and David Essex's baby blues. Oscar's Best Song of the year? 'The Way We Were'. From 1969 came 'Albatross', from 1970 'All Right Now' – *déjà vus* all over again. Capital Radio opened up shop and doubled the golden oldies quota overnight. Even Bowie succumbed, killing off Ziggy Stardust, metamorphosing into Aladdin Sane then paying tribute to his roots on *Pin-Ups*, the first authentic collection of pop covers to top the UK album charts.

This was also the year I woke up. Courtesy of Percy Podmore's history class, I discovered that the Commies and the IRA had a point, sound ones at that. When the latter fired their ire at Harrods and Westminster Hall, confusion outscored outrage by about 10 to 1 (Please sir, if a war can be 'The Troubles', does that make the Holocaust 'The Nuisance'?). Courtesy of Watergate and Cambodia I cottoned on to the fact that politics bore even less relevance to honesty and honour than Stork did to butter. Oil crisis or no oil crisis, the unions overdid it, imposing candlelit *soirées* with a slide-rule and providing the then Education Secretary with the stick she would subsequently wield to beat the have-nots when she entered No. 10: even partial power corrupts absolutely. Monty Pythonitis broke out among the crew of a Royal Navy frigate whose idea of a good wheeze comprised lobbing carrots at an Icelandic gunboat. Centuries of White House neglect prompted a band of Native Americans to seize hostages at Wounded Knee, in turn persuading Marlon Brando to reject his Oscar for Don Corleone in protest at his country's degradation of Sioux and Apache. Famine in Ethiopia but no Live Aid; civilian massacres in Mozambique but no embargos on Portuguese men o' war. Then came 6 October: not just my mother and my sister's birthday but Yom Kippur, Day of Atonement, holy day of holy days. Egyptians and Syrians descend on Israeli soldiers in mid-repentance as the buggers pray in their bunkers. This was the moment the mask came off. Some were spared. That clever chappie Picasso had had the prescience to pop his clogs in March, and Tolkein took the hint just in time. The Sixties were over. O levels were less than a year away. It was about time this hopeful romantic got real.

The zeitgeist, though, was captured by the mega success of Pink Floyd's *Dark Side of the Moon*, electronic mood music for manic depressives that brightened the three-day week no end by inferring we were all potty. 'Hanging on in quiet desperation is the English Way' indeed. Notwithstanding Ian Botham, Elvis Costello and the three Ps – Dennis Potter, Reggie Perrin and punk – that line set the tone for my England in the remainder of my Seventies. In January 1974, both the permissive society and the so-called youth rebellion were blamed on Dr Spock (fancy letting children get their own way). By then, significantly, The Rolling Stones, Led Zeppelin and The Who had all rocked their last definitive roll. The decline was just as apparent further afield. In Brussels on 17 May, a year after Cruyff, Krol and Co had walloped them 4–0 in the first leg of the Champions' Cup quarter-finals, Bayern Munich deposed Ajax as the czars of European football: an ominous sign. In high summer, Brazil went into the World Cup with studs upraised and West Germany won the bulbous new Stanley Rous Trophy at the expense of Holland's more soulful brand of Total Football. Not inappropriately, the dream died in Munich. Characterised by nihilism (Sid Vicious, Travis Bickle) and kitsch ('Bohemian Rhapsody', James Last), the Seventies had divorced the Sixties and conceived the Eighties. How fitting that they should have opened with *Performance* and closed with *Apocalypse Now*: from the gangster as star to war as showbiz. Eventually, on 4 May, 1979, came the fateful substitution: Thatcher for Callaghan.

Continuing the theme of frightening images, we come to that abiding Seventies' mystery, *A Clockwork Orange*. Not since the end of 1973 has it been legal for British cinemas or VHS-owners to show Stanley Kubrick's apocalyptic vision of London, a merciless Metropolis where Rossini and Ludwig Van collide with parades of soulless tower blocks and re-programmed thugs in bowler hats and mascara. The Thieving Magpie meets suburban rape. Alex and his droogs had surfaced on screen in New York in 1971, arriving in London the next year and not going on general release here for a full twelve months after that. Soon after it hit the provinces, a 17-year-old Dutch girl was raped in Lancashire by a gang chanting a version of 'Singin' in the Rain' that owed rather more to Kubrick than Kelly.

Further instances of 'copycat violence' provoked widespread outrage in council halls and beyond, driving the director to withdraw the film from UK distribution. As recently as 1993 Warner Brothers sought, and were granted, an injunction preventing Channel 4 from screening a *documentary* on *A Clockwork Orange* (the Court of Appeal, to its credit, reversed the verdict). As I write, the video – a Dutch import of which I fortuitously stumbled upon in Camden Market – is freely available in the vast majority of the Western world, from the FNAC Musique on Place de la Concorde to the rental shop on 108th and Broadway, New York. But not in the land in which it is set. Do starched top lips really conceal such indiscriminate rage? Or is it merely shame?

For all that, *A Clockwork Orange* had a considerable impact on English culture. Much as a first-rate peacenik wimpoid such as myself is loath to acknowledge it, it was all too easy to understand how Alex and his droogs made violence fun, or, better still, a viable response to repression. I did once get sufficiently protective about my racial origins to own up to them to a ruffian in a crombie, whereupon his fist felt the full might of my nose. Never, however, have I felt more physically aggressive than that night I emerged blinkingly from the Harrow Granada. Mind full of horrorshows and balletic ultraviolence, I headed for the bus stop aiming rhythmic boots at an imaginary victim: 'I'm sing-in' in the rain (kick, kick), just sing-in' (kick) in the rain (kick, kick) . . .' If it could have that effect on a fairy, surely it cannot be stretching coincidence to connect scenes of this type, however tangentially, to the record 180 arrests that scarred the opening day of the 1973–74 League season. According to Chris Lightbown of *The Sunday Times*, a respected expert in the field, the hoolies' heyday lasted from 1968 to 1971. I'm not so sure. From the Shed to the Stretford End, the tribes ritually gathered, skinheads and suedeheads and smoothies, bovver boys united by club loyalty, by a notion of superiority through muscle, through hardness, of aggro as a giggle.

A Clockwork Orange also burrowed into the fashion world. Eyeliner became *de rigueur* for every aspiring Beatle or Rolling Stone. Glam rock woz 'ere, albeit not to stay. The first stirrings had occurred at the Camden Town Roundhouse on 22 February 1970. Second on the bill to a herd of hairies known as Fat Mattress, David Bowie and his new band, the even more honestly dubbed The Hype, were anxious to make their mark. Despite reaching No. 5 in the charts with 'Space Oddity' four months earlier, 23-year-old David Jones from Bermondsey was having a job persuading Joe Public he was the bee's knees. Described at school as 'a complete exhibitionist', Jones/Bowie went for something completely different, reinventing himself as Rainbowman – lurex tights, silky blue cape, knee-high pirate boots. Drummer John Cambridge was Cowboyman – frilly shirt, 10-gallon hat; on guitar, Mick Ronson, aka Gangsterman, slinky in Bowie's silver suit. Looking on was the Jewish imp from north London, Mark Feld, aka Marc Bolan, catching the mood as a Roman legionnaire complete with plastic breastplate from

Woolies. 'Some chroniclers have described glam rock as a reaction to the sexual freedom of the Sixties,' observed Bowie's biographers, Peter and Leni Gillman, 'but The Hype's costumes were a projection of David and [then wife] Angie's even less inhibited ideas.' In 1970, the punters were rather more inhibited. 'We died a death,' Bowie would concede. One flutter of Alex's black widow of an eyelash and the kiss of life was in full swing.

Graduating from assisting dad on his window-cleaning round in Walsall, Noddy Holder exercised his Lennonesque larynx as lead singer of Slade, his calling card a top hat festooned with mirrors. 'The first time it was for a stage effect. I wanted it to be like a mirror ball and light up the audience. But I only wore it two years, '72 and '73. The idea was that when we went on *Top of the Pops* we wanted to stand out. We wanted people to say in the pub, "Did you see them Slade last night? They're mad, they are".' The condition spread to football. Until 1971, Best and a smattering of other daredevils had been alone in growing their hair, still less daubing it with anything but Brylcreem and Vaseline Hair Tonic. Now every Bob, Dave and Kevin who fancied himself was preening and grooming and pampering. Chubb should take such pride in their locks.

'In the Seventies,' as that self-confessed peacock Frank Worthington sees it, 'football became part of the pop industry. I used to go to a lot of pop concerts and shows and got to meet a lot of the stars. There is still a common bond, an affinity with one another, that stems from back then, because footballers are frustrated pop stars and the pop stars are all frustrated footballers.' Rodney Marsh ventures a step further. 'To be brutally honest, it felt bigger than being a pop star because you had the whole range. You had young girls who went to the games to see the players, you had married women that would come up to you, you had men admiring you for being an athlete. Actors would want to come and watch you play and sit in your company. It was really bigger than pop because it was everybody.'

To an extent, those Saturday afternoon Cavalier–Roundhead tussles replicated those in the parks and alleys. Slade started out as a skinhead band, the antithesis of glam. Saxon perceptions of manliness threatened by all those simpering hippies with their tresses and dresses and stoned-out excesses, jasmine jossticks and Incredible String Band albums, the skins cropped their skulls, befriended Doc Marten and Ben Sherman, and got off on the bonking rhythms of Prince Buster and Desmond Dekker. Football followed suit. Those nancy-boy strikers with their bellbottoms and unisex parlours had it coming. 'Oo yew screwin', John? Callinmealiar, John? Fancy a new nose, John?' If Norman 'Bites Yer Legs' Hunter never used that precise phraseology before attempting to skewer a victim's thighs, the drift was much the same. Just as queer-bashing helped usher the end of glam, so the Hunters (and the Smiths and the Harrises and the Storeys) scythed the gender-benders off the pitch, the gender-benders in this case being anyone caught with Cossack hairspray in their handbag. Bubble-perms, oddly enough, were acceptable. Then again, the first player associated with that style was Kevin Keegan, epitome of industry and derring-do. Whoever heard of a poof wearing Brut?

Worthington, too, detects a causal link between pop's brief dalliance with androgyny and the rise of the hatchet man. 'All those hard men are from the old sort of values, aren't they? They were brought up a certain way, but things changed. The Bowies and Sweets made becoming or looking like a girl more acceptable, but you will always have those who are totally against anything like that and go the other way. The Tommy Smiths wanted to be more macho than ever. I was playing for Leicester one day and we were beating Leeds 1–0. I was down by the corner flag, hemmed in by Johnny Giles, so I flipped the ball over my shoulder and over his head. He just turned to me and said, in a very cold, calculating, matter-of-fact sort of way: "If you ever take the piss out of me or Leeds United again I'll break your legs".'

Just as glam soon faded, usurped by Barry White's bloated butchness and the asexual allure of The Wombles, so English football quickly turned its back on exhibitionism. A combination of the three Rs saw to that: Ramsey, Revie and repression. 'When Orwell said that the English were the gentlest people on earth,' John Osborne reasoned in 1965, 'he meant the people who were actually *on* the end of Wigan Pier. He didn't mean the people who run it. For the voice of English violence is the voice of the threatened profit, of those who believe in the virtue of "getting on", "leaving things alone", yet are possessed of the greedy desire to order the lives of all, and especially those who are young, sexually immoral or who simply speak out of turn. And, most of all, those who appear to be all three, and are paid large sums of money – the thing the bourgeoisie care most violently about – and become rich and famous for their transgressions.' The Angry Youngish Man was defending David Frost at the time; a decade later it could easily have been Worthington or Marsh, Hudson or Bowles.

So what can we conclude about the Seventies? Maybe the following scenario will help. Christmas 1993. A gaggle of Where-Are-They-Nows gather in an ITV studio for a televised debate entitled *The Trouble with the Seventies*. In the chair sits broadcasting's very own be-denimed Dorian Gray, Michael Aspel, star of autocue, *Ask Aspel* and *Crackerjack*, on the verge of being exposed as a cuckolder. The cast list covers most of the bases: Cynthia 'Madame Sin' Payne and the hacks' hack, Derek Jameson; original Page 3 Girls Nina Carter and Jilly Johnson; an original Sex Pistol, Glen Matlock; Helen Morgan, that doe-eyed Welsh swooner who resigned as Miss World because she didn't much fancy a starring role in a divorce petition. Sally James still had huge boobs, Paula Wilcox could still melt hearts at a hundred paces with a coyly whispered 'Geoffrey Bobbles Bon-Bon'. Aspel has a dart at the TUC, asking Jack Jones whether 'all those beers and sandwiches at No. 10' achieved anything. The reply is craggily pointed: 'Um, well, industrial tribunals, collective bargaining, redundancy payments . . .'. Nice one, Jack.

Self-mocking chunters greet the roll-call: stack heels and tank tops, cheesecloth shirts and loon pants, Jelly Tots and Aztec bars, space dust and spacehoppers, rock operas and *Rock Follies*. Titters accompany Jenny Hanley's admission that she went bra-less on *Magpie*, ditto the ad for Denim, the aftershave 'for the man who doesn't have to try *too* hard'. Cue nudge-nudge wink-wink interlude: frustrated troilism in *Man About the House*; Sid James letting rip with the World's Most Salacious Laugh one last time in *Bless This House*; Mr Humphries announcing his availability in *Are You Being Served*?; Larry Grayson complaining about the draught.

That darts a nd snooker were the only examples deemed worthy of mention by Aspel and Co neatly encapsulated English sport in the Seventies. This, after all, was the decade in which 'our' representatives, unfairly entrusted with upholding a nation's self-image, taxed as never before the mythical native aptitude for gracious losing. For once, they had oodles of practice. For the first time in five decades of one-sided rivalry, 'our' cricketers lost Test matches at home to India and away to New Zealand. For the first time in any decade since the turn of the century, 'our' mucky ruckers failed to win either the Triple Crown or the Five Nations' Championship. For the first time, period, qualification for the World Cup proved beyond the scope of 'our' footballers. By way of emphasising the depreciation, this particular pratfall was repeated four years later. Similarly, in 1973, six years after Benaud and Johnners and Arlott had guided me through my inaugural summer of flanneled foolery, England went to India and lost an official Test series for the first time in my experience, then repeated the dose against the West Indies.

The outstanding conglomeration of British talent in the Seventies? The Welsh rugby union team. Ginny Wade won a Wimbledon singles title, Tony Jacklin a US Open, but the best of British individualism was confined to the Celtic rangers: Jackie Stewart, Mary Peters, Ken Buchanan. 'The way I see it,' Willem Dafoe's Sgt Elias tells Pte Charlie Sheen in *Platoon*, 'we've been kickin' ass so long it's about time we got our ass kicked.' To Sgt Elias, 'we' was the USA, the ass-kickers the Vietcong. Oh, had Messrs Perry and Croft possessed the nerve (or, more important, the licence) to make Captain Mainwaring lay the same rationale on Private Pike.

Perspective, irritatingly, sprang from Jonathan King, that self-publicist supreme who once had a sizeable hit under the pseudonym of Shag. 'The curse of the Nineties and Eighties, and the trouble with the Seventies,' opined the Cambridge-educated *kitschmeister* behind 'Jump Up and Down Wave Your Knickers in the Air', a smug grin on legs in graduation gown and baseball cap, 'is the curse and domination of the Sixties.' The Sixties teased us with trailers for a nicer planet – peace and love and guilt-free sex, equal rights for women, blacks and the young. The Seventies sloshed us with the cold flannel of cynicism. Come the Eighties, the only waves Britannia ruled were the morally treacherous waters of advertising.

Cutting back on the flesh-pressing as radio and TV offered a more ego-friendly soapbox, politicians, those selfless folk responsible for shaping our future, perfected the quick sell: first slogans, then soundbites. Even football had its euphemistic catchwords: 'competitive', 'committed', 'professionalism', 'professional foul'. Four days before the 1974 General Election, John Osborne – now Middle-Aged Malcontent – set his stall out in *The Observer*: 'I shall vote Labour once more, but with even emptier heart than usual. Like the historian, our politicians use the language in a manner in which it is impossible to seek the truth. With their ritual incantation of phrases – as if they were *things* – like "Inflation", "National Unity", "Priorities" and "Social Contracts", they only conceal the nasty reality of the awful brutishness of most of English life today . . . Buy shoddy is the trick of all parties.' Tim Bell and the Saatchi brothers, men steeled in the cut-and-thrust of the detergent market, would soon be plotting election campaigns and shaping our destiny, a tomorrow of aspiration on the never-never.

The Seventies, Jonathan King declaimed, 'was the decade of the marketing men', as his bank manager would doubtless concur. 'Punk was fake. I was the original punk because I believed you could sell the public anything, from the *Rocky Horror Show* to Terry Dactyl and the Dinosaurs. Malcolm McLaren, Johnny Rotten and Sid Vicious were all actors.' Face a paler shade of crimson, sideburns more hairy thicket than shag-pile showroom of yore, Noddy Holder's retort was succinct: 'Jonathan is talking out of his backside as usual.' Well, not entirely. In marketing, everything is transient, disposable. In the Seventies, fads came and went like cuddly toys on Brucie's conveyor belt, testimony to the deftness of the commercial manipulators.

Ironically, football's reluctance to market itself left the job to the tabloids, lengthening the lifespan of the maverick militant tendency. Glam, punk and anarchic comedy were even briefer detours on the way to Middle-of-the-Road Hell. All the best English 'social realism' sitcoms had expired by the mid-Seventies. To that cinematic dream weaver par excellence, Terry Gilliam, the visual masterchef who sharpened its cutting edge with – according to *The Guardian* – 'collages of Edwardian prurience under assault from psychedelic illogic', even Monty Python had little or no lasting effect. 'I really don't know if we've done anything that changed anything, ultimately,' he reflected recently. 'I kept thinking that Python was going to open the floodgates of similar comedy. But I don't think it's happened.' As an American, Gilliam must have realised why. Risking making a prat of himself is not exactly high on the average Englishman's list of priorities.

Roger Scruton, that self-styled intellectual foxhunter and a man not known for his equanimity who once decreed the French Literature section of the London Library to be his favourite smell, argues that, since we cannot always find satisfactory solutions to dilemmas, compromise is obligatory. Brave indeed are those who spit in the face of compromise and ride roughshod over realism, who resist suffocation and scorn embarrassment, who eject fear and insert life. Regrettably, happy as we are to draw inspiration from them, we demand more of them than we do of ourselves. The Mavericks elicited more hypocrisy than a would-be woman priest. We treasure them because they embraced risk, because they dared *not* to give a damn, because, most of all, they dared on our behalf. The moral of Seventies England seems clear: hubris never pays.

Chairman Alf and The Godfather

'In Hungary we make love to the ball and we sleep with it. The English eat it.'

Florian Albert, former European Footballer of the Year

There are certain thoughts an Englishman is best advised to keep to himself. Like 'I wish that bomb had got Maggie' or 'God bless America'. Or 'That Olivier geezer was rubbish'. Neither, above all, does it do to suggest that the 1966 World Cup was the worst thing ever to happen to our national game. But there, it snuck out. Perhaps I can redeem myself by citing the second-worst thing ever to happen to English football: Don Revie succeeded Alf Ramsey.

For most English chaps in their mid-30s, and not a few chapesses, 1966 was *the* annus mirabilis. Was there ever a kinder, blinder Russian than Bakhramov? Did a net ever billow quite so bounteously as the one Geoff Hurst tested for tensile co-efficiency in the dying seconds at Wembley? What other breed could have adopted as plug-ugly a hero as the dentist's dreamboat and prototype Eddie Edwards, Norbert Stiles? It was the year of Yellow Submarines and Pretty Flamingos, of Sunshine Supermen and Happy Jacks, of Sunday Afternoons and Fridays on My Mind. It was the year when the workers had all the best lines: Bob and Terry, Alf and his Silly Old Moo, Harold Steptoe and his Dir-tee Ol' Maaaan. It was the year of Alfie as well as Alf, of three British nominees for Best Actor (Burton, Caine and Paul Scofield) and Best Actress (Liz Taylor, Vanessa and Lynn Redgrave), of Oscars for Scofield and *A Man For All Seasons*.

Yet in other respects it was a discouraging passage for the budding

27

anglophobe. Cassius Clay splattered 'Our' 'Enery's eyebrows all over Highbury. Garfield Sobers wined merrily at the expense of our cricketers. An Aussie, Scobie Breasley, won the Derby. The Beatles played their final gig, in *America*, not to mention having their trailblazing thunder stolen by a bunch of Californian beach bums and a Jew from Duluth. Evelyn Waugh died, Brady and Hindley went down. A Canadian bought *The Times*. At Yuletide, mums, sisters and grans were in a state of abject lust, the object Tom Jones, who spent the whole of Advent at No. 1, whining on about how green the grass is in South Bloody Wales. Skimpy reward though it was for all that endeavour, there wouldn't even have been a Jules Rimet Trophy had Pickles the mongrel not proved more efficient than our beloved bobbies, and I bet he had an Irish grandmother.

Yet Nobby, Mooro, Banksy and the rest of the World Cup Willies made up for all that, didn't they? Long-term considerations – and hindsight, naturally – decree otherwise. Video has uncorked a whole mass of worms of which the 1966 World Cup, as an event, prompts more squirming than most. A stale Lambrusco compared to the Château Rothschilds of '58 and '70, only Italia '90's *vin très ordinaire* has done more to paralyse the palate. A Euro carve-up, depriving us of a full vista, it was also a triumph of defence over attack, destruction over creation. If Eusebio, Albert and Chislenko glittered, Banks, Wilson and Moore glowed. Confronted by the soft-shoe shuffle of Pele and Garrincha, the Bulgars and Portuguese perfected the Hack, indulged by suspiciously weak referees. The stylish Hungarians, repeatedly undermined by inept goalkeeping, were duly ambushed by the Russians. The Italians were welcomed home by a squadron of flying tomatoes after being mugged mid-strut by North Korea's Pak Doo-Ik (whose name always sounded like something Akela would bark whenever the 16th Edgware cub scout troop assembled for a spot of dibbing and dobbing). Neither for the first time nor the last, Uruguay and Argentina stained their flags with abysmal self-control.

Against such an obliging backcloth England would have done bloody well *not* to win. As if using the same changing pegs for every match were not enough of a push-start, they were handed an additional leg-up in the quarter-finals by an officious German referee's intolerance of Antonio Rattin's over-zealous tongue. Any fule knos the decisive third goal in the final bounced on the line rather than beyond it, yet had Helmut Schoen not permitted his respect for Bobby Charlton to smother his faith in the young Franz Beckenbauer as a matchwinner in his own right, even that might not have mattered. The bottom line, of course, was that these descendants of Adolf, Herman and Josef could never have been allowed to win in a million millennias, hence the Soviet linesman.

In the short term, Chairman Alf was vindicated in his decision to stick with Hurst and Roger Hunt instead of recalling Jimmy Greaves. The price, though, was far too steep, the inference all too obvious. Football is science, not art. Get shot of the clever dicks, bring on the automatons. Skill? Been there, done that. 'On the one hand,' Bobby Charlton sympathised, 'Alf had Geoff and Roger who could be relied upon to sweat cobs, and on the other Jimmy, a fantastic finisher but a moderate team player. Alf did what he thought would be best for the team. Mind you, if we'd lost, he'd have been condemned for the rest of his days.' We've granted Alf a couple of decades' worth of suspended sentences, so why not start now? Sir Bobby, too, is due a blast of perspective. What was it that Best said about him? That he was 'the kind of guy who gets up in the morning, looks in the mirror, smiles, and then says to himself, "Thank fuck that's over with for the day".' How can a player who scored 44 goals in 57 games for his country, who in seven seasons between 1958–59 and 1964–65 topped the First Division scorers' list five times, then did it again after his last cap, who still holds seasonal records at Chelsea and Spurs, be a *moderate* team player? What greater contribution can one footballer make than to find the net more frequently than his peers? Jimmy Greaves drowned his anger by pickling his liver; Hunt – who got so fed up with the press campaign to restore Greaves he advised Ramsey to get himself another fallguy – ended up in haulage, Hurst in insurance. Greaves was eventually reborn as Greavesie, Eric to Saint's earnest Ernie, Salt of the Earth, Man of the People. Do we detect a moral here?

'Pleasure in English sport,' *Esquire* magazine suggested, 'is still by and large the satisfaction of the result.' With all due deference, bollocks. Ken Barrington and Geoff Boycott were dropped by the Test selectors for scoring centuries that whipped spectators into a frenzy of *ennui*. English cricket may have been teetering on the brink of haplessness over the course of the past decade, but you try getting a ticket for a one-day international at Lord's. English tennis may have gone a long way past haplessness but that doesn't prevent the All England Club from making a tidy packet at Wimbledon each June, nor Jeremy Bates from being hailed as a national hero for reaching the last 16. Shortly before the final Christmas of the Sixties, Wembley Stadium staged a chorale of catcalls after Jack Charlton had scored the only goal of a dog of a game against Portugal. Come in the fuddy-dudderers of Lancaster Gate, continually fretting over whether Paul Gascoigne's farts project the correct image. Correct as in truthful, as in being a fair reflection of both the male species and The Englishman Abroad? Of course they do.

Between 1968 (30 million) and 1986 (16.5 million), League attendances as good as halved during a period that saw English clubs – and, of course, their Celtic additives – claim eight European Cups, three Cup-Winners' Cups and ten Fairs/UEFA Cups. This can be attributed in part to something every bit as downright evil as hooligans and all-day TV and shopping centres, every inch as malevolent as Alex and his droogs: Boring Football. Manchester United were watched by more paying spectators in 1974–75 than any other team in the League. The fact that they were in Division *Two* that season emphasises both the durability of the attraction and the reason for it. Even without Best, Law and Charlton, the club stood for something more than success: the promise of artistry and enchantment, of rabbits being pulled out of hats. For the majority of this period, furthermore, they continued to be the biggest crowd-pullers despite producing nothing of the sort.

During the career of Belfast's neon scion, Northern Ireland failed to reach the final stages of a World Cup let alone win the damned thing, yet George Best now commands £1500 a night for lounging around in front of packed houses at the Hippodromes and Shaw Theatres of this world, trading one-liners with Rodney Marsh. If the result was all, why would the Mavericks – only one of whom, Charlie George, managed to win a Championship medal – be deified by Sky Sport and Fantasy Football League, by *The 606 Show* and *There's Only One Brian Moore*? Or be so in demand on the after-dinner circuit? To my generation they embodied what we fondly imagined to be the spirit of our youth, and these homages will ensure that our children get the message. They were exceptions to a totalitarian rule, the memories they stir nothing if not selective. 'In England,' Marsh apprised a Florida TV audience in 1979, 'soccer is a grey game played by grey people on grey days.' Right on, brother.

The Seventies were actually more grisly than grey. Ramsey's Wingless Wonders begat Revie's Robots. Curl up in bed with a dossier. You've Got To Sweat A Bucket Or Two, Boy. Mental agility was sacrificed at the altar of physical toil. Off-the-ball lung-bursting bred faceless pragmatism, repression incarnate. 'To Alf's way of thinking,' claims Malcolm Allison, 'skill meant lazy.' A misanthropic passion held sway: black hearts, no soul. Those who lamented England's misfortunes against Brazil in Guadalajara were allowing nationalism to cloud their judgment. The world's most irresistible attack budged the world's most immovable defence, simple and just and beautiful as that. Sure it was close. Had Jeff Astle set his sights on goal instead of Row F, it would have been a draw. By the same token, Banksy did deny Pele with the Second Greatest Save Ever (not even that could top Jim Montgomery's incredible double stop to confound Trevor Cherry and Peter Lorimer in the '73 Cup final). Besides, Gerson wasn't playing. On the night, right smote might.

Trouble was, in the post-'66 twilight world of English football, might did most of the smiting. Matt Busby conveyed his distress to *The Observer* in 1969. 'The way things are going alarms me deeply. Hard men are nothing new in football. What is new and frightening about the present situation is that you have entire sides that have physical hardness for their main asset. They use strength and fitness to neutralise skill and the unfortunate truth is that all too often it can be done. Of course, there are really great players who cannot be subdued all the time, but their talents are seen only in flashes and they have to live dangerously. George Best survives only because his incredible balance allows him to ride some of the impact of some of the tackles he has to take. Because of their heart and skill, he and other outstanding players in the league can go on giving the crowds entertainment. And it's true there are still a few teams who believe the game is about talent and technique and imagination, but for any one you'll find ten who rely on runners and hard men.'

The growth of the hard man attained malignancy in the early Seventies. Of course it was more than mere coincidence that the reign of glam should have covered the 1972–73 and 1973–74 League seasons, when the hard nuts' thirst bordered on the unslakeable and the professional foul entered the dictionary. Upon receiving *Standing Room Only*'s 1994 Platinum Parrot Award for All-Time Worst Tackle – Graeme Souness will have felt a mite miffed – Tommy Smith was asked if the contemporary game was as 'hard' as it was in his day. 'No one gets stuck in,' he moaned, tongue not obviously in cheek. 'It was a man's game back then. In the Sixties and Seventies you got stuck in, you went home with a few bruises but you enjoyed it. We're getting like the continentals. One touch and they're off to intensive care.' What made that World Cup exit at the hands of the Poles all the harder to bear was what seemed like England's deployment of the foul as tactical tool. Allan Clarke set the ball rolling by clattering into Tomaszewski after 40 seconds; Roy McFarland capped a night of fear by attempting to divest Lato of his shirt when the winger was clean through, earning a booking, no more. Cheating is usually the first resort of the inadequate; that someone as able as McFarland was prepared to stoop so low did not so much take the biscuit as dunk it. Not that the FA suffered unduly: Lancaster Gate's profit from the evening was a cool £153,350, nearly half the overall annual surplus on the international match account.

By the end of the 1973–74 season, Best had dribbled his last dribble in the First Division and Sir Bobby had been retired for a year. Bobby's *frère* Jack found the pace too hot and *he* had a little black book. Were they trying to tell us something? In 1973–74, some 1,107 goals were scored in Division One: 30 per cent down on 1963–64 and 10 per cent down on 1983–84. The PFA announced its inaugural Player of the Year that term, and the winner was . . . Yup, you guessed it, Norman Hunter. Blending style and stiletto, Leeds romped off with the Championship. Most symbolically of all, Manchester United were relegated. Hillsborough and Bradford aside, the saddest scene I've ever seen on an English field of play occurred at Old Trafford on 27 April, the day Denis Law met his Medusa. Having backheeled the goal destined to send his old muckers down, the enormity of the action sinks in as Colin Bell rushes over for a cuddle. The face clenches, turning to stone, the guilt all-consuming. On pour the crowd, off trots dignity. The hoolies achieve their aim, forcing an abandonment, only to be snookered when the result is allowed to stand. A case, for once, of the lawmakers obeying spirit rather than letter.

The nadir was near. When Bill Shankly finally came around to conceding that life and death might well be as important as the game he graced, he bade adieu at the 1974 Charity Shield match, the first to be played at Wembley. Kevin Keegan and Billy Bremner paid their respects with a brawl and an unscheduled shower. In the *Charity* Shield? What were these guys like when they did it for real? Not that they were alone. That same broiling afternoon – so steamy Bremner and Keegan dispensed with their shirts as they left the field – Johnny Giles, midfield maestro and possessor of 'a sometimes fierce capacity to look after himself' (© Brian 'Diplomatic' Glanville) warranted a decent stretch at Her Majesty's Pleasure for one undetected assault.

That 1973–74 was the first season of three-up, three-down may permit some comprehension, yet the aggro had raised its fist with even greater malice aforethought the previous season. Take a random period, 2 April to 14 June 1973. Between those dates alone, the FA Disciplinary Committee, a body jostling for minute space in every sense with the likes of the Match and Grounds Committee, the Benevolent Fund (Rota Committee) and the Registrations and Permits Sub-Committee, managed no fewer than 36 sittings. There were three such confabs covering the same period in 1963, a far from angelic time during which,

Lancaster Gate records report, 'Mr K. Ferguson of Blackburn Rovers FC was suspended for seven days for giving an incorrect name to the referee when being cautioned'. The sum total of disciplinary meetings for 1953 was 18. Even if statistics of this ilk do say more about referees than players, many of whom were upbraided for lack of deference, it still seems reasonable to conclude that the 1971–72 clean-up campaign was not a conspicuous success. Not that Sir Harold Thompson and his Oxbridge cronies at Lancaster Gate were much help. Despite producing a sheaf of bonafide medical certificates, Exeter of Division Four were fined £5,000 for having only nine fit players; mighty Leeds received a perfunctory £3,000 suspended fine for years of accumulated violence.

Another interpretation was furnished by Professor Percy M. Young. In his illuminating 1975 joint venture with Derek Dougan, *On The Spot: Football as a Profession*, he makes an abrasive counsel for the defence. 'We may as well start with the first complaint of the ignorant. That is, that football is more violent than it ever was,' was his opening gambit in a chapter entitled 'Thoughts on Rough Play'. 'But to be truthful the worst excesses are to be found outside the British Isles.' Now there's an unusual way of abdicating accountability: blame Johnny Foreigner. The footballer, he maintained, has 'the opportunity to get rid of some of his inborn tendencies to violence by the combat and physical conflict which is his profession. There is obviously a very thin borderline between what is fair and what is unfair. Thin, because defining what is in the one category and what is in the other is nearly impossible.' In other words, Professor Young appears to be saying, the thigh-high tackle that arrives later than the second post is not readily distinguishable from the tangle of honest feet. Get real.

Those 'inborn tendencies to violence' surfaced elsewhere on the opening day of the 1973–74 season, when unparalleled arrests were made on a host of League premises. As the season progressed, so the pitch invasion became hip. 'This is the Maggie May generation,' proposed Chris Lightbown, 'the kids that got so fed up with school that they just walked out, with truancy rates of 30 and 40 per cent. These kids have lost the fear of authority, and there is no barrier that they won't walk through. The pitch was sacrosanct to my generation, whatever we did off it, but to these kids, invading the pitch is peanuts.' Yet, however insignificant their influence might have seemed when set against social deprivation, limited horizons and innate machismo, there can be no doubting that the bovver boys on the park encouraged their counterparts on terrace and train. Osgood, Marsh and George hung on to their manhood by getting their retaliation in first. 'The only way to get back at them,' a defiant Best once observed of the gentlefolk whose apparent *raison d'être* was to marmalise his legs, 'is to make them feel so inferior that they never want to play another game of football in their lives.' Making thugs feel inferior, unhappily, is a self-defeating exercise. The more you gnaw at their already limited self-esteem, the higher the price your body pays.

Breaking spirits as frequently as legs, football *was* more violent in the days before the tackle from behind was banned. You know a sport is rotting when the ability to handle oneself becomes more relevant than one's ability to handle the ball, when the willingness to click through the turnstiles consequently demands courage rather than desire. When their gods are tapping ankles and throwing left hooks *and* getting paid for their trouble, why should those who finance the church see anything untoward in their own antics? Witnessing casual violence a giant step on the road to committing it? Was that not the defence's excuse in the Bulger case? This sounds like the mating call of the bleeding heart, I know, but football cannot expect absolution for the cold-blooded terrorism of the Cold Blow Lane faithful or the Inter-City Firm.

Onfield friction also had its genesis in the game's spiralling rewards. Manchester United's rout of Benfica had cued an extraordinary run for English clubs on the continent, expanding representation in Europe and galvanising gate receipts as it deluded us as to the true state of affairs. In March 1970, Martin Peters claimed a slice of Britain's first £200,000 transfer fee; by February 1979, freedom of contract was with us at last and Trevor Francis had become the first player to cost a million – a 400 per cent rise in nine years. During the Sixties, by comparison, the ante had been upped by 65 per cent. Not unnaturally, the pressure to justify price-tag and wages, which had been building since the abolition of the maximum wage in 1961, went into overdrive. Fear had become the motivating force.

In addition, the transfer spiral was ultimately responsible for the formation of the Big Five, the ruling class of Liverpool, Manchester United, Everton, Arsenal and Tottenham, the rich kids who could pay for success with American Express. Between 1952–53 and 1965–66 there were nine different League champions and 13 different FA Cup winners, in the six seasons from 1966–67 to 1971–72, six different League champions and six different FA Cup winners. Over the past 20 years, the Big Five have accounted for no fewer than 17 Championships/Premierships and 15 FA Cups. Before the start of the 1973–74 season, the Stoke chairman, Albert Henshall, sensibly proposed that the spending power of any club 'should be limited to £250,000 in any one season . . . it is grossly unfair that the chequebook rules the game.' Unfortunately, Mr Backhander had joined the negotiating table, rendering takers somewhat hard to find. Not that everyone grew fat on the proceeds. For the vast majority of players who had started out in the Sixties, a pub in the country was the extent of their ambitions. True, Hamburg would have signed Bowles instead of Keegan had Germany held a broader appeal for Stan than the White City, but the truth was the Barcelonas and Milans were not really interested back then. The one Maverick to cash in was Marsh, and he had to go to the States to do it. When Arsenal won the Double, George, the boy who made it possible, was entitled to no more than a pocketful of loose change from the club's service-related bonus scheme.

Which brings us to the chairmen. Demanding regular ego massages and unswerving fidelity in return for impatience and contempt, these were the gentlemen responsible for converting our grounds into Indigestible Food Zones. On a good day, the Stamford Bridge burgers were 10 per cent pure beef: there are more advisable methods of soothing tempers. In 1957, not long after Northern Ireland had won on English turf for the first time since Archduke Ferdinand met his maker, the Derby County manager, Harry Storer, inquired of the Barnsley chairman and then Football League president, Joe Richards, what his credentials were for being a national selector. When Richards boasted that he had been watching the game for more than half a century, Storer was primed for the kill: 'We've got a corner flag at the Baseball Ground. It's been there for 50 years and still knows absolutely nothing about the game.' That said, the chairmen knew full well how to milk it. The open tombs of Bradford and Hillsborough will forever bear witness to their avarice, the greed that made Thatcherism possible.

The chairmen's chief representative, Alan Hardaker, the Football League secretary who contrived to get his office shifted to Lytham because Preston was too far to commute, was despised by fans as well as players. Here was the misguided fellow responsible for introducing those essential baubles known as the Watney Cup and the Texaco Cup: to him, World Cups and European Cups were irrelevances. Here was the kindly soul who detested the press while using newspaper print as the medium for his message, who 'wouldn't hang a dog on the word of a professional footballer'. Yet for all his advocacy of a basic wage, his condemnation of 'ridiculous demands by players', even the knockdown £2 million he charged Littlewoods for the fixture list, Hardaker was never more than a juice man for the mob. 'Soccer is run by second-rate con-men,' Eamon Dunphy contended in 1973. 'Petit-bourgeois, frustrated small businessmen.'

'The ideal board of directors,' stipulated the ever quip-ful Tommy Docherty in 1977, 'should be made up of three men – two dead and the other dying.'

Malcolm Allison, who stood head, shoulders and chest above every other English coach of the period but who probably should have given management a wide berth, points the finger at his own kind. Now in his late 60s, Big Mal was once the Human Fedora, the Flash 'Arry who taught Ron Atkinson everything he knew about the art of swank but left out all the bits about taste. These days Allison and his wife Lynn reside in the trilby-only village of Yarm in Yorkshire with Gina, their four-year-old daughter. The ardour, though, is no less fierce. 'The system didn't kill the players; the people who run the system killed them. I'm talking about the coaches and the managers. The FA wouldn't know. They wouldn't understand. That's the greatest tragedy that's ever happened – our Football Association. We've got organisers that can't start the Grand National and a Football Association that forgets about Hitler's birthday when arranging a friendly in Germany.

'The deterioration of English football, which to my mind started in 1975, was down to the managers and coaches. We had a school of coaching at Lilleshall that started up after the war. Three hundred managers and coaches being taught how to teach, eating together, drinking together, talking about football. In that group was a phenomenal person, Allan Brown, who was Burnley's manager when they won the League in 1960 and got to the Cup final in 1962 – a brilliant man, a brilliant coach. There weren't many teachers like him. But when Charlie Hughes took over, things changed.'

Rodney Marsh amplifies the point. 'Hughes once said that Brazil have got it wrong because they pass the ball too much! When English football is being run by people like that, what chance have we got?'

'What baffled me,' continues Allison, 'was that all those outstanding players I watched when I was growing up had different ideas and could contribute and weren't asked. Mannion was a brilliant first-time passer, Finney a left-footed outside-right. Tommy Lawton was brilliant in the air, Stanley Matthews was brilliant at running at people. Joe Mercer weighed about ten stone and he was a brilliant tackler. I'm not saying they would all have made great coaches but they had experience and knowledge to pass on. But nobody used them. The waste. Take Stan Cullis. Look at all that success he had when he managed Wolves. Once he was 55, no one ever spoke to him. It's the waste, the waste of knowledge.

'I go and watch players today, in the Nineties, so-called good players, so-called midfield players, and three-quarters of the time they're running between the game. They are neither good defenders nor good attackers. They don't really know what they have to do and there's no one there to tell them. The reason the Dutch were so successful was that they began concentrating on their youngsters in 1958, teaching them from eight to sixteen. The Italians have learned how to control the ball, it doesn't run away from them as it does from us. Football should be an education. I go to schools to teach kids and all they say to me is, "When can we play a game, when can we play a game?". So I tell them: "As soon as you finish training". Football is a lesson, a subject, a business. I saw Cruyff training as a 12-year-old: the tricks and things he learnt. He became a great link player *and* a great individualist.

'There's no such thing as natural ability. Three hundred million Chinese and none of them play football. Your teacher comes along and he says to you, come here, you can do this and do that, you can practise this. If you run with the ball this way you'll be quicker by two yards. If you do this this way you'll be able to protect yourself when you've got the ball. If you do this this way you'll be able to kick the ball further than any other kid in class. All of a sudden, after about a year, instead of not getting a kick he's one of the star players – because he was the one who wanted to learn. The most important thing in life, in anything, is your teacher. The problem is, there aren't enough teachers, I mean football people who teach. The coaches that are doing the job are really concerned because they know they don't know much. All these mavericks, Rodney, Stan, Ossie, Charlie and so on, would have made better use of their undoubted talents, been more consistent, had it not been for bad teaching. Some people need driving. There's a difference between motivation and self-motivation. The ones who've got self-motivation reach the top and the ones who need motivating, when the motivator is not there, they don't do it.'

Marsh argues that English football went into decline from the moment boys started asking managers to sign their autograph books, a trend he first noticed during the early Seventies. Self-importance of this nature was undoubtedly part of it, but can-carrying is primarily the lot of the national manager. Since his claims to expertise purport to have at least some basis in fact, and since he is the trendsetter-in-chief, he is the individual in sorest need of a bulletproof vest. Not for him the weekly showcase trials, the endless fear of dismissal. Yet for all the self-important posturing and incoherent strategy (60 different players in 38 games; 160-odd line-up changes, only 78 per cent of them imposed; to sweep or not to sweep), I felt sorry for Graham Taylor. Who, after all, can say with any certainty whether his former post or John Major's present one (as I write) is the least enviable in England. Why else would the poor bugger have contemplated suicide? Has self-disgust scattered our sense of proportion? Is lambasting the manager not akin to hauling the Egyptian coach before his local magistrate for failing to anticipate the tactical substitution that brought about the parting of the Red Sea? To an extent, yes. That, though, is the nature of the beast. It goes with the salary.

Summonses are hereby issued to Chairman Alf and the ghost of Don 'Readies' Revie, aka The Godfather, for that most heinous of crimes: murdering flair. Had Alf not made the initial dagger thrusts, the coaches would never have taken up arms and Charles Hughes would never have been allowed anywhere near impressionable young boys. 'We've all followed Ramsey,' his Welsh counterpart, Dave Bowen, acknowledged in 1973. 'The winger was dead once you played with four defenders. Alf saw to that in 1966 and it just took the rest of us a little longer to understand.' George Raynor, manager and director of Sweden's climb to the 1958 World Cup final, was more succinct in discussing the Dagenham Girls' No. 1 Pied Piper. 'There's no substitute for skill, but the manager's job is usually to find one. Ramsey obviously found one.' Revie fostered skill at Leeds yet nullified it in his ruthless efforts to snuff it out in opponents. Gary Sprake, whose legendary capacity for clanger-dropping should not preclude recognition of a perceptive brain, saw him as 'knotted with fear'. 'He believed that international players could be controlled and manipulated minute by minute. A lion taught to jump through a hoop is no longer a lion.' David Miller was also referring to Revie, but it could just as easily have been Ramsey.

Admittedly, the contrast between managing at club and international level is daunting, the divide accentuated all the more in England by the knackering domestic programme and the nifty line in unco-operative bloody-mindedness modelled by the League managers. Confirmation was forthcoming every time Revie's mealy mouth narrowed into a slit of exasperation, pushing that spade-like chin ever deeper into the mud of self-pity. Miljan Miljanic, once coach to Yugoslavia, Real Madrid and Chelsea, outlined the dilemma with refreshing clarity: 'The club manager selects his tactics according to his players, the international manager his players according to his tactics. The club manager is less concerned than the international manager with the creative part of the game; his concern is to motivate players at regular, short intervals, even when they do not feel like playing. The club manager can command; the international manager can only seek co-operation. The club manager selects players for their form on the day; the international manager has to have a long-term vision on little practice or evidence. The club manager is pragmatic; the international manager should be concerned with the broader development.'

Unfortunately, Revie was never sure about his tactics, Ramsey wasn't interested in creativity, and neither seemed to give a hoot for broader development. Not that the common ground ended there. Both were weighed down by modest roots and matching insecurities. Both were cunning strategists, the military metaphor all too appropriate. Blatantly ripping off a Hungarian blueprint, the so-called 'Revie Plan' enabled Manchester City to outwit Birmingham in the 1956 Cup final, the author mimicking Nandor Hidegkuti's pivotal role as a deep-lying centre-forward. Hailed by Billy Wright as 'the finest full-back with whom I ever played', Ramsey, meanwhile, devised the modified 4–2–4 that won the 1961–62 League title for Ipswich. By withdrawing his wafer-thin mint of a Scottish winger, Jimmy Leadbetter, to the left side of midfield, Ramsey opened up more space for the central strikers and began killing off the wide men.

Then there were the blind spots, the darkest occupied by the young and the free-spirited. The conservatism was stark. Ramsey saw fit to keep Alan Hudson and Colin Todd waiting, breeding resentment, Revie doing likewise in the case of Trevor Francis. Both bleated that the quality of the available manpower was against them, yet both were control freaks quite prepared to dispense with their prize blooms if it meant keeping the garden spick and span. While Ramsey was comfortably the more decisive, he could never make up his mind about that tricksy-dicksy Liverpool flanker Peter Thompson, a late exclusion from consecutive World Cup squads. Revie could never decide whether to go with wingers or target men, zonal marking or man-to-man. Before a critical World Cup qualifier against Italy in November 1976, he scrutinised the opposition eight times, then made six personnel changes and was fortunate to leave Rome with a 2–0 defeat, to all intents and purposes costing England a role in the 1978 finals. The back four had never been seen in unison; two of the three midfielders – Trevor Cherry and Brian Greenhoff – were defenders by calling. Giacinto Facchetti called it 'the worst England side I have ever seen'. Not that the immaculate full-back stopped there. 'They were disorganised, confused, had only modest ability and, most surprising of all for a team from England, they seemed to have little heart for the battle.' In 29 games Revie fielded an unchanged side precisely once. Graham Taylor was not alone in having an unshakable faith in his own shilly-shallying.

The concept of the good loser was mutually alien. After failing to persuade Ray Tinkler that that charming Tony Brown might just have been a teensy-weensy bit offside when he scored the goal for West Brom that handed the 1970–71 League crown to Arsenal, Revie trudged back to the Leeds dugout, head cast theatrically to the skies, eyes screaming 'Why me?', a man carrying his own coffin. 'Four of those goals came from outside our penalty area,' Ramsey fumed after Puskas and his fellow artists had decorated the Wembley pitch with their indelible watercolours. 'We should never have lost.' Had he played for Bon Accord in another era, he would presumably have traced all 36 Arbroath goals to an inefficient offside trap.

To Geoff Hurst, Ramsey was 'the most patriotic man I've ever met'. Others saw him in a less complimentary light. 'Ramsey pulls the strings and the players dance for him,' sniped Bob Kelly as early as 1964, shortly after becoming an ex-president of the Scottish FA. 'He has theorised them out of the game. They mustn't think for themselves. They have been so brainwashed by tactics and talks that their individual talent has been thrust into the background.' 'Stalag Lilleshall' was the players' pet name for their World Cup training HQ, 'one shandy and you're history' the gist of one vital pre-tournament pep talk. So highly did Ramsey value the men who took ball-winning to such unpalatable extremes, that he put his job on the line during the 1966 World Cup when urged by the FA to drop Nobby Stiles, who had done his level best to deprive a French forward of a kneecap or two. Ramsey also saw fit to award Peter Storey 19 caps; 19 years would have been preferable.

Revie was even more at one with the rakers, the knobblers and the dead-leggers. Who else can be held responsible for the white corpuscles of 'professionalism' that flowed so virulently through the arteries of his Leeds sides? The Elland Roadsters of 1965–1974 were truly schizoid, formidable in both the English and French sense. On the one hand their frequently sublime interpassing evoked nothing less than Serge Blanco's comment about having to 'think about the other person's pleasure'. On the other they dealt out pain with all the coldness of a croupier fingering a marked deck. Intimidators and ref-baiters *par excellence*, bookings outweighed the early baths because the guilt was so evenly spread. If there was a line to cross, every man jack was aware of its precise whereabouts. Better, surely, for eight canny buggers to step out of bounds once apiece rather than two silly buggers four times. For years I was convinced that Paul Madeley, the Action Man who really had worn every shirt from 1 to 11, had been far too busy, not to mention far too squeaky-clean, to dirty his hands. Then again, he did go on to make the odd squillion in property. The irony was that Leeds faltered at the final hurdle far more often than they cleared it.

'The thing with Leeds,' proffers Allison, exasperation manifest, 'was that they were cynical. It wasn't just being stronger and stopping the other team, it was cynical. There was no need for it. They were the best team in England, a great side, but greedy, greedy. That was the nub of it. A lot of what Leeds did was premeditated, and I would think that made Don Revie an unsuitable man to manage England. A lot of professionals would agree with that even if the FA didn't.'

For most non-Tykes, Revie's Leeds demanded grudging respect and defied genuine affection. When Derek Temple, Everton's speedy if lightweight winger, was carried off following an almighty collision with the Leeds full-back, Willie Bell, Les Cocker, Revie's hard-bitten spaniel of a trainer, instructed the survivor to stay down and let the crowd cool off. Seeing Bell prostrate, Revie hastily summoned another stretcher. 'Get your own fucking stretcher,' barked back one of the ambulance attendants. Revie had only just left Elland Road when Bremner and Keegan traded blows in the Charity Shield: his ethical standards did not disappear overnight.

At the time, nevertheless, I felt sorry for Leeds. In my neck of the woods, with the exception of Bobby Grossmark (who subsequently met Glenn Hoddle on the road to Damascus and duly embraced the creed common to most North London Jews, Spursism), they were detested by everyone and his sister's budgie. Then again, I also felt sorry for Soames Forsythe. Leeds were the bridesmaid's bridesmaid: in the space of ten years they were runners-up five times in the League, three times in the FA Cup, once in each of the Euro tourneys. There were afternoons of pizzazz. Eddie Gray *en route* to the decade's most breathtaking individual goal, pirouetting past six Burnley defenders, a couple twice just to ice the cake. 'When he plays on snow,' enthused Revie, 'he doesn't leave footprints.' If Eddie had gone out on the razz a bit more, sown a few more oats, been a touch less steady, we might not have noticed Georgie Boy had gone walkabout for good. Then there was the awesome power of Peter Lorimer, uncorking a 30-yard thunderbolt against Manchester City: rising then dipping in a devilish parabola beyond the humungous Joe Corrigan, who may have strayed two yards off his line. At most. Giles himself, whose passing implied an aptitude for threading needles with one arm trussed behind his back. Be all that as it may, the Godfather and his soldiers deserved every ounce of their persecution complex. Upon taking on the national job, Revie (and his PR lackies) played up the sense of togetherness he had generated, the 'family' atmosphere. More Corleone than Partridge.

Ramsey and Revie both inculcated in the majority of their charges the kind of unquestioning obeisance more readily found among the whackos of Waco. In Ramsey's case, this apparently extended to some of his superiors, albeit not the FA, whose Corinthian sensibilities were not so much rattled by the Eastender's success as compressed into a ball of barely pent-up disdain. The season Ramsey took Suffolk into the European Cup, Eric Steel, one of the Ipswich directors, suddenly resigned. The manager, he insisted, was 'negligent' (a reference, one assumes, to his disinclination to bother with the youth team), the board 'a bunch of Ramsey's yes-men'. To attract commitment of this order was no mean feat for a couple of blokes who gave the distinct impression that they would rather have spent their working hours down an unlit pit. That way they could have chanced a smile and not a soul would have had to know. While Osgood and Hudson were putting on the glitz during Chelsea's 1970 FA Cup quashing of QPR, even Clouseau could have spotted Ramsey in the packed West Stand. Hemmed in by a host of animated, appreciative visages, he was the one bearing the strongest resemblance to a recently bereaved basset hound.

Obsessiveness, that reliable indicator of fear, was another common denominator. While Revie had his lucky pinstripes and rabbit's feet, a newly married Ramsey, attested Brian Glanville, once bustled down a narrow White Hart Lane corridor and failed to detect the presence of his bride. They also shared a certain, um, sleight-of-hand. For some reason, Ramsey persisted for many years in stating that he had been born at Parrish Cottages in 1922. *Who's Who* and *The Sunday Mirror* fell for it, so too the publishers of his book, *Talking Football*. Only *Debrett* – naturally – got it right: Five Elms Farm, Dagenham, 22/1/22. Pretentious, *quoi*? Arthur Hopcraft had a right old snigger in *The Observer*. 'Alf Ramsey, the dignified, the aspirer after presence, could not, I am convinced, give false information to the book of the Peerage. Not Sir Alf.' No doubt an early appearance on *What's My Line* had left its mark too. Alf had won 31 England caps yet not one member of the panel untangled his line, even without blindfolds.

Ramsey's desire to leave his past behind was as fervent as Martin

Guerre's. To some, disguising dropped aitches is a betrayal, to others a career move. Hopcraft reckoned he was 'more careful of his aspirates than his answers'. Not long after being appointed England manager, Ramsey bumped into an erstwhile Tottenham colleague on the train to London. The latter, a proud cockney sparrer, sniffed the air and caught a whiff of an accent that had just undergone a manicure and pedicure. 'Come off it, Alf,' was the response. Unfortunately, for all those elocution classes, Ramsey found communication another kettle of cod altogether. His biographer, Max Marquis, regarded him as 'inarticulate, fluent but unable to communicate with any precision', which had a good deal to do with a predilection for two-syllabled words when one was more than enough. Whenever *Sportsnight* broadcast an England game, obligatory watching was confined to the post-match interview. Andy Woodend, Ian Reed and I would tot up how many times Chairman Alf uttered 'most certainly' and compare notes the following morning. Chairman Alf was always top of the Form 305 'Things We Wish They Would Say' chart: 'Most certainly we were crap . . . most certainly I should have played Osgood/Greaves/Marsh/Old Man Steptoe/Robert Dougall . . . most certainly Argentinians are jolly fine fellows . . . most certainly Bobby Moore and I have a non-Platonic relationship.' Quite why he didn't insist on being called Alfred remains one of life's imponderables. Perhaps he didn't want to surrender his street cred.

In truth, the hysteria generated by Revie's desert desertion now seems unfairly overblown. At least Judge Cantley had the presence of mind to overturn his ten-year ban, the heftiest ever imposed by the FA, on the grounds that its chairman, Sir Harold Thompson, should never have chaired the tribunal. Be honest. If you knew millions of people were reading unflattering remarks about you over breakfast every day, even if you did deserve two out of every three, wouldn't you be tempted by the thought of earning a few extra shekels in a land a very long way away? True, £340,000 was a lot of extra shekels, ten times Revie's FA wage. 'I know people will accuse me of running away,' he told *The Daily Mail*, 'but the situation has become impossible.' Thompson, he would later lament, 'treated me like an employee' (perish the thought) whereas 'these Arab Sheikhs treat me like one of them.' David Miller didn't offer quite so much sympathy for the devil, but then he was working for *The Daily Express* at the time. 'I thought his final departure was a pathetic capitulation to Mammon,' he fumed in his account of the 1978 World Cup, 'sacrificing honour for riches in a way which made one feel sorry for him not having the guts required for high office.' Honour? Not that Miller – nor many other members of the pressbox fraternity – had objected too forcefully when Revie was appointed.

It is difficult, nonetheless, to quarrel with Miller's belief that 'there always seemed to be a trace of the hustler in the background'. Bernard Shaw's allegations of an attempt to bribe him prior to the 1972 Leeds-Wolves Championship decider may not have been proven, but Allison wasn't taken in. 'Of course there was something in that, and of course they didn't prove it. It was crooked. When I was chasing the title with Manchester City in 1972, there was this crooked game at Ipswich. Revie gave their centre-forward, Rod Belfitt, who used to play for Leeds, £15,000. Ipswich were 2 to 1 against and they bet it at the bookmakers. Leeds won 2–0 and they got four-and-a-half grand out of it. Four-and-a-half grand, in *them* days. Revie used to leave three hundred or four hundred quid in the referees' room, in an envelope, and they could take it or leave it. I'm just talking about a little bribery.'

In revealing that he had personally raked in a million pounds or more in commercial revenue for the FA during his tenure as England manager, Revie was at pains to point out that not so much as a threepenny bit had reached his own pockets. Indeed, Bert Patrick, the chairman of Admiral, was insistent that Revie had not creamed a farthing from the £250,000 England kit deal he negotiated to such suspicion and derision. Well, it was pretty dodgy. The shirts were the most aesthetically displeasing since Mr Bri met Mr Nylon, the sock tags naffer than a skinhead in hot pants. The answer to the charge of vested interests was unequivocal: 'I've never taken a penny from a sports goods firm in my 15 years at Leeds, nor since I took the England job. If it had been money I was after I would have stayed at Leeds.' Maybe, maybe not. Richard Langridge – then marketing director of the company responsible for the one and only Stylo Matchmaker, a boot of purest Gucci compared with the Made in Woolies of the poncey Gola White – was present when Revie signed a contract to promote the Stylo boys' range subsequent to his installation as England manager; the Leeds players' pool had previously struck a deal with the same firm.

In 1975, his first full year as an FA 'employee', Revie addressed the nation thus: 'Some players don't know how lucky they are. They should go down on their hands and knees every night and thank God they are doing something which they love and are being well paid for.' At this very juncture, the England manager was holding out for some pin-money – a £200 fee in exchange for a free slap-up lunch at the *Rothman's Football Yearbook* launch and an opportunity to spout a platitude or two. In 1976 Revie distributed a circular advertising his wares for seminars at the knock-down price of two hundred quid a session. Yet, try as they might, no one could pin a thing on 'Readies', barring, that is, gross treachery to Queen, country and infrequently beautiful game.

The force with which the doo-doo had hit the fan first became apparent when England went to Berlin for the second leg of the 1972 European Championship quarter-finals. Inspired by a two-goal deficit, Ramsey took the enterprising step of adorning his midfield with Hunter and Storey, a pair of Mr Magoos in visionary terms, their task to exterminate Gunter Netzer with prejudice *in extremis*. Opting for pride over glory, neither, mercifully, was forthcoming. In the estimation of the German manager, Helmut Schoen, an inexpert whinger at the worst of times, the goalless stalemate was engineered by 'brutal' English methods, an accusation supported by the not inconsiderable award of 27 free-kicks to the hosts. Ramsey declared himself 'satisfied and proud'. Within a couple of months Schoen's schonest were pissing all over the Soviets in the final with a bravura display of what the catchphrase artists would subsequently dub Total Football. Although Netzer's move to Real Madrid and subsequent loss of form would prompt more pragmatic tactics in the World Cup, Schoen had evidently learned a lot since 1966. By persisting with his own form of ten-man rugby, Ramsey had demonstrated merely that his loyalty to certain players was more than matched by a fixation on blinkers.

'Maybe Alf did hold on to certain players for too long,' concurs Roy McFarland, 'but then he did have to replace a number of world-class players at the same time.' But for those inconvenient slip-ups against Poland, Allison maintains that, come the Real Thing, England would have reached 'the semi-finals at least'. McFarland is more realistic. 'We could have done well in Germany, what with Tony Currie coming through as he was, but to be honest, we got left behind a bit when the game moved on, particularly in terms of the introduction of the sweeper. And no, I don't think it was complacency.' Some were less sure. The first issue of the Lancaster Gate in-house organ, *FA News*, to be published after that Wembley stalemate contained some strong words from the new FA secretary, Ted Croker. 'There are far too many elderly men being asked to do more than is reasonable in administering football. This is not just a personal opinion, as a report was prepared five years ago by the Chester Committee on all aspects of football and this was their considered opinion and recommendations were made to ease this problem, but, so far, they have not been implemented. It is time we had another look at that report in many aspects of football and accept that it was perhaps unfortunate that it was published too soon after we had been successful in the 1966 World Cup, and, therefore, could be said to have been complacent.'

At face value, Ramsey's overall record was nothing to sniff at: 69 wins and 17 defeats in 113 matches, equivalent to 165 points out of a possible 226. However, strip away the 23 wins in 34 encounters with British opposition and some of the polish fades. Between the 1966 and 1970 World Cups, in fact, leaving aside games against Northern Ireland and Wales (seven wins, one draw), England's record was anything but immodest: won 12, drawn nine, lost four. I can't even think of a handful of post-'66 victories that linger with any sense of joy. A 5–0 Wembley frolic against France on Terry Cooper's debut in March 1969, the second half against the Scots on the same ground two months later, the 2–1 scrapes in Montevideo the following month and Moscow in 1973. The games that stick fastest were those valiant knee-bowers against Brazil in Guadalajara and Rio, and against the Germans in Leon. When the going got rough, the tough got weak. When it came to shitting and busting – qualifiers, sudden-death, extra-time – it was bust all the way after the 1967 European quarter-final second leg in Spain (in the interests of even-handedness, I feel obliged to relate that the homeboys were seen off with an 80th-minute strike from Spiny Norman). Florence, Leon, Wembley, Chorzow – four defeats and a sodding draw. The Swiss, Bulgarians, Romanians, even the Welsh, escaped Middlesex with a point. Yet in 1972, when Terry Neill hoofed Northern Ireland to their first success at Wembley for 15 years, Ramsey had a cast-iron alibi: for the first time since the Bakhramov 'n' Dienst Show, not a single World Cup Willie was on parade.

What made that funeral in Berlin all the more sombre was that it had been prefaced by a first leg in which England's shortcomings had been laid bare by Netzer, the Borussia Baryshnikov: 29 April 1972 was the day Alfism got its comeuppance as the Moenchengladbach passmeister's cream mane jigged winsomely in the Wembley evening breeze, more emancipated than the average bra-burner. Footloose and fanciful, Netzer had licence to express, locating and liberating colleagues time and again with the disdainful strut so envied and despised by League managers. A definite flash bastard: preening here, prancing there, every touch dabbed with a vain flourish. And why not? There was a magnetic precision about his passing, from 40 yards or four: weight, timing, angles – the lot. England, more by luck than judgment, were still level at one apiece with six minutes left, yet, for the first time in half-a-dozen years of urging on my so-called representatives, I was happy in defeat, relieved that two late goals had done the opposition justice. All right, so the lads hadn't had a fixture since December, and Roy McFarland, the most mobile and astute central-defender at Ramsey's disposal, had withdrawn through injury, leaving the declining Bobby Moore, a marker of space rather than men, to plug the gap. Excuses, schmexcuses. When I went to bed I dreamt about being tried for treason by a jury comprising Ken Baily, Enoch Powell and Alf Garnett.

What intensified the teeth-gnashing was the conviction that, if there was no one on hand to compare with Beckenbauer and Muller, we did have our own Netzers, our own Hoenesses and Heynckeses. Released from captivity by that most aptly christened of men, George Best, a veritable bevy of English ball-playing beauties were high-stepping their way into folklore: the Munificent Seven, aka the Mavericks – Stan Bowles, Tony Currie, Charlie George, Alan Hudson, Rodney Marsh, Peter Osgood and Frank Worthington. Unlike Duncan McKenzie, the one contemporary compatriot worthy of occupying the same Olympus, each made at least one appearance in full national colours during the Seventies. Indeed, Marsh came on as a late sub for Hurst during the Netzer Show, and was actually picked to start the Berlin fiasco. None, though, was ever wholly trusted either by Ramsey or Revie, the first two England managers to be accorded sole selection rights.

Currie won 17 caps (in three spells spanning eight seasons), Marsh nine, Worthington eight, Bowles five (under three managers), Osgood four, Hudson two. George barely made it past the hour on his one appearance. Understandably, this disproportionate allocation provoked a degree of hostility. 'When I was at Derby,' relates Charlie George with more than a hint of satisfaction, 'Tommy Docherty called me into the office and said that Ron Greenwood wanted me to play for the B team and I said: "Well, you phone Ron Greenwood up and tell him C is for Charlie, C is for class and I don't play for no fucking B team." Tommy phoned up the FA while I was there and he told them. Looking back, I opened my mouth when I shouldn't have. If I'd kept it shut, who knows? But you can't change what you are.'

Marsh enjoyed more consideration than the rest – seven successive appearances, an all-time Maverick record – and he despised pretty much every minute. The Mavericks' combined 46 caps are as many as Mick Channon aggregated on his tod and barely half the 84 stashed away in Ray Wilkins' attic. Each was given a chance, an opportunity to fail.

'Butch' Wilkins knew the score. He was 17 when I first clapped eyes on him, wispishly slim, waspishly energetic. The potential would have been obvious to a short-sighted ostrich. As a distributor he could have played Williams off against Ferrari and named his price. Goals were infrequent, but when they came, such as the bodacious 50-yard lob that damaged Hull beyond repair at the Bridge in March 1977, the *longueurs* felt worthwhile. That season, glory of glories, it was this now 18-year-old mannish boy who skippered Chelsea to promotion. He'd already turned out for England by then. Roy McFarland remembers the first time: 'We were playing Italy in New York to mark the 1976 Bicentennial and I was on the bench, injured. At half-time we were 2–0 down and the boots were flying, but he wanted the ball all the time, this kid in his first international. He had a lot to do with us coming back to win 3–2.' Astute, adventurous and seemingly wise beyond his years: what more could you possibly ask for? Hell, you even forgave the swot in him, that straighter-than-The-Six-O'Clock-News protective wrapper that prohibited idolatry.

Sadly, having matured so swiftly, Butch mellowed early and settled for the armchair. He came to exude a conservative consistency that delighted the Greenwoods and Robsons and depressed anyone not enamoured of squandered endowments. Joe Public came to scoff, to sneer at his peerless mastery of the square pass, of crab-ball. He seldom did anything wrong in an England shirt, but then rarely did he do much of a positive hue. By hedging his bets, eliminating error at all costs, he always did just enough to hold on to his place. So it was that Glenn Hoddle, the man Greenwood and Robson should have built their team around, was so often on the periphery, even when he was in the team. Wilkins could have been a contender and ended up a shrewd bum with a career plan. 'He should have been a Socrates,' avers Marsh, 'but he ended up playing these little passes, like Nobby Stiles. He became a continuity player. You couldn't leave him out because he never gave the ball away, but he never did anything. He was a much better player in his mid-30s than he allowed himself to be in his 20s.' It took the challenge of playing in France and Italy to stir the loins anew, and it cannot be denied that the Rangers of west London and Glasgow both benefited from his professorial probing. As an international player, nevertheless, Wilkins compromised.

Having spent his apprenticeship alongside those wastrels Osgood and Hudson, it would be fairer to blame the system that bred Wilkins, the ethos that bequeathed Len Shackleton as many caps (five) as Jeff Astle and Bryan Robson nearly twice as many as Hoddle. How long did Bobby Robson dally before giving Gascoigne his head? Why didn't Graham Taylor play Matthew Le Tissier against the Dutch? The Mavericks were unusual only in as much as they suffered concurrently. Seldom have so many been so distrusted by so few. Then again, envy is the Englishman's Uzi.

As with so many Englishmen gifted the ability to simplify the unnecessarily complicated, the Mavericks fell foul of that envy. They scared managers with their quest for freedom – from fear, convention, boredom – and petrified them when they attained it. Next to moderation, compromise was the last thing of which you could accuse the Mavericks. As a consequence, their dilemma in the international context was threefold. Selfless anonymity had been the cornerstone of the Ramsey régime; their naked exhibitionism ran in the opposite direction. Worse still, bar Osgood, their long, unruly hair made them look like poofs, the Wizard of Os compensating with sideburns that endlessly proposed betrothal to a sandpapered chin. Each folicle out of place was a snook cocked at Lancaster Gate, an affront to the crewcut machismo of the common or garden back four. None of the Mavericks, more significantly, was adept at licking bottoms, least of all bottoms belonging to those with insufficient matter up top to appreciate the diversity within any collective. Irreverence and daring were their bywords, safe options anathema. Charlie was the south, east and west of the North Bank, Rodney and Stanley lords of the Loft, Peter the Wizard of Os. Alan rose from King's Road knave to Renaissance Man of the Victoria Ground. Tony trotted out at Bramall Lane to the strains of 'You Can Do Magic'. If Frank was too active a rolling stone to ascend any one local throne, his network of touched hearts spread all the wider.

It would have been unnatural had the life-affirming manner in which these men practised their craft not traversed the touchline. Their reputations, furthermore, were only partially unwarranted, even if they were irrelevant to their capacity to do their jobs. Which is why, for all their knowhow, none of them has ever held down a management post in the upper echelons of the League. They were the Lairds of Laddism, disruptive influences one and all. Unclean, unclean. Not that they worked overtime to dispel that image. Hudson, Currie and Worthington liked a tipple, Bowles a flutter. George was the yobbo who scrapped with photographers and threw V-signs at spectators. Osgood fell in love once a week with women bearing scant resemblance to his spouse. Marsh was a swank.

So what, wondered another party animal, Peter Storey. 'From the first time I kicked a ball as a pro 19 years ago,' he reflected in 1980, 'I began to learn what the game was all about. It's about the drunken parties that go on for days. The orgies, the birds and the fabulous money. Football is just a distraction – but you're so fit you can carry on with all the high living in secret, and still play the game at the highest level.' Storey, it must be said, went a tad too far. Not content with head-butting a 67-year-old lollipop man, he was also found guilty of controlling prostitutes, counterfeiting gold sovereigns and stashing illegal porn mags in the tyres of his car. His point is still pertinent, though. Bobby Moore, no Mother Theresa himself, would frequently argue that nothing a player did off the field should matter so long as he did the business on a Saturday.

Citing these peccadilloes erected a handy smokescreen. In the mid-Seventies, Alan Ball and a business acquaintance conceived the bright idea of forming The Clan, a syndicate comprising the League's more notorious attractions, the aim to generate extra income through various promotional ventures. Among the founder members were Osgood, Hudson, Ball and Allison. The press piled in for the launch, held, it scarce needs adding, in a plush London eatery with a hint of spivviness. Neither Osgood nor Hudson can remember a thing about it after that. 'I reckon it, er, lost a bit of steam,' recalls Hudson, dimly. 'I definitely don't remember making any money.' Ball felt for them as much as himself. 'What is it that makes a player a "bad boy" in the eyes of the soccer bosses? It's not the much-publicised drinking sessions or the newspaper articles or the TV outbursts. It is simply that those in authority, and managers in particular, just do not know how to handle players who will not conform to their regimented ideas of running a football club. Players of exceptional talent have complete belief in their own ability and, as a result, they do not need a manager holding their hands for them every day and night . . . The "bad boys" fear no one, they fear no situation, they fear no institution. Fear is a terrible thing in this game. It turns good players into mediocre players, and average players into bad ones . . . I know all the controversial characters, and I don't hide the fact that I am one of them – Hudson, Osgood, Stan Bowles, Malcolm Macdonald, Charlie George. I know what the jealous people say when another headline appears: "There he is again, that flash merchant, shouting his mouth off, letting the manager and the rest of the team down. Who does he think he is?".'

Discarded by Revie after half-a-dozen outings – like Emlyn Hughes, he unaccountably slithered from captain to outsider – Ball snarled back, slamming Revie's next squad as 'a bunch of donkeys'. He apologised for this indiscretion 'but only because it didn't apply to all of them personally. I still think the analogy was apt. Without realising it, the players in his squad were becoming the robots he was looking for.' Players like Hudson, Currie and George were 'not the sort of men who would happily play bingo for hours on end or spend all afternoon on the putting green. We wouldn't take dossiers seriously. We became annoyed at repeating dead-ball moves 20 times because someone was too thick to understand it the first time. We just wanted to get on with the job of making England great again. And we would have done it. But Revie was frightened of us.' Is it any wonder that not one of the Mavericks has a son who has taken up the family trade?

Ray Wilkins, interestingly, has since put his finger on a few more home truths. 'Generally speaking, players don't analyse themselves and their game enough. That's why we lack the technique of foreign players. It's a matter of pride. An individual knows what's wrong with his game, knows what's required to put it right. He shouldn't need telling to go out and improve his weak foot or make his first touch better. To be the best you have to work at it. When I was at Chelsea I'd go out with John Hollins after training and we'd hit 50 balls at each other using both feet, outside of the foot, curving, chipping, lobbing them. When I was at AC Milan we spent 20 minutes every day juggling with the ball as part of our warm-up exercise. We had to keep it in the air all that time. It gave you a wonderful feel for the ball and marvellous close control. When people say "It's all very well talking about the Italians, but they have a lot more time in Italy", they miss the point. The fact is the Italians make more time because their first touch is so good. There are signs that things are improving in our soccer but there's still a long way to go.'

In Italy, added Wilkins, 'you were put on a pedestal and they kept you there'. Now there's a novel way to behave. 'For me the saddest happening in sport in recent times,' he continued, 'was the retirement of David Gower. Jesus wept, why? He is still a great player, a unique entertainer. I compare him to George Best. That same extraordinary talent. And he wants to pack it in. I don't understand it.' Maybe our ingenue should have pondered a trifle harder. See, we don't take too kindly to the extraordinary in these parts. Too good for the ordinary are we? Well, la-di-dah. If a chap thinks he's God Almighty, how can he know his place?

Not that easily when exposure is at unprecedented levels, particularly for the fixated and/or anally retentive schoolboy. In 1964, an NOP survey indicated that 44 per cent of Englishmen over the age of 16 watched football at least once a week. The World Cup almost doubled that even before TV multiplied the options. Enter ITV's Sunday regional answer to *Match of the Day*, *Star Soccer*, subsequently rechristened *The Big Match*. By the early Seventies, a week in the life of armchair anoraks and purists alike could comprise six weekend League fixtures – usually all Division One – plus midweek League Cup, FA Cup and/or European ties. Barring European and FA Cup finals, it was highlights all the way, easily the soundest method of concealing the fraying knickers of a game so fast and furious as to be incapable of sustained quality for 45 minutes, never mind 90. And to think TV was deemed the enemy.

In 1969, meanwhile, *The Sun* had gone tabloid, flogging mucky parsons, Page-3 Scanties and transfer tattle six days a week. The periodical industry went bananas, spurred on by the reinvention that year of *Match of the Day* and *The Big Match* as technicolour spectacle. (The night *Match of the Day* was first broadcast in colour – Chelsea 3 Man City 1 – I actually expected our portable black-and-white to serve up brown mud and royal blue shirts. When it didn't, I screwed up my eyes and that seemed to do the trick.) Already undermined by *Goal*, a slightly brasher part-colour weekly, perennials like *Football Monthly* were shoved off their plinth by the advent that same year of the even brassier and glossier *Shoot!*. According to one long-serving editor, Peter Stewart, *Shoot!* was the first such magazine 'to be aimed deliberately at the young'. It glamourised football, he averred, 'in a way that hadn't been seen before'.

Celebrity columns, centrefolds and cut-out-and-keep League tables proliferated alongside that wondrous mine of information, the Q&A. Thus did we discover Worthington's aptitude for piss-taking. 'Biggest disappointment' changed down the years from Revie's appointment as England manager to 'not getting the lead part in *The Incredible Hulk*'; 'Miscellaneous likes' from bird-watching to 'browsing around hardware stores'. That was how I discovered that Alan Ball's wife Lesley was as worthy of a piece of my heart as Brigitte and Ursula. I had the pleasure of bumping into the Divine Mrs B at Osgood's Hampshire golf club some 25 years later: I'd spent the previous day poring over a pile of old *Shoots*, so it must have been a case of wish-fulfilment. I felt compelled to come clean and advise her of my affliction. 'Hope I'm not too much of a disappointment now,' she replied gently. 'Not at all,' I spluttered, 12 again and blushing madly, and meaning every word.

Notwithstanding Julie Welch's wittily elegaic *Those Glory Glory Days*, Matthew Sturgis was right to point out, as he did in *The Independent on Sunday*, that this was the era 'when football imposed itself upon the schoolboy consciousness'. Force-feeding was in. While a half-hour football soap called *United* failed to dislodge Annie Walker and her regulars from the top of the ratings, *Quiz Ball* ('I'll take Route One, David' – 'Good luck, Bob') had become a firm favourite, if only for stressing that goalkeepers are not as maladjusted as they are cracked up to be: no one had the beating of West Brom's gaunt, upright minder, John Osborne. Alf Garnett had his West Ham, Bob Ferris and Terry Collier their Newcastle. Thingummy out of *The Dustbinmen* – you know, Gerry, the worried one from *Coronation Street* – looked ready to top himself every time Manchester City lost. Roy Race, Jumbo Trudgeon and Blackie Gray were granted a free transfer by *Tiger and Jag* (née my beloved *Tiger and Hurricane*, home of GP driver Skid Solo and wrestler Johnny Cougar) and started up their own comic, *Roy of the Rovers*. *Scorcher and Score* broke ground with 'Billy's Boots', 'Bobby of the Blues' and countless other strips concerned exclusively with muddied oafing. In 1970, Esso dispensed with Green Shield stamps and gave away plastic World Cup coins with their economically sound gasoline. Then came football's first meaningful foray on *Top of the Pops*, 'Back Home'. Did anyone ever look less at home in a bow-tie than Nobby?

Pride of place went to *The Wonderful World of Soccer Stars*. Thrust upon an unsuspecting populace at the outset of the 1968–69 season, this series of stickers, five to a pack, introduced 15 members of each of the 22 First Division clubs. On the reverse was a thumbnail sketch-by-numbers. A goalie was invariably a 'doughty custodian', full-backs 'keen in the tackle', centre-backs 'towering' and 'good in the air', midfielders 'scheming' and strikers 'powerful'. Yet for those of us who spent our lunch breaks trading like Wall Street dealers in relentless pursuit of civilisation's remaining pork belly – 'Tell you what, a Neil Young and a Peter Grummitt for two Sam Ellises and a John O'Rourke plus a full set of Monkees cards, *with* the original bubblegum' – a complete album was our Holy Grail, our Lost Ark and our Dead Sea Scrolls. It became our *Hitch-hikers' Guide to the Galaxy* of Seventies football, enabling instant proximity to our heroes. A World Cup edition came in due course, bringing Tostão's gammy eye and Gianni Rivera's suaveness into our lives, whereupon the event itself turned photos into indelible memories. Courtesy of Best rather than Ramsey, football had indeed become glamorous. The most staple-strewn midriffs belonged to the Mavericks, the fourth estate's bread and fodder.

Yet the early Seventies also produced the first backlash: *Foul*, 'football's alternative paper' (as it styled itself) and forerunner of *When Saturday Comes* et al. Edited by a scrum of Cambridge graduates, it hit the newsstands in October 1972, 'the name,' as Phil Shaw noted in his definitive fanzine history, *Whose Game is it Anyway?*, 'a deliberate parody of magazines like *Shoot!* and *Goal*'. The first cover shot was indicative of the tone: Bobby Moore elbows an opponent, an adjoining 'bubble' caption reads 'Who Says We're Just Pretty Boys Then?' *Foul*, asserted Shaw, 'kicked against the frightening and frightened football of Revie and Ramsey'. Originally typewritten, the majority of its 34 issues were typeset and distributed, suitably enough, by the same company that handled *Private Eye*. Stan Hey, Steve Tongue and their chums put it to bed for the last time in October 1976; a month later, England's World Cup trail ended in Rome. Strapped for cash and unable to defend a libel action, the timing was said to be coincidental. All the same, it was as if they had accepted the futility of the struggle.

History overflows with What Ifs. What If the Brighton bomb had got Maggie? Would the need for *The Big Issue* be quite so pressing? What If that cultured midfielder Jimmy Adamson, the man first offered Walter Winterbottom's job, had decided that he could handle the pressure and that managing his country's football team was a piece of piss? Or Joe Mercer had been given a team to run rather than merely look after? Chances are:

(1) I would never have been able to boast that George Cohen had a Jewish grandad (there were rumours about Martin Chivers, but Mordecai Spiegler, Avi Cohen, Ronnie Rosenthal, Barry Silkman and Mark Lazarus are the only Football League players of the past 30 years whom I know definitively to have been Chosen Ones);
(2) So long as they bribed the ref to ensure they kicked off in every game, England would have won the 1974 World Cup with the following 3–3–4 formation – Shilton; Todd, McFarland, Beattie; George, Hudson, Currie; Marsh, Osgood, Worthington, Bowles;
(3) Matthew Le Tissier would be up where he belongs. Dream on, son, dream on.

'I try to provide entertainment on the field to help distract people from their worries, even for 90 minutes. If only society could do that for eternity.' That soundest, most idealistic of bites came courtesy of Eric Cantona, the Premiership's one maverick. During the golden hour of the Seventies, there were more English footballers capable of distracting us than we deserved, albeit less than we would like to remember. As an antidote to the world according to Chairman Alf and the Godfather, the Mavericks were potent indeed. Unfortunately, the recurring theme of English football in the Seventies was all too transparent: Who dares loses.

Gunning for Trouble

We 'ate Arse-nal an' we 'AYTE Ars'nal
We 'ate Arse-nal an' we 'AYTE Ars'nal
We 'ate Arse-nal an' we 'AYTE Ars'nal
We are the ARSE-nal – 'AYTERS . . .'

Self-loathing. Right-thinking Englishmen hate Arsenal because we associate them with most of the characteristics we would rather our heroes did without, traits all too abundant in our daily lives. Sensible, orderly, restrained. Risky as a Status Quo riff, romantic as Victor Meldrew in mid-strop. Marinello, Petrovic, Nicholas, Limpar – what *were* you thinking of? Brady – how could you? Highbury is the Camelot of the civil service, a court of convention. The marble halls don't quicken the pulse, they deaden it, locking it into a time warp where Empire is intact and every man not only knows his place but is damned proud to be there. Try the Neutral Test. Sky broadcast live coverage of a game between Arsenal and another English club, neither of whom you support: who do you shout for?

In fairness, Arsenal were unfortunate. There we were, grooving to the samba of Pele and Gerson, still in thrall to the concept of football as physical art, expectations soaring. Brazil had completed their Mexican tap dance less than a month earlier. In the Hall of Fame of Thankless Tasks, following that was up there with that poor sod who was scheduled on the Olympic long-jump runway directly after Bob Beamon, and wisely gave it a miss. Perhaps Hardaker and his cronies at Lytham St Anne's would have been better off doing likewise with the 1970–71 season. Instead, Arsenal went out and won the Double, the second club so to do if we discount Preston, as well we should. After all, the North Enders' competitive fixture list in 1888–89 totted up to a mere 27 outings, barely 40 per cent of Arsenal's 64. Indeed, given Tottenham's 49 games in 1960–61, Liverpool's 57 in 1985–86 and Manchester United's 62 in 1993–94, Bertie Mee's infantry have good reason to consider their achievement the most glorious of all.

One minor problem: ranged alongside the Prozac of Tottenham, Liverpool and United, let alone Brazil's magic mushrooms, this lot were pure, uncut Mogadon. Since the Second World War, mention of Arsenal had evoked those thoroughgoing Thirties thoroughbreds, Alex James, David Jack and Cliff Bastin, waving wands in shorts roomy enough to house a papoose or three; Herbert Chapman and Tom Whittaker; the modest cigars and the hint of genteel grandeur. Having ended a fallow decade and a half by carrying off the Fairs Cup the previous spring, the 1970–71 model, setting as it did the trend for the dispassionate acquisition of silverware over the subsequent two decades, simply rammed home the message sent by Brazil: English football lacked joy. Thus did jealousy beget mass wrath.

With one exception. Charlie George, the Johnny Rotten of the park. Lofty, leggy and decidedly lippy, that stringy, dark beige mane singled him out as a horse for another course. Had he not broken an ankle in two places at Goodison Park in the act of scoring on the opening day of the 1970–71 season, we might have been more forgiving of his club. After all, by the time the tasty geezer from Holloway finally returned against Portsmouth in the fourth round of the FA Cup, six mind-numbing months had meandered by. Plunk, plunk, fizz. In Cup and League alike Charlie proved an instant pick-me-up, making and taking chances with astonishing alacrity for a 20-year-old. His was the fulminating drive that clinched the Double at Wembley, his the most solipsistic act of celebration ever enacted on Middlesex soil: flat back on the sacred turf, eyes to the skies, arms at quarter-to-nine and three-fifteen, Christ awaiting deliverance from the cross. But for him, the Double would not even have been a single. As with Liam Brady, it seemed criminal that such audacious impertinence should have been surrounded by so much regimented, cheerless efficiency. As odd couples go, even Keith Harris and Orville had their work cut out competing with Charlie George and Arsenal.

Not that Charlie had much option. The youngest of four and Bob and Elizabeth George's only boy, his earliest memory remains Coronation Day. Not content with garbing their two-year-old in red and white, Bob and Elizabeth pinned a card on his chest identifying him as Jimmy Logie, the Arsenal and Scotland alumnus. Another one-cap wonder. Home was a five-room council maisonette on the Holloway Road: on Friday afternoons, with a half-decent pair of binoculars, you could spot the Highbury groundsman touching up his lines. 'Supporting the Arsenal wasn't strictly a family thing,' Charlie avers. 'My cousin, Horace Woodward, played alongside Bill Nicholson at Tottenham, and I think my dad was originally a Tottenham fan. My brother-in-law took me to Highbury one day and after that it was the norm.' Only an Arsenal junkie calls his fix *the* Arsenal.

Those 'I Love Charlie' badges adorning the lapels of a thousand crombies in 1971 celebrated Charlie more for where he came from than what he did. The wealthy, after all, rarely shop at the local supermarket. A couple of years ago, or so the North Bank regulars fondly imagined, he might have been standing next to them. Jostling, urging, cajoling. Hurling the same taunts at the away enclosure, guzzling down the same tepid hot dogs. Letting go. He was one of them, and now he was their representative, an MP with street cred. Hindered as much by a clash of philosophies with Bertie Mee as by his own volatile combativeness and the unscrupulousness of others, Charlie would make just 113 appearances for Arsenal in five seasons, and ultimately spend most of his career in loyal opposition. For all that, the Gordian knot remains tightly ravelled. The boy became a man at Derby County, but the image is forever Highbury. 'The first time I went back there with Derby I'd just scored four goals in a European Cup tie against Real Madrid – and we'd lost. All my mates were there, my whole family. This bloke come running out the North Bank with a bouquet of flowers. 'Fucking hell!' I thought to myself. You get all goose-pimply. That's what I call appreciation. Even when I go to games now I still get a chant.'

'He felt a good time on the North Bank was actually getting into a fight,' observed Maurice Gran, a Holloway Comprehensive classmate who tells the tale of a Cup tie at Peterborough when Charlie nipped into a bakery and half-inched a tray crammed with cream buns, which he duly delighted in throwing indiscriminately at anyone sporting a blue and white scarf. 'We always used to stand round in the playground talking about our ambitions and he said his ambition was to play for Arsenal and score the winning goal in a Cup final that is one of the thousand best. And he did it . . . he's done it and that was the undoing of him. It should have happened to him later.'

There are not too many restaurants outside the West End that can attract a full house on a chilly Monday evening in January. One such is

The Oslo Court, secreted in the bowels of a posh if vaguely tatty apartment block located no more than a Pat Jennings punt from Lord's. So well hidden, in fact, that, for all my 19 years in the area, its existence had totally eluded me. Then again, it is a division or two out of my usual league. If Daisy's voice reminded Jay Gatsby of money, those jabbering away inside reeked of Amex gold cards and Swiss bank accounts. Here a cooing pair of City dinkies and an Egyptian family reunion, there Nigerian dignitaries and dicky bows, and sharp suits doing sharper deals. The cuisine, predominantly French, is adequate, no more, the middle-aged waiters stealing the show with their bustling bonhomie, scuttling between the closely grouped tables like worker ants in bow ties. As culture shocks go, meeting Charlie George in such uptown surrounds was not unlike bumping into a Getty in a chippy.

That said, from Maître d' to barman, the staff greet him as they might a kid brother on parole. He hadn't shown his face for a year or two. Much as he has a weakness for fine cuisine, the pockets no longer extend quite this far. The pub in the New Forest, the marriage to his childhood sweetheart: both ancient history. The garage in King's Cross – liquidated the previous autumn. Charlie's principal means of support are a regular Saturday public relations gig at the Arsenal Museum and the odd TV appearance. He lives in Hackney, plays golf as often as he can, trains at Highbury a couple of days a week, and is contemplating trying for an FA coaching badge. Every Arsenal home game finds him perched in the East Stand. In nearby Mountgrove Road you can get a full English breakfast for £2 at the Charlie George Café, where the walls are littered with Marilyns and Stans and Ollies, images of its namesake mysteriously conspicuous by their absence. Charlie, unquestionably, is still smitten. 'Frank [McLintock] played for Leicester for a long time, but he would say he's an Arsenal supporter now. There's something about the club. I don't know what it is, but as you walk in that stadium you've got the bust of Herbert Chapman and the whole place just hits you. You go down the dressing-rooms and it's something else. I graduated from the terraces to the pitch and now I go back there and I'm always made to feel welcome. I still get a buzz.' Well, I suppose mass-murderers have wives too.

Neither as lean nor as long as memory had dictated, Charlie cuts a smart, almost elegant figure. Trimmer and receding though it is, that mane still dusts those clothes-hanger shoulders, the only outward indication of rebellious youth. The second finger on his right hand is stumpy, the legacy of a spat with a lawnmower in 1980. At first he is all beams and *badinage*, but once we get past the baked avocado and the

Chianti kicks in, a sombreness takes over. Serious-minded, thoughtful, he laments the ills of English football with the muted despair of a parent whose child has been missing too long to encourage optimism. The past is not a country he relishes visiting. Reminiscences are delivered in a deep baritone, Norf London a la mode, tinged with resignation. Defiant words fail to stem the undercurrent of regret. 'I never lose sleep over it' is a phrase that crops up too frequently to be completely convincing. Behind a pair of those goggle-specs that turn ordinary menfolk into Emerson Fittipaldi, the eyes are sad when they are not vacant. Above and beyond all this, though, is the profound sense of nobility.

'One thing that annoyed me was that I wasn't given more than one chance to play for England. I don't care who you are you have to have at least seven to ten games at international level because it *is* different. You cannot say I was not an international player because I only played 60 minutes. Revie picked three central strikers, Keegan, Stuart Pearson and myself. To me, Stuart was a lovely player, but he couldn't lace my boots. Very limited. I don't want to be disrespectful but I don't think he could lace my left boot, let alone my right. So there was no wide man. I ended up laying behind those two but I just didn't know where I was supposed to go. None of us knew where we were running. Everything got cluttered up. We did score just before the interval, when Kevin and I were involved in the build-up to Stuart's goal, but at half-time it was pointed out we needed someone wide on the flanks to provide the crosses so essential for a player like Stuart to play back to goalscorers coming from behind – myself and Kevin. "I want you to go down the wing," Revie said to me. I told him I wasn't a winger and that was pretty much it. A left-winger, Gordon Hill, came on about 15 minutes later and that was the end of me: as I came off, Revie went to shake my hand and I went, "Fuck you," and went straight up the tunnel. He never said a word to me about my performance. I've watched the game over and over again and I was as good if not better than 80 per cent of 'em.'

Frank McLintock accuses system before player. 'It annoys me when players don't achieve all they can. Charlie definitely didn't. He should have been one of the greats, should have played regularly for England. He should have wised up before he did. All the rebels had a very fixed idea of how the game should be played. Must be all too easy when you've got that much talent. They took liberties. It was all "bollocks to that" and "who's he to tell me what to do?". Foreign players are more dedicated. They realise there's a fortune in it for them so they don't do anything to the detriment of their career. The problem is, we're stereotyped in this country. We make players into all-rounders.

We tried to turn Hoddle into a Bryan Robson. If all these maverick characters had played anywhere else they'd all have won more than 40 caps.'

McLintock is in no doubt about Charlie's attributes. 'He could play as a double centre-forward or an attacking midfielder. He was very skinny at first but he filled out, and with his range he was best suited to midfield. Tremendous vision, tremendous shot – when did you ever see him tap one in? Some of the things he did in training reminded me of Best. We'd just look at each other in amazement.' Bob Wilson remembers one particular training routine wherein he would hoof the ball in the general vicinity of Mars and challenge Charlie to kill it. 'He always did. He was the touch of genius in the side. He was born with similar gifts to Best and built like Cruyff – incredible thighs, whippet-like top.'

'He could do the unpredictable,' admired George Graham, 'hit crossfield balls of 30 or 40 yards, no problem.' From a purely footballing perspective, Graham is also certain where the flaw lay. 'His biggest failing was that he never got involved enough in a game. He'd play for five or ten minutes then disappear for 20 or 30.' Ay, there's the nub. Or at least it was with Bertie Mee and his fellow disciples of work rate, the wonder drug that allows athletes to pretend they're footballers. Within six months of sealing the Double, having just made a remarkably swift recovery from a cartilage operation, Charlie was dropped. Mee did not actually use the word 'lazy', of course, but the inference was unmistakable. 'I feel that once he superimposes a higher work-rate on his outstanding individual ability,' explained the manager, 'he will be back in the first team.' Instructed to at least look busy, Charlie went on the offensive. 'I know I'm not getting into the game enough. It isn't that I'm not running. I'm trying to find space all the time. But I'm being pushed back into defence. Instead of someone marking me, I'm the marker.'

Infuriation lingers. 'People here always question your temperament. Does he work hard enough? They always said that about me. That Charlie George, he's lazy. But the team is made up of 11 different players. You've got your runners, your tacklers, your workhorses and your gifted players who are going to win you games. All those abilities have to be utilised. Trouble with this country is that as soon as we see anyone with ability we want to knock them down. We want to curb people's enthusiasm because it might go astray. But look at Brazil. It was nice to see people with such great talent win the World Cup the way they did in 1970. The talent they had was just phenomenal. It was unhealthy. Pele, Rivelino, Tostão, Jairzinho, Clodoaldo, Gerson – oooh, that left foot. It was frightening, wasn't it? I know there was that period in the Seventies when Brazil adopted a harder, European style, but, generally speaking, you know, even when they get beat, the philosophy is never really going to change. Our football is never going to change the world but, the way they play, they could.

'The hardest thing in the world is to get that talent. All right, it's got to be used in the right way, but we seem to want to put a ball and chain round it and keep it there. "He's got to do this for the team," they say. But if someone's got ability he should be told to get out there, take this bloke on, take that bloke on. If you lose the ball, you lose it. There are ten other players in the team. So what if he beats someone three or four times and knocks it in the net, so what if he does that once a game or once every two games. We just want to keep that talent suppressed instead of nurturing it and suffering it. Look at most of the great occasions in football history, the vital goals: the players who make those moments have had that special talent. Gerd Muller was a great six-yard player, but what did he do besides that? What do you say to him? "Why don't you chase back?" He'd laugh at you.'

Charlie's attitude to money mirrored this cavalier *modus operandi*. 'Obviously, the money was nice, but I never really thought of football as the money. I enjoyed it, it was a good way of earning a living. I've always been the same as Stan [Bowles]. Never invested a penny. Money is spent. Money has never been my god. I think I could have utilised my name a lot more than I did, but I just didn't fancy it. As soon as I finished I just wanted to get home to the family. I did do a bit of dabbling, mind. I had a column in *The Daily Express* the year after we won the Double. I was also good mates with a *Daily Mirror* photographer so we used to get a few shots in the papers, including one of me as Gary Glitter, complete with eyeliner and thigh-high boots. I even recorded a single, 'A Love Song for My Lady', but it was never released. There was an advert for eggs, "E for B and Charlie George", but I never had the foggiest what that was about and nor did anyone else. I've gambled a lot – horses, dogs, you name it I've probably done it. I wish I'd never gambled.

'Mind you, I always moaned about my wages at Arsenal. Because of my age I was at the bottom of the loyalty-based bonus system. I was on peanuts. I left there and doubled my wages straight away. I was so determined to get away I gave up my signing-on fee by demanding a transfer. Derby paid one hundred thousand quid for me and I didn't see a penny. Dave Mackay couldn't believe how easy it was to sign me. I was naïve. All I wanted to do was play football. Looking back, I wish I had gone abroad when I was young. I would have been appreciated more, for sure. I'd be a wealthier man than I am now. But when I went to play for Bulova in Hong Kong, although I was earning good money, it meant nothing. I didn't enjoy it there so I went home. I could have gone to Zurich when I was at Derby. They called one Saturday while I was in Australia with my wife and daughter. I think they'd just been beaten by Liverpool in the European Cup semi-final. Derby had given me permission to play for St George's in Sydney: it was 21 hours by plane to Zurich. I didn't fancy the flight or the club but I had to do it. We all went to this hotel where we met the club officials, and I decided to make such outrageous demands that they'd have to turn me down. I asked for a Mercedes car, a flat. You name it, I asked for it. Then I said I was going upstairs for a shower and they could let me know when I came back down. They agreed to everything. I had to think quick. "Tell you what," I said, "I'm going home now, phone me at this number tomorrow and I'll tell you what I've decided." When they did ring I just said I was staying put. Just didn't fancy it.'

Charlie knows full well that wilful spontaneity was as integral to his charm as his undoing. 'Has it ever struck you that if Charlie George wasn't a brilliant, sensitive, temperamental footballer, he'd be a long, thin, lank-haired, loud-mouthed yob?' Thus wondered a caption under a *Daily Express* mugshot of Charlie published in 1972. The Gazza of his day, no English footballer of the Seventies stimulated such extremes of emotion. Distorted both by the fourth estate and his own incautious tongue, reviled by those who had only ever met him via cathode ray or newsprint, the King of Highbury wore a ragamuffin's crown. Abdication then freed him from the ties that bind, from the handcuffs of conformity. He found a supportive new court at Derby; by the end of his first season there, the Fleet Street flunkeys were voting him the second-best player in the League. He was 27 when he sustained the knee injury that made him half the player he had been: it seemed only proper that it should have been inflicted, however accidentally, by Ray Kennedy, a fellow member of the Class of '71. In the era of Chairman Alf and The Godfather, Charlie was the most predictable of victims.

Not that the hostility was wholly unjustified. Despite the North Bank's assertions to the contrary, there were two Charlie Georges. Dr Charlie was an absolute lamb. 'He would really gee us up in the dressing-room at Derby,' notes Roy McFarland, 'but then you'd look at his changing peg and he'd have shoe trees for his boots. When he was getting changed you'd see him folding his socks. Most players fling everything on the floor.' 'Charlie is never different, never moody,'

Susan George asserted following their marriage in December 1971, nine years after their first date. 'Honestly, no one believes me. You'd never know if he was playing for the first team or for an amateur club. I've never known any tension with Charlie – he's not like that. He doesn't ever come home and think, "Oh, the game. I must go to bed at nine o'clock." We're not "in" on the "in scene" or partygoers. We go to the same places and have the same friends. I know it sounds draggy but it's true. We decided over a drink one Sunday to marry on the next Thursday. We wanted it to be our little wedding. My mum and dad and brother came, and Charlie's dad and his sister and brother-in-law. We went to Grosvenor House for a meal then to the Talk of the Town to see Bruce Forsyth, and Shirley Bassey was at the next table. It was quite a nice evening.'

Mr George, in contrast, used to grab his shinguards and pick a target. Insolence and aggression were intrinsic to the onfield persona. 'He was the lad off the North Bank,' asserts McLintock, 'full of brashness and cockiness. He was very outspoken, even when it came to the manager. Even at 17 he didn't show much respect. To him, everyone was a wanker.'

Bob Wilson saw another side. 'There was a façade to him. He was all bluff. He was quiet in the dressing-room. At half-time I'd gee him up. "What about that ball I hit from 70 yards?" he'd say. He would cling on to that one moment. He was a very complex character.'

'He also had a bit of a temper so he liked to tackle,' adds McLintock, 'to prove himself as a man. He was very dynamic and went in very hard. He was very volatile, it made him the player he was. If someone threatened him he wouldn't shirk.'

So was this a protective mechanism, a route to survival in a thuggish climate? To a degree, yes. Provocation, from opposition and crowds alike, was freely available. That ankle Charlie fractured at Goodison at the outset of the Double season certainly forewarned of the company he would be keeping. 'Although I'd been brought off during the first leg of the Fairs final in Anderlecht and Ray Kennedy came on and scored, I was the one who played in the home leg. Then I had a good pre-season. I felt great, ready for my first season in the first team. Then, in the very first game, you score and the keeper fucking breaks your ankles open. I'm not sure whether it was an accident or not, but put it this way, if Westie [Gordon West, the Everton keeper] had come out with his hands it wouldn't have happened, would it?' By the same token, Charlie's admiration for Leeds betrays the lack of innocence. 'Most people thought Johnny Giles was a dirty bastard. Yeah, Leeds were dirty, but they were professional about it. I admired them for it. They had it down pat, the way Revie organised them. If there was trouble it wasn't one player involved it was all fucking 11 of them. I loved that.' Neither was Charlie's other cheek for turning. 'If they kick me or one of the others,' he revealed in his *Daily Express* column in March, 1972, 'well I just nut them. I call it me "flick". It's a joke among us at Arsenal . . . it means being brought up in Holloway where it's tough and you learn from the pram to nut people who pick on you.' He was fortunate to escape with a warning from an FA Disciplinary Committee conveniently anxious to brush reality under the carpet.

Those vengeful urges nevertheless cost Charlie any chance of becoming the first player to turn out for two English Double-winning teams. Vigorously defending their League title, Derby were a week or so away from an FA Cup semi-final against Manchester United when Stoke came to the Baseball Ground for a League fixture. 'Dennis Smith was going down the line to clear the ball and it sort of entered my mind to go over there and get stuck in. It wasn't macho or anything. It was just like when someone hits you at school. You go looking for them. Fortunately for him he got out of the way just as I was coming at him and I can remember hitting the floor, hard. I pulled my shoulder right out. I never found out for another three weeks that I'd fractured my elbow too. But that was beside the fucking point. You want to go in and do someone, you know what I mean, and come out worse.' Without Charlie, Derby faded in the closing furlongs and wound up empty-handed.

The mutually affectionate relationship between Charlie and the Derby faithful surprised many. Four years earlier, after all, the Baseball Ground had been the scene of a ghastly FA Cup fifth round tie against Arsenal, a Tourneur-scripted Hammer flick that earned notoriety via a mere gesture from the man who earned the visitors a replay. *'Where's your handbag, where's your handbag, where's your handbag, Charlie George, where's your ha-and ba-ag, Char-lie George?'* The taunts were incessant. When Charlie slotted in his second goal, tying up the scores, he sprinted over to the source of the abuse, came to a halt and flourished a double Harvey Smith. 'GROW UP, LAD!' howled *The Sun* above a shot of Charlie with digits pointing heavenwards (*The Express* contented itself with a quieter 'Time to grow up, George'). 'What the hell is Charlie George playing at?' continued *The Sun*, the same esteemed arbiter of decorum that would one day soar to the heights of 'Up Yours, Delors'. 'What on earth is he trying to prove? It was stupid, thoughtless, dangerous. A foolhardy gesture to cheapen the reputation of Arsenal and devalue the name of football. It could also have sparked off a riot. We say that Charlie George the genius is acting like a jackass.' Quite rightly, the FA let him off with a warning.

Charlie is unrepentant. 'The Derby fans were giving me terrible stick. Suddenly, Sammy Nelson went down the line and hit a cross-shot. The ball bounced out to the edge of the area and I smashed it into the roof of the net. My immediate reaction was to run from one end of the pitch to the other, sticking my fingers up at them. It wasn't meant to incite trouble. Anyway, even if I did offend people, they must have liked it because they kept coming. I was always the one they had a go at when we played away from home. Whether it was because I had long hair, or I was flash, I don't know, but they knew I could play. Then again, I always knew I could play. I didn't need anyone to tell me. I was very self-assured, even when I was a young kid. I did what *I* thought was right. Whether it was right or not didn't make any difference. I was always my own man and always will be. I didn't cultivate a brash image, it was just the way I was when I did my job. If you could do the job you were cocky, and arrogant with it. I was brash, I was arrogant. I used to take the piss out of people, make mugs out of them. Sit on the ball, kneel on the ball. Sure it wound people up. You got whacked back but you just accept it, don't you. The funny thing is, for all the total, absolute abuse I gave them that time, when Dave Mackay took me there I built up a rapport with the Derby fans straight away. We always enjoyed a laugh and a joke. If you scored you showed the people paying your wages some affection. People who score then immediately run back to the centre-circle might as well be fucking dead. You've got to give something back. When I'm working at the Arsenal on a Saturday I get people coming up and saying how they appreciated the way I played. That's nice.'

Loudly as he exhorted Eastham and Baker, Skirton and Haverty, Charlie's role model was Denis Law. 'I remember him as a youngster playing at Highbury for Manchester City, 5–4 to Arsenal I think. He scored a hat-trick or something. He'll do me, I thought. Different. I loved the way he wore his cuffs rolled back. I don't think I ever consciously tried to be different: I just wanted to be myself.' Schooldays in Holloway brought plenty of lip and negligible education. While Bob Wilson was still on amateur forms, he took Charlie for PE and found his hands full. To the rest of the class he was 'Mr Wilson'; Charlie preferred a 'How ya goin', Bob?'. Not that that dissuaded Wilson from throwing the 13-year-old in with the 15-year-olds, so blatant was the contrast between Charlie and his peers. Frequently ejected from class for one bit of rank insubordination or another, he was eventually expelled. Next stop Hugh Myddleton in Clerkenwell. 'It's no good looking at me, I'm going to Arsenal,' he advised his careers officer. 'I hated school, hated it. I wish I'd had an education now, but you can't go back, can you. That's why I made sure my daughter went to a private school. Not that I wasn't given the chance: I just didn't learn anything. I started training over at the Arsenal when I was 12 or 13, couple of times a week. The scout was George Male, a lovely man and also a great player. I thought it was just the norm, that when I left school I'd go to Arsenal.'

'It was obvious,' Male would reflect. 'This kid had got it. All the confidence, all the touches were there already. It was just a case of waiting and watching for him to reach the age when we could approach him.'

The goals flowed at Youth and Combination level, a hundred in three seasons. At 18 Charlie made his League debut at home to Everton. Bob George's proudest hour had come on Christmas Day, 1926: a hat-trick for Islington Boys at Highbury. The potential was said to be there, but ambitions in that sphere were soon overtaken by realism and a foreman's job with Gestetner. The odds against scaling the top of football's greasy pole are always forbidding. By the time the first team beckoned for Charlie, his employers estimated having spent £77,000 in order to ferret him out. During the course of the 1965–66 season, Arsenal's 27 scouts attended 1,836 school matches across the UK. Sixty of the boys were selected for summer trials whilst another 80 Londoners began attending training, Charlie amongst them. Directed by chief scout Gordon Clarke and his assistant Ernie Collett, the operation cost £16,000, comprising payments and expenses for scouts in addition to fares, kit and accommodation for the kids. At the end of term, nine of the locals were offered apprenticeships. The next 12 months were given over to training – Monday, Tuesday and Wednesday plus Thursday morning – with lectures and instructional films breaking things up on a Thursday afternoon, followed by a game for the third or fourth team on Saturday. Unaccustomed to so much running, Charlie threw up on the first day. Wages and allowances (digs, travel, equipment, insurance and medical attention) totted up to £28,000. After a further year, the nine were duly whittled down to six: two had their contracts cancelled, a third turned pro and was promptly handed a free transfer. The remaining trio also signed as full-time professionals and rose to the Combination side, whereupon one was sold, leaving Charlie and Eddie

Kelly. Running a reserve team ran to £51,000, the total outlay of £95,000 offset by the £18,000 raised through selling ex-apprentices. From 1960 to 1969, Arsenal took on 86 apprentices: ten graduated to the first team. In order to get to Charlie they claimed to have sifted through 40,392 aspirants.

So Charlie landed a 40,000-to-1 shot. 'My father made it possible, his enthusiasm made it possible. He was a working-class man and playing football can be expensive. I loved him, he was my idol. When I came back from Hong Kong he was dying of cancer: once I lost him there was no interest in the game for me whatsoever, so I gave up. You know . . . I mean . . . losing him was . . . what does football mean? Football doesn't mean anything. It doesn't mean nothing. I'm pretty sure he was proud of me but he never gave me a due. He would tell my wife I played well. I'd come off after a game and I'd say, "How'd I play, Dad?" and he'd say, "yeah, all right," which was probably great, really.'

Don Howe, the Arsenal coach, was beside himself, likening Charlie to a Bobby Charlton with Greavesian instincts – and that was *before* he made his senior début. 'We had been looking for a truly gifted player to complete the team,' enthused Bertie Mee. 'Suddenly we realised that in young George we had all the flair and instinct of the man for whom we were searching. Star quality oozed from everything he did.' Mee 'hand-picked' Charlie's early outings, 'so that he wouldn't burn himself out before he matured'. Displaying a precocious sense of occasion, he collared national attention during the climactic stages of Arsenal's 1969–70 Fairs Cup campaign, the quarter-final against Dynamo Bacau and the semi against Ajax bringing four goals. He was a consistent force in the home leg of the final against Anderlecht, Kelly, John Radford and Jon Sammels accounting for the three unanswered strikes that overturned a 3–1 deficit and earned Highbury its first pot since the 1952–53 Championship.

Compared with Leeds, Arsenal were pristine in thought and deed. Sure, they harboured in their midst one Peter Storey, that apotheosis of the anti-footballer. Frank McLintock and Pat Rice, moreover, were as forthright as any when a man had to do what a man had to do. Yet even when Bob Wilson was diving at the feet of opposing forwards in order to slake his thirst for muddy laces, the dirt seldom stuck. As befits the team dynamo, sweat oozed from George Armstrong as if pumped out by some high-octane garden sprinkler, yet somehow, despite that scruffy moptop, he always looked neat and tidy, shirt tucked precisely into shorts, socks tied tight. Hair clipped just so, never mussed, even if it did look as if it had spent the night under a fruit bowl, Peter Simpson was Highbury's John Steed, an unflappable defender more familiar with perspicacity than perspiration.

Any defence that concedes just six goals in 21 home assignments has to be a bit useful: reinforced by the Storey stiletto, that was certainly the basis of Arsenal's consistency. Owing his initial call to Charlie's broken ankle, Ray Kennedy was Radford's powerful abettor on the front line, a teenage tank a stride or two away from the elegantly perceptive playmaker who would emerge at Anfield. Equally strong in the air and nimbler than he looked on the ground, Radford was an even greater triumph of toil over touch, even if he did clutch his cuffs. My favourite member of the supporting cast was Kelly, a sleek, energetic Scottish midfield plotter adaptable enough to play sweeper when Arsenal had their fleeting dalliance with Total Football. In a similar mould was the boyish Sammels, a chubby McCartney facially, the starlet who never quite progressed as he should and was driven away by the crowd that once swooned to his every feint. George 'Stroller' Graham, a gifted striker at Chelsea now manoeuvring just behind the front men, was the same only much, much more so. Graham also had the classiest hairdo, a rectangular, perfectly symmetrical, oily black number barely distinguishable from the one adopted by Alain Delon's Marseilles hood in *Borsalino*. The Award for Imaginative Folicle Sculpting, however, went to McLintock's crinkle cut. Shirt liberated from elasticated waistband, Charlie, needless to say, was the only one whose hair dared creep below that sacrosanct collar.

Arsenal prospered during Charlie's enforced idleness in the autumn of 1970, their attacking focus symbolised by an avalanche of headed goals, yet only once did they enchant the senses. When Liverpool came to Highbury at the end of November, the hosts spent most of the afternoon foundering on a well-organised Mersey rearguard, Storey's presence in a No. 8 shirt offending the soul as well as the eye. These, after all, were the days when a number had value, when it meant something, when most positions had a corresponding numeral, a direct and automatic translation. Okay, so Roger Hunt's No. 21 and Martin Peters's No. 16 in the World Cup final had shown that certain liberties could be taken, as did Bobby Charlton's No. 9, but No. 6 was still left-half and Bobby Moore, No. 7 right wing and George Best. Peter Cormack had yet to escape Hibernian: the idea of a midfielder pretending to be a centre-half had yet to be hatched. What right did Storey have to impersonate an inside-right? Then, thankfully, came some 'gorgeousity' from the substitute, Graham. Pressure by Radford and Kennedy forced the Liverpool defence into some intricate, hurried close passing ten yards outside their own box. Sammels stole in to rob Ian Ross and find Graham to his left. Drawing one defender, Graham flicked the ball disdainfully to his right, back to Sammels, who lobbed over the hulking, statuesque Larry Lloyd in the centre of the area. Graham continued down the inside-left channel and volleyed with his right, the ball looping in a parabola above and beyond the leaping Ray Clemence. Bill Shankly screamed offside, albeit none too convincingly.

Lucky Arsenal? Not really. It was the one-dimensional nature of the scoreline that started all that tosh. Take Southampton on 27 December. The second dimension that afternoon was Eric Martin, the visitors' Fred Flintstone of a keeper and proprietor of a pair of sideburns that bore an uncanny resemblance to those thick, left-handed ticks Mr Latham scrawled in my composition book to express approval. Undeterred by a snowstorm, Martin had an absolute blinder, securing a goalless draw when Arsenal might have won by six or seven. In a similarly frustrating bout with Manchester City on 6 February, Arsenal filched the only goal with five minutes left, yet should have had a dozen, so completely did their own vigour smother the threat of Bell, Summerbee and Lee. Charlie had just proved his fitness by scoring twice in that comeback Cup-tie at Portsmouth: this was his showcase. The next afternoon, the capital's armchair millions finally discovered what all the fuss was about.

The overture was frantic, grotesquely one-sided. Arthur Mann flung himself across goal as if in training for a bungee jump, clearing Armstrong's effort off the line with Joe Corrigan well beaten. A couple of minutes later the giant keeper – you had to have been a Martian not to know that, at six-foot four, Corrigan was the tallest player in the League – soared to tip over after Kennedy had chested down McNab's chip and hooked a waist-high volley with his left. Armstrong's corner almost deceived Corrigan: when Radford headed the rebound past the stranded keeper, the ball was cleared off the line as the referee blew for a foul. Then Corrigan swooped low at the near post to deny Sammels as he latched on to Radford's flick. Then he blocked Kennedy's header after Charlie had taken possession on the edge of his own D, cruised upfield and found his man with the outside of that radar scanner of a right foot.

What ensued was a bit like watching Mike Tyson belting the living daylights out of a punchbag. Charlie intercepted a Francis Lee pass in the left-back position, ten yards outside his own penalty area, sauntered on, mane flapping in the gusty breeze, then released Armstrong on the left wing 20 yards inside the City half. Armstrong returned the favour, laying the ball in for Charlie, running through, to head across to Radford on the left edge of the area. When Radford's cross was blocked the ball ballooned out to Rice, who centred once more. Again it was cleared, but again Armstrong and Sammels were closing people down. Back it came to Storey for a cross that arrowed in towards Kennedy and Radford at the far post. Corrigan dove at two sets of feet, and when the ball emerged from the mêlée George Heslop, whose underpopulated scalp made him a dead ringer for Bobby Charlton's grandfather, plunged to head off the line. Referee Gow was so puffed he blew up for an imaginary foul on the keeper.

For the best part of 90 seconds, Arsenal had battered away. Not one City instep had made clean or effective contact. The only comparable spell of sustained pressure I can ever recall was the build-up to a stupendous try by Mike Slemen for the Lions in South Africa, forwards and backs interweaving with such dexterity and intuitive anticipation that not one opposition hand got to grips with the ball for fully two minutes. This, though, was the scattergun approach, relentless in its intensity, restricted in scope. In the middle of an England training session, Des Anderson, one of Don Revie's assistants, would subsequently contend that Charlie was 'two steps ahead of everyone else', which is precisely how he came across that afternoon. It took a defender, Simpson, to unpick the lock. Surging from his own half, he spotted a gap yawning between Corrigan and the far post and unleashed a speculative cross-shot that the keeper could only parry: Radford poked it in. Charlie was first to the scene, leaping into Radford's arms and saluting the crowd with upraised arm. 'The new Charlie George,' drooled Jimmy Hill on *The Big Match*, 'reminds me of Johnny Haynes. Look at that with the outside of the foot!' Cut to a 40-yard lofted pass to Kennedy after wrongfooting Oakes on the halfway. Close control, balance, sleight of foot, the boy had it all. Malcolm Allison remembers it well. 'Charlie was spraying passes all over the place that day. It was the one time I ever saw him go looking for the ball instead of waiting for it.'

Defeats at the Baseball Ground and White Hart Lane were overcome by Arsenal's rigour at Highbury, that win over City the second in a run of nine successive victories that would carry them to the title, a sequence that yielded a mere 13 goals. The samba was exclusively Charlie's province. Adrenaline-a-go-go in front of a crowd of 62,087, he turned the faucet full on against Chelsea, themselves fresh and frisky after a 3–1 drubbing of Leeds. Neighbourly it was not. Storey crunched Hudson during the initial exchanges and received an irreverent grin in return. Ron Harris arched his eyebrows in baffled innocence when pulled up for another foul: 'Went for the ball, ref, promise.' Pausing between some argy-bargy of his own, Charlie supplied the *divertissement*. Dummying over Armstrong's low cross, he made space for Kennedy to rifle home a shot. Later, intercepting John Dempsey's ill-directed header, he hared down the inside-right channel then pulled off the double-bluff, feinting to pass inside then doing so the instant the defender committed himself. This found Radford on the edge of the Chelsea box, back to goal, who in turn played it straight back into Charlie's path. Now running right to left, he sent a first-time pass towards the far side of the area where Kennedy chested down and drilled just inside John Phillips' right-hand post.

Charlie's most telling stroke, however, occurred at home to a moderate Newcastle. Booked in the first half, the game was still goalless when, roving from right to left across the front edge of the Magpies area, he shot against one defender with his right, controlled the rebound, evaded another challenge then drove, left-footed and off-balance, past Ian McFaul. That same afternoon, Leeds lost at home to West Brom and Don Revie donned his world-is-against-us grimace. Arsenal were top – on goal average – for the first time that season. When they played West Brom a week later, this time at The Hawthorns, they came away with a point, the margin by which they would finally edge out Leeds. Charlie fashioned both goals: a shot from outside the box cannoning off the keeper for McLintock to convert the rebound; foot under the ball for a lofted through pass to the unmarked Storey. One day off and back they came, to be undone by a controversial Jack Charlton goal at Elland Road. Leeds, though, had dropped points at Huddersfield and Newcastle that month. Take the last two games and the job was done.

Arsenal's ninth 1–0 win came against Stoke on 1 May, their tenth and last at White Hart Lane 48 hours later. With two-and-a-half minutes to go, Charlie chased a ball that seemed certain to be Cyril Knowles's, then curled in a low pass with the outside of his left foot for Radford to shoot and Pat Jennings to punch away. Armstrong collected on the left side of the area, near the byeline, and crossed for Kennedy to power home a header as emphatic as any Tommy Lawton ever nutted. Resplendent in grey suit, blue shirt and white tie with shiny speckles, Charlie stood second in line to McLintock when Arsenal were awarded the freedom of Islington, the mayor lauding them for their 'success, their consistently high standards of sportsmanship and the pleasure they brought the people of Islington'. Shame about the rest of the country.

The FA Cup final was the following Saturday. It was the nearest Arsenal had been to a home tie, having traipsed from Yeovil to Fratton Park to Maine Road to Filbert Street before the semi-final against Stoke, whose 5–0 victory at the Victoria Ground in September had been the catalyst for Eric Morecambe's Saturday night jibes. Villa Park was where the 'lucky' tag stuck fast. Scenting Wembley for the first time in their history, Stoke went ahead when Storey's clearance cannoned in off Dennis Smith. Charlie's intrusions at the other end had hitherto provided Arsenal's knockout punch, most vividly against Manchester City, but it was he who gave away the second, casually underhitting a back pass for John Ritchie to nip in. Beginning when Storey rammed in a loose ball from the edge of the box, the revival was completed in injury time, the same player defeating a virtually motionless Gordon Banks from the spot after John Mahoney had handled McLintock's goalbound header. Strikes from Graham and Kennedy wrapped up the replay. Lucky Arsenal? Only in as much as they were fortunate to possess players with so much energy, selflessness and willpower.

On the morning of the final against a Liverpool side hovering between dynasties, Charlie was violently sick. Not that this was an unusual activity. 'I used to be sick before every game at Arsenal. It was just nerves. I couldn't eat. I used to burn up so much acid in my body. Just nerves. Funnily enough, when I went to Derby, it never happened. Crazy, isn't it? I suppose it could have been that I wasn't playing for my own club anymore. When I went to Derby I used to have a fag before the game. After the first year there I was even more relaxed. Christ knows why. Frank [McLintock] always used to say I was under such pressure at Arsenal because I was the local lad, and I was. If we played good it was down to me, if we played bad it was down to me. At the same time, I was fortunate that the fans never had a go at me, even when I played like a complete plonker.' The vast majority of the participants attained plonkerhood that afternoon. Fatigue and heat conspired to ensure an enervating affair only spared anonymity by its final chord. In extra-time, Steve Heighway deceived Wilson at his near post to quicken the Mersey beat, whereupon Kelly's worming apology for a drive proved almost as deceptive as Graham's claim to have applied the final touch. Time for rabbits to be plucked. Tightly marked, Charlie is fed by Radford then immediately sidefoots back. Radford carries the ball down the left, halfway betwixt the Liverpool area and inner part of the centre circle, then rolls it inside for Charlie, now a stride or two outside the box, a couple of yards left of centre. A short wind-up, a biff with the right. While Ray Clemence is still insistent that the ball kissed Larry

Lloyd as it whooshed past his right hand, he at least has the decency to acknowledge that it might not have made any difference. To the jury of red- and-white bobble hats there was no might about it. A marriage had been consummated.

But for that, it seems certain Charlie's official paymasters would have got shot of him long before they did. From that moment on during his tenure at Highbury, the lows outnumbered the highs, excesses such as that Baseball Ground salute tolerated because he was a good box office draw. At Wembley the following May, Allan Clarke of Leeds had yet to head the only goal of a noxious Centenary FA Cup final when Charlie's drive crashed past David Harvey for the bar to intervene. On the eve of the next season, Charlie, now living in comfort and comparative peace in Enfield, was placed on the transfer list at his own request, the asking price £300,000, a British record. Eddie Kelly and John Roberts joined him in the window. All three felt the disparity in wages and bonuses unduly favoured the older squad members. None, though, would be allowed to leave until 'suitable replacements have been found'. 'Once upon a time,' Geoffrey Green wrote disapprovingly in *The Times*, 'it was unthinkable that such a thing should even cross the mind of a player at Highbury. When the first man to do so hit the headlines in the 1930s – George Drury was the player concerned – it was said that the standards of Arsenal would soon begin to decline.' Roberts, Green contended, 'can be absolved ... since as an established full Welsh international he feels frustrated with reserve football for much of a season. George and Kelly on the other hand are reaching out into the club kitty ... It will serve both right if they are kept kicking their heels on the sidelines for a spell. Both, after all, achieved their present stature through Arsenal. Both seem to have forgotten that fact. As for George – for all his small triumphs that have brought publicity – he has never struck one as the type of player to do the name of Arsenal justice.'

Roberts left for Birmingham when Jeff Blockley was secured as a replacement in central defence. Uncovering another Kelly, let alone another Charlie, was a somewhat stiffer task. Charlie was in and out of the side over subsequent weeks. A booking against Manchester United in his first full outing was succeeded by another after he rose from the bench in the 74th minute against Chelsea, appeared to trample on Ron Harris and precipitated a 12-man brawl wherein he exchanged knuckle sandwiches with Steve Kember. If the press reaction was histrionic – *The Sun* reported that Harris, who was quite content to 'forgive and forget', had been rushed to hospital after 'a series of demented kicks in the chest left him coughing up blood' – Denis Hill-Wood, to his credit, was more broad-minded. 'I feel Charlie has been attracting a lot of unfavourable publicity because he is Charlie George,' maintained Arsenal's Old Etonian chairman. 'The referee took no action when he was supposed to have trampled on Harris. I see that Harris himself says it was nothing and the trouble only arose when another boy went for Charlie after that . . . It's true that Charlie is very excitable, but I don't believe that there is any vice in him. He's just dreadfully keen. Coming on near the end of a match is always difficult. Charlie was probably frustrated at having to sit and watch. I would hate him to go and I am sure he wants to stay.'

At first, Hill-Wood's words appeared perceptive. By October Charlie had signed a new contract. By November he was off the list and in the England Under-23 party, something of a mixed blessing for the *enfant terrible* who had so repeatedly professed himself more interested in club than country – and meant it. To Mee this constituted 'recognition for the fact that he has now matured in his attitude and behaviour . . . it has taken a tremendous conscious effort on his part. Indeed, he has lost a little bit of sparkle in recent matches through biting his lip to stay out of trouble. This is an attitude which has become part of his self-conscious. I'm sure we will soon see all the potential he has shown blossom totally. He had to create a new image and he is well on the way to it.'

Over the next two years, however, Charlie was on the bench as often as he was on the field. Compromise was dimming the spark, the rift between manager and problem child was widening. A fresh start was imperative, but when Arsenal at last agreed to release him shortly before Christmas 1974, the assassination of his character was so complete that Chelsea, Manchester City and Derby immediately scoffed at the £250,000 tag. At that figure, 'the most skilful footballer in Britain' (according to Johan Cruyff) was worth £100,000 less than Bob Latchford, the strictly head-down, one-paced target man for whom Everton had broken the British transfer record the previous February. The Derby manager, Dave Mackay, spelled out the general consensus: 'Charlie could become one of the world's great players, but I'm not prepared to pay big money to find out.' Charlie, Mackay continued, needed to 'apply himself week in, week out . . . I admire the boy's skill, and I hope it works out for him. It will be one of football's tragedies if he drifts into being just another player.'

By the time Mackay interrupted his summer holiday to discuss terms and persuade the Derby directors to change their stance, Charlie was so eager to get away he had voluntarily waived his 5 per cent cut.

The fee, more significantly, was now £100,000. Quite a bargain for the man Mackay believed could help transform English champions into European ones. Charlie's enthusiasm for Mackay was such that he accepted a lower basic wage than Tottenham had put on the table. The relief was immense. He hadn't been sleeping properly for weeks. At 24, he was metamorphosing into a grumpy old git. 'Bert [Mee] and I seldom speak to each other now,' he had confessed to *The News of the World* after a Football Combination game in January, 'and we'd both be better off if he sold me. I just don't understand why he's not playing me regularly. It has to be because he has something against me but I honestly don't know what it is. I admit that a couple of years ago I was hard to handle and gave Bert problems. He did me some favours in those days and I'm grateful, but I'm completely different now. I'll tell you just how much I've changed. Alan Ball had a go at me in a paper last week. Said he was sick about my name being bandied about when Arsenal lose and that I was only good for one game a month. That was unjustified and unfair. I protested to Bert about it and let it go at that. But a couple of years ago I'd have had a right go at Bally. Instead, I said to him: 'Thank you very much for that.' He didn't even look me in the eye. I get on well with the the lads at Highbury. John Radford and Geoff Barnett live near me and we have a drink at weekends. I don't go round upsetting any of them. There are some good kids coming along in the reserves, but they're inexperienced and they're making me look bad. I'm sticking passes about and they aren't seeing them. I'm wasting away and I'm only 24.'

Leaving Susan and baby Karra in Enfield while he went house-hunting, Charlie found a new place to dwell in the Derbyshire village of Littleover, far from Highbury's Heartbreak Hotel. The next phase of the rebirthing process saw him re-emerge with the bubbliest perm ever conceived outside the wardrobe department of *The Black and White Minstrel Show*: goodbye Nijinsky, hello Charlie the Giant Poodle. Forging 'an almost telepathic relationship' with Kevin Hector, Charlie revelled in the freedom Mackay granted him by floating him behind the strikers: 'Dave never really told you how to play. He gave you respect, treated players like adults. He drank himself.' Voted Midlands Player of the Year, Charlie's *pièce de résistance* was the left-footer on the run that launched a hat-trick against Real Madrid in the second round of the European Cup. He also scored in the Bernabeu, where Derby lost 5–1 to concede a thrilling tie 6–5: 'I must be the only player who ever scored four against Real Madrid and still finished on the losing side.' As Roy McFarland recalls, 'Charlie soon showed he cared, that he was relieved to be at Derby.' 'I know how difficult it must have been to leave Arsenal. I used to watch Liverpool and they were the only club I wanted to play for.'

Bruce Rioch was pleasantly surprised to find that man bore scant resemblance to myth. 'I had this image of him being a long, lanky-haired cockney, arrogant and self-opinionated, but nothing could be further from the truth. A very, very quiet man, a good pro. I enjoyed every second I ever played with the fella.' For Mackay, he had 'all the qualities. He was brilliant in midfield because he had a marvellous first touch. He could receive the ball on the centre spot, hit the outside-left with one sweeping pass with his left, and with his right hit the outside-right. How many players could do that today? None, I would expect.' A key factor in Tottenham's double-winning collective before a twice-broken leg supposedly reduced his effectiveness, Mackay became Clough's onfield orchestrator when the latter, together with Peter Taylor, dragged Derby from the crypt at the end of the Sixties. Mackay used to bet team-mates £50 that he could hit the bar from the halfway line six times out of ten – and clean up. To him, the Charlie who bestrode the Baseball Ground during the 1975–76 season was 'the best all-round front player in the game . . . the way he is playing puts him on a par with Johan Cruyff.'

Bobby Charlton had long since anointed Charlie as his successor in the national XI. Don Revie, or so it appeared, was in his corner now. 'There is little doubt that Arsenal's success [in 1970–71] would not have been possible without George,' the England boss informed readers of *The Evening Standard*. 'They were a well-organised, fit and determined team and George was the joker in the pack . . . [He] returned at a time when their stamina and concentration – the attributes which had kept them in the title reckoning in his absence – were beginning to fade . . . after that season George failed to mature as a player, due to his attitude towards the game. His talents were wasted by temperament. Mee has been criticised for letting him go but he had no option. I would probably have done the same. Considering his background, I thought Derby took a risk when they signed him. But that appears to have been a turning point in his career – he has since erased most of the doubts which many managers, including myself, had about his football character. Provided he continues to make a genuine contribution as a team player he will become one of the finest forwards this country has ever seen.'

Yet Revie's decision to cap Charlie against the Republic of Ireland in September 1976 can be interpreted as little more than a sop to the manager's myriad critics. What better way to get them off your back than pick the people's choice for a meaningless friendly sandwiched between World Cup qualifiers, shove the right-footed so-and-so on the left of two other central attackers then sit back and watch him vanish? 'Charlie George's first England appearance ended in humiliation at Wembley last night,' reported Brian Scovell in *The Daily Mail*, one of Revie's few allies. 'And rarely can an international debutant have been pulled off sooner. Ten out of ten for behaviour but not more than three out of ten for performance – 46 minutes had gone by before he made his one and only tackle. In the Revie phraseology he failed to close anyone down. He had started well. His first touch was a raking 25-yard pass, but he made only two more such passes. Mostly, he did the easy thing, settling for short balls to the nearest man. He made 30 passes in all, 23 on target. He had two shots, one blocked, one wide. His only solid contribution came with England's goal in the 43rd minute when he freed Keegan for the England captain to supply the cross from which Pearson scored. When Gordon Hill came out George took it in the right spirit – holding out a hand to Hill. Don Revie stepped forward to pat him on the back. "Do you want to sit on the bench or have a bath?" asked Revie. "I'll have a bath," said George.' (Charlie, of course, records the conversation as having been a teensy bit more abusive, but we'll let that pass.) 'He strode off to the dressing-room along the dog track,' continued Scovell, 'a sad and lonely figure.' An hour after the game he reappeared, signed a few autographs and attended the reception. Asked if he was disappointed, he said: "Not really. It was my first match, wasn't it?" He added: "Their full backs were coming through a bit".'

'Don Revie never really had a settled side,' confirms Roy McFarland, 'so I can't understand why Charlie didn't get a second chance. In any case, you would have thought a player in his first international would get to complete the full 90 minutes.'

More than a year passed before Mackay's successor at Derby, Tommy Docherty, summoned Charlie into his office to inform him that Ron Greenwood had invited him to play for England B. It took him all of 30 seconds to decline. 'It was an insult,' affirmed Docherty, 'like asking Cruyff to go on trial for Lincoln City. It was a slap in the face.' McFarland concurs: 'He had nothing to prove.' 'Why should I, at 27 years of age, have to travel with an England reserve side?' Charlie argued in *The Sunday Mirror*. 'Why should I have to prove what I can do? It's just not on when I know within my heart that I should be the man leading the full England side against the World Champs. Maybe that's part of my trouble. I don't believe I'm second best to anybody. I know I'm first class. The best forward in England at the moment. And, because I've had the guts to turn round and tell the FA just that, I realise that C will no longer stand for Charlie, C will mean crucifixion. Crucifixion for my international career. I'll probably never be chosen for England again. I've nailed myself to a cross for all time. But it's a cross I'm ready and willing to bear. Because the only B I'm interested in is B for bloody honesty. I didn't want to be a cheat or a liar. I could have left it till the weekend before the match, then pulled out with a phoney injury. Others have done it before. Not me. Others have run away when they were dropped. Like Kevin Keegan. And Paul Madeley wouldn't go on an England tour because his missus didn't want him away from home. They've been forgiven. I doubt if I will because I'm supposed to be one of football's problem boys. I'm not a problem boy. I'm not a big-head. I'm a bloody good player.'

Bob George was unable to comprehend the fierceness of his son's pride. When he rang, Charlie was unable to discuss it. 'The funny thing was that Ron Greenwood had once been so keen to sign me for West Ham that he was ready to hire a plane to push a deal through. I was at Trent Bridge watching a Test match: it was only when I returned home that I knew what had happened. Ron had phoned and spoken to the missus. "I want to sign him," he'd said. "Will he be in later tonight? I can hire a plane and come up." He never did. I never spoke to him about it. Derby turned down whatever offer he made and that was that. A pity really. I wouldn't have minded playing for West Ham or Ron. I never could understand why a man who obviously thought so highly of me when he was a club manager should downgrade me at international level.' On reflection, Charlie regrets his haste. 'Yes, I did feel insulted but it was probably one of those times when I should have swallowed my pride and gone and got on with it. Perhaps I would have been picked for the full side after that, but that's all hindsight now.'

If Charlie did himself few favours, the fates were willing accomplices. On a wet night in October 1977 he had suffered a depressed fracture of the cheekbone when the minicab speeding him to Litchfield for treatment ploughed into the central reservation on the A38 between Derby and Burton, hurling him into the windscreen. When Liverpool came to the Baseball Ground the following March, the roof caved in. 'I went up for a ball with Ray Kennedy and he caught my knee on the way down. Pure accident, but my knee ligaments were badly damaged and I had to have the cartilage out. I knew it was bad as soon as I hit the ground – I couldn't get up.' Derby's subsequent decline was not unrelated. Nine months later, Docherty shipped Charlie off to the Spa for Crocked Stars, Southampton, and was probably lucky to get

£350,000. After a dispute over hire purchase arrangements, contracts were signed in a refreshment room at St Pancras.

'I only signed players who were knackered,' confirms Lawrie McMenemy, the silver-tongued Southampton manager who had persuaded Kevin Keegan to exchange Hamburg for the South Coast. 'They had to be cheap because we couldn't afford anything else.' At the time, McMenemy portrayed the acquisition as a personal triumph. 'It's no longer a question of which ones are supposed to be the fashionable clubs. These deals are now a battle between managers and their personalities. It's about selling yourself as the manager someone like Charlie would want to play for.' McMenemy had given it the big sell, picking up Charlie at a London hotel, driving him back to stay at his home then spending most of the following day outlining the benefits of leaving the Midlands. 'He knows his temperament won't worry us,' he assured the media. 'I spelled out what I call our after-sales service. We give real help in finding the right house, the right school for the kids, the right home help if it's needed. We keep taking an interest.' Soon, however, McMenemy was taking rather more interest in Charlie's physical condition than he had hoped. 'It was only when I saw him working out with weights, trying to strengthen that knee, that I realised he'd been such a great player that he'd lost confidence because he wasn't 100 per cent, because he couldn't do the same things anymore.' With calf trouble compounding matters, Charlie made 15 appearances in his first 12 months at The Dell. 'I've seen Charlie George play' proclaimed a badge in circulation at the Milton Road end: not until August 1979 did Charlie score his first goal in Hampshire. McMenemy felt obliged to placate the sceptics. 'People think Charlie's arrogant as a person because he can be arrogant on the field but he's not. He's a lad who needs encouraging and this has been a difficult time for him. We want him back but only when he can be effective for us.'

A return to the top table beckoned the following season when Brian Clough, who had expressed considerable interest in Charlie when Derby originally put him on the market, signed him on loan to bolster his Champions' Cup-chasing Nottingham Forest squad. Clough, in fact, had twice made enquiries about Charlie when he was managing Derby, once going so far as to stir a slumbering Bertie Mee on a Friday night with the words 'How can you sleep on a Friday night?'. 'Charlie George,' the Sherwood svengali now pronounced in his *Match Weekly* column, 'has been one of the most gifted players on the football scene in the last ten years. He's never ever consistently produced the goods but, to be fair to him, he's not been in a side that has given him a chance of doing just that. Perhaps he needs a bit of luck, perhaps he needs the right kind of management.' The respect was mutual. 'The man was a complete one-off,' marvels Charlie. 'No one could copy or do what he did. He wanted the game played right.' In one of the more dazzling unions of English talent ever assembled under one roof, Charlie briefly linked up with Stan Bowles and Trevor Francis. 'Stan was tremendous, a great player, a great person. Well, my type of person, anyway. A good laugh to be with. Cloughie used to change things round quite a bit because Forest had so many talented players they could utilise them in different positions. Sometimes Stan played midfield and I played up front with Trevor dropping back. Another time I'd swap with Trevor.' After a month, Charlie refused to prove his mettle by accepting an extended trial, reasoning he had done enough for long enough to be worth a place in the first team. Clough changed his mind before Charlie did and that was that.

Back at Southampton but now sidelined by a groin injury, Charlie had his one-sided argument with the lawnmower. By the time Susan rushed him to the Royal Hampshire County Hospital, not only had one finger been decapitated, two others were hanging by a thread. Happily, the damage to them was solved by needle and thread. At the end of the 1979–80 season Charlie and Susan cancelled the family vacation in Majorca. 'I trained every day at home with weights to build up the leg muscles that had been wasted because of my knee injury. I went on a two- or three-mile run every day. When we reported for pre-season training I must have been the fittest player on the staff.'

Someone was going to have to pay for all this inactivity, and that someone was Jack Spencer, a photographer from *The Eastern Daily Press* dispatched to cover Southampton's trip to Carrow Road. 'I was going through a bad spell with injury. So when I did play, every game was a bonus. There was more than a bit of tension about the game, too, and it all built up inside me just to explode in that moment when the ball went towards the photographer with us a goal down and just seven minutes left to play. It was a corner for them and normally a photographer would either push the ball into play or just leave it alone. This one did neither. Instead he picked it up and when I went towards him to get the game moving he made to keep it. I just snapped. Of course I shouldn't have. Any of my real mates will tell you it was right out of character.'

The day John Lennon was shot is engraved on the memory: '10 December 1980, my day out at Norwich Magistrates Court.' Charlie was fined £440 for assaulting Spencer and given a lecture on the art of the role model. 'A trip to a football match has become the occasion for violence and hooliganism,' intoned the chief magistrate. 'You carry an enormous amount of responsibility.' In addition, Charlie was fined a week's wages (around £400) and suspended for seven days. His team-mates clubbed together to contribute £200 of the court fine. 'They weren't saying "you were unjustly treated",' a typically candid Charlie reasoned a couple of years later. 'What they were saying was: "You're our team-mate, you got in trouble – will this help?" I'll never make any excuses for what I did that day. Even now I can still hardly believe it all. It was stupid, the most regrettable incident of my whole career. It meant a lot of worry for myself and my family and I suppose the club. It also gave the anti-Charlie George brigade a field day. I could hear them saying it: "I told you so, I told you what he was like." It must have been my state of mind at the time. I'll never forget the incident or the court case. If my career had ended before that game I suppose I would be remembered for the Cup final goal I scored for Arsenal against Liverpool in the Double year. Now I'm not so sure. I don't think I'll ever be allowed to forget what happened that day.' Had the incident occurred in N5 instead of Norwich that might well have proved to be the case.

As the body continued to rebel, the rebel waned. A £90,000 move to Bulova meant setting up home in the Kowloon Holiday Inn with Susan and Karra, now eight. Charlie missed his scheduled début with a calf strain. Forty-five minutes before kick-off the following weekend, the PA announced that he had ricked his back. Nine thousand-odd spectators reportedly 'erupted', lighting bonfires and baying for refunds while peppering the arena with fruit and cans. 'Where is Charlie?' wondered *The Sun* in October 1981. 'I'm here, aren't I?' Charlie apprised John Sadler. 'Holed up in my bleedin' hotel and that's no funny business. I really am injured and can't wait to start playing. It's still football. It's another country, another challenge. I like something new. English clubs know me, but nobody tried to buy me.' The Bulova coach, Ron Wylie, was confident Charlie would woo the locals anew: 'Once he's fit he will show the people out here he's in a class of his own. With his skill he'll be a sensation.' By February the contract had been cancelled, 18 months ahead of schedule; Charlie had made seven appearances. 'His style of play did not suit Hong Kong,' explained Wylie, unhelpfully. Mel Blyth, another erstwhile Dell favourite, had recently baled out, complaining that it was impossible to afford decent housing and warning others not to succumb to the lure of quick lucre.

When Charlie arrived home to find his father dying, the desire drained away. He rejoined Derby in March, helping them stay in Division Two at the end of a season that saw five points cover the bottom ten clubs, whereupon he was released in what the club described as 'an economy measure'. Brighton invited him to join their pre-season tour of Holland but negotiations fizzled out. Enter Dundee United, only for Charlie to rupture a calf muscle and miss the entire 1982–83 campaign. Bobby Gould, a fellow Old Highburian, brought him to Coventry on a month's loan the following July, but the sell-by date had long since passed.

These days, the goal is management. 'I didn't use to think it was for me but I'd like to get involved, start at the bottom and work my way up. The likes of myself, the Osgoods and the Curries, the Bowleses and the Hudsons, we've all definitely got something to offer and until people like us are brought back into the game I think English football could be suffering for a few years to come. I don't quite know what the preliminary coaching badge entails but if you pass that you go to Lilleshall for the full badge. At the end of the day, what have you got to lose?'

Genuine, self-critical, philosophical: Charlie George is all of these. 'I've learned a lot over the last few years, what to say, what not to say. Before I always did what I wanted. At times I would probably have been better off if I'd have listened to Sue. She would suggest things but I would never listen. I always fancied running a pub so that's what we did when I packed in, but after a while I began wishing we'd never got it. Working together all the time – it's the best way to get a divorce. I've known Sue since she was 13 and I was 14. We grew up together. We were married for 16, 17, 18 years, whatever it was. Sue was still running the pub when I came back to London and went into the garage business with a friend of mine in King's Cross. Eleven months ago we went into liquidation. Because Karra went to school in Hampshire she stayed with Sue, but she comes to visit. When she was young we went to Littleover and then to Winchester, so I thought it wasn't right to thrust a young girl into the London scene. Looking back, though, I wish she'd come back with me. I took her to the Arsenal last Saturday. The stadium is fantastic. It's very different from when I used to stand up there but we've got to change with the times, ain't we?'

Has Charlie? 'Yeah, I think so. I never really used to think about anything directly. Whatever I did was spontaneous. I still don't know why I laid on the floor at Wembley. Afterwards you thought what a prat you'd made of yourself but it was just done on the spur of the moment.' *Carpe diem quam minimum credula postere* – Seize the present, trust tomorrow e'en as little as you may .'Tis the maverick creed. Had Arsenal not won the Double, would Charlie have benefited? Probably even more than the rest of us.

Blue Was the Colour

'Chelsea are the most unusual of clubs. They have never done what every other club was doing at the same time as every other club was doing it.'

Ralph Finn – *A History of Chelsea FC*, 1969

Finding a football club worthy of support was once as much about obligation as choice. Local loyalties, travel constraints and, above all, family tradition. Then television broadened the horizons, emphasising defeat as failure.

Mine was a circuitous route to partiality. A Glasgow dentist in possession of about three and a half teeth he could call his own, my paternal grandfather had played the odd game for Queen's Park yet professed to despise all sport. A year or so before his death – I was nine at the time – he caught me reading the back page of *The Sunday Express* inside the Mc to Mo volume of the *Encyclopaedia Britannica*, and instantly made me promise never to turn to the sports pages ever again. As I hovered outside the dining-room the next morning, secretly watching him pray, I swear I heard him mutter something along the lines of: 'And while you're about it, Lord, I would greatly appreciate it if you could please, please convince that grandson of mine that Henry Moore is more important than Bobby Moore.'

A boxing addict until Ali retired, golf was the only ball game ever to inflame my father's limited passion for athletic competition. To this day he remains a sucker for all those clean, well-behaved chappies and their well-pressed strides. It was therefore up to the maternal branch of the family to supply the lead. In 1966 my mother's father, an East End doctor with a lifelong yen for the Orient (Leyton branch), plonked me down in front of the Everton-Sheffield Wednesday FA Cup final and proceeded to inform me about the death of his late brother. On Boxing Day some years before, it transpired, Uncle Sonny had been so excited by a Chelsea goal against Arsenal that he suffered a massive heart attack. There was no choice.

Peter Osgood once saved the life of a friend of mine. Camden Town after midnight. Stirring from his semi-stoned slumber as if his buttocks had just been tattooed by an over-zealous anaesthetist, Jeff shook like the San Andreas Café in the throes of a bad day on the faultline. In the next breath he kicked out with both feet, sending ashtrays, mugs, cans and Fruitella wrappers flying off the stained pine coffee-table. With equal suddenness, he jerked back in the settee and froze, complexion turning rapidly from russet-brown to ghostly grey. Seconds later, the pallor was closer to a shade Dulux could have retailed as Sheet White. The hands followed suit. 'Oh no,' screeched Agnetha as she bent down and seized Jeff's limp right hand, a shaft of pure terror streaking across those habitually breezy Scandinavian features. 'He's freeeee . . . zing,' she stammered, each vowel drenched in panic. 'Call an ambulance, call an ambulance, call an ambulance.'

Jeff had ingested mushrooms before, but this time the magic had been confined to resurrecting demons. For what seemed like an eternity and a half but was probably less than three minutes – hallucinogenics do tend to treat clocks with disdain – he sat bolt upright, eyes blank, mouth cast in a deathly grimace. Every now and then he appeared to enter semi-consciousness, only to drift back into stupor almost immediately. And so it went on, him floating between purple dragons and terra firma, us unsure whether to call an ambulance or let him ride the waves. Agnetha decided reassurances were in order. 'We love you,' she intoned over and over again, as if chanting a mantra. 'I love you, we all love you, everybody loves you.'

'I love you too,' I chipped in with rather less conviction, 'and I only met you three hours ago.' A feeble attempt to relieve the gloom, granted, but fortunately coinciding with a lucid moment, eliciting the merest flicker of a smile. 'Peter Osgood,' I announced, trying to sound as chipper as possible while recalling an earlier conversation in the car wherein Jeff had owned up to a teenage passion for Chelsea seemingly at odds with his Herefordshire-based youth. 'All my mates went for United so I decided to be different,' he had explained then. 'Chelsea had so much style at that time – Osgood, Cooke, Hudson, lots o' flash.

Football was fun then.' Fun was the last thing on Jeff's mind right now. 'Remember Ossie's sideboards, eh?' I blithered on. 'Must have made his kneecaps a bit itchy.'

Jeff's eyes glistened. The lips parted, creasing at the corners, powerless to defeat a treasured memory. 'Yeah,' he mumbled, 'and what about that bloke who could throw miles?' Coherence was returning. 'Hutch . . . Hutch . . . Hutchinson. Remember . . . when he threw it and Webby headed it in at Old Trafford? Brilliant.' Before the next wave transported Jeff back to day-glo hell the life-affirming strains of a chuckle could be heard.

Season 1969–70 was unquestionably the maddest, gladdest, grooviest in the history of Chelsea FC, and Old Trafford the final, perfect cadence. FA Cup winners for the first time, third in the League, but more, much more than that. It was Alan Hudson's first full season, Charlie Cooke's last consistently effective one and Osgood's finest since his broken leg. Together, for one glorious term, here was the Smoke's riposte to Best, Law and Charlton. Football as swank and twirl, Stamford Bridge the catwalk. At 18, Alan, the boy from the neighbourhood with the airbrushed locks, was the roamer and provider, anticipation and awareness uncanny in one so callow. Cooke was the stooping Scottish winger with the ball stapled to his instep, sinuous slaloms the house speciality. Whenever Chelsea were leading with ten minutes or so left, the word went round: 'Give it to Charlie'. Peter was the King of Stamford Bridge, matador's instincts fusing with the playmaker's vision to make him the most complete striker in the land. Born on the day Clem Attlee announced that Britain would vacate India, the independence of spirit was only fitting. His then manager, Dave Sexton, touted him as the British Di Stefano; ever one for the outlandish comparison, Sexton's predecessor, Tommy Docherty, sincerely believed he could have been as effective a progressive sweeper as Franz Beckenbauer. The ego, however, craved the goalscorer's adulation.

With an average gate of 40,818, more than 5,000 up on Tottenham, Chelsea took over as the capital's biggest draw in 1969–70. Dickie Attenborough was on the board, the luvvies and Lear-jetters thronged the stands: Leonard Rossiter, Tom Courtney, Ronnie Corbett, Michael Crawford, Dennis Waterman, Judy Geeson, even Henry Kissinger. John Cleese, Marty Feldman and Eric Idle stood side by side. 'When Dickie brought Steve McQueen down to the dressing-room,' Peter insists, 'it was the proudest moment of my life.' Shortly before kick-off against Leicester in 1972, Jimmy Hill turned up in the dressing-room accompanied by Raquel Welch, who had specifically asked to be introduced to Peter. 'Lovely lady, but I don't think she really knew who I was.'

'I think all those celebrities, the whole King's Road scene, was a response to the football,' contends Dave Webb. 'Like Manchester United, Chelsea attracted the neutrals, people from outside the area. With Chelsea it was different because there's no real affinity with the people who actually live in the council blocks down the World's End. The footballing types went to Fulham, the showbiz types to Chelsea. They wanted to be entertained. They would stand up and applaud a nice movement, or a piece of individuality. Sometimes you don't have to be successful to play a part in things. These days, however well you play, defeat seems like total failure, but that didn't really start happening until the mid-Seventies. Before I moved to Chelsea in 1968 I was travelling by train to an away game for Southampton when I met this fanatical supporter of theirs, Maxwell Morrison. He told me that the Chelsea fans hadn't minded losing to us 6–2 a few weeks earlier because that was Ossie's first game back after his broken leg and he scored a wonderful goal. They forgave the six goals because Ossie gave them one little bit of magic. People wouldn't accept that today.'

Roddy Doyle, one of Webb's 'neutrals', freely confesses to having done 'a lap around the garden' when Peter equalised at Old Trafford. 'The greatest moment of my life, better than winning the Booker Prize.' Supporting Chelsea, he reinforced, 'prepared you for adult life'. What better way to learn how to handle disappointment, or derive pleasure from the smallest successes, than to be tantalised by a club that promises so much and delivers so little? What better way to acquire the hopeful romanticism that tempers fortune's sting? To John Moynihan, author of that seminal ode to the football nut's endless virginity, *The Soccer Syndrome*, the Chelsea of his youth resembled 'a beautiful woman pursued relentlessly over a number of decades, who throws out excessive hints over dinner that consummation is only ninety minutes away, but never allows herself finally to be possessed.' Who could possibly ask for more? The most intoxicating of women make you feel like a first-form twerp with a heart of potty-putty and cheese dip for brains. The lack of requitement renders the fervour all the more intense. You tolerate anything, forgive everything. Sparks of encouragement assume near-mythic proportions, first exaggerated, then logged in some Comfort File to be retrieved in times of existential despair. The Chelsea of my pubescence was basically Ursula Andress in shin pads.

The matchmaker was Tommy Docherty, the pithy, vinegary Scottish extrovert under whose managership Chelsea gained promotion from Division Two in 1962–63, easing out Sunderland on goal average after pounding Portsmouth 7–0 in their final fixture. Rebuilding the side around Terry Venables and giving youth its fling, less than two seasons had elapsed before the Doc was inspiring his 'wee diamonds' towards an unprecedented assault on four major trophies. No matter that only the League Cup was actually won; a point had been made. Chelsea, at last, had the wherewithal to mount a sustained quest for honours.

True, they had enjoyed 32 uninterrupted years in the First Division before finishing bottom in 1961–62, 28 points constituting their lowest tally in the top flight to date (1978–79 would yield 20). One (losing) Cup final and one Championship in 60 years, however, doth not a glittering past make. Celebrating the club's 50th birthday in due style though it did, even that lone title was pock-marked: in the entire history of the 22-club First Division, no side has ever topped the pile with fewer points than Chelsea's 52. Between 1963–64 and 1971–72, on the other hand, they made off with both major domestic cups as well as the European Cup-Winners Cup, their lowliest League placing ninth, the mean nearer fifth than sixth. There were further Wembley appearances in the FA and League Cup, two FA Cup semi-finals and a Fairs Cup semi-final play-off loss in Barcelona. Docherty's feet had started itching in 1967 but his successor, Sexton, had picked up the baton in sure, imaginative fashion. Not only had Chelsea survived all those snide George Robey cracks, they were now in considerably ruder health than the music halls. *Au revoir les* Pensioners, *bienvenue les* Blues.

Built like a young poplar and blessed with an ease of movement that suggested castors had been glued to his feet at birth, Peter Osgood was the siren-in-chief. The son of a Windsor bricklayer, he had entered the trade himself upon leaving school with six O-levels. As captain of Berkshire Schools he had a trial with Reading but failed to make anyone sit up. When Arsenal sent him a letter inviting him to another, he ripped it up, reasoning Highbury to be an unlikely proposition for a Reading reject. At 17, his footballing horizons extended as far as Spittal Old Boys, whereupon an uncle, Bob Snashnall, wrote to Chelsea to inform them of his abundant skills and request a trial. Hendon was the distant venue, amateur forms the prompt reward from the youth team manager, Dickie Foss. 'Normally I only played for them on a Saturday but I remember being let off early one Wednesday to play in a Junior Floodlit Cup final at Upton Park. John Hollins was the captain and we were 2–0 up from the first leg but they had Johnny Sissons and Harry Redknapp and hadn't been beaten at home for years. In the end we won 3–1 and I scored two of them. Clutching my little shield, I caught the milk train and got home about 2 a.m. Next morning my father opened *The Daily Express* and saw the headline: "New boy Osgood scores two goals". He was so proud. It was lovely. Of course, I was back on the site an hour later. To be honest, I enjoyed the blend.'

Within three months Peter had signed full-time. Injuries created an early opportunity in a League Cup tie against Workington, wherein he scored twice, leading to a productive close-season tour to Australia during the course of which his wife, Rose, gave birth. Recollections are blurred: 'The day I got the telegram, I sat in a bar in Manley and got absolutely pie-eyed.' So taken was Docherty that he shunted Barry Bridges, an England international, out to the right flank to accommodate the 18-year-old father at centre-forward. Docherty raved about 'his casually deceptive amble . . . that sinuous shift which took him past an opponent who, left with a baffled look on his face, turned to gaze almost in awe'. Backing his judgment, Docherty guaranteed Peter ten consecutive games in the first team 'no matter how you play', an unusual step and a refreshing change from the patronising, distrusting attitude towards youth espoused by the preponderance of League managers. 'Peter is one of those natural players a manager hopes and prays for all through his career . . . he is destined to be one of the all-time greats.' Bastin, Lawton, Matthews, Finney, Greaves—Docherty invoked them all when claiming that Peter had the same 'elusive stardust which heralds the greatness to come'. By the time the trial period was up, Docherty's seemingly excessive enthusiasm had spread far beyond the Brompton Road. In the Fairs Cup at home to Milan, 35 yards from goal and blocked by four visiting defenders, Peter feinted to volley with his right, removing Maldini from the equation, then pushed the ball forward with the left and arrowed home a low, meticulous drive. A playoff was required, the power struggle between Docherty and Venables having reached breaking point in the interim with the latter being transfer-listed and dropped. Peter assumed the orchestrator's role, made an early goal for Bridges and collapsed with exhaustion after Harris had decided the tie with a prescient call at the coin-toss.

Sometimes the appreciation emanated from unexpected sources. Gliding across the muddy morass at Turf Moor, a gazelle on skis, Peter evaded four challengers before rounding off a solo sally of such outrageous panache that even the Burnley keeper, Adam Blacklaw, applauded him back to the centre circle. On an icy, sand-strewn surface at Anfield, he engineered the biggest upset on FA Cup third-round day. Roger Hunt put the holders ahead after 91 seconds, Peter equalised with a thumping header from a corner and Tambling converted an eminently deserved winner to round off a display hailed by the ever-effusive Docherty as 'the greatest and most satisfying performance since I took over'. The highlight was the sudden injection of pace that swept Peter from deep inside his own half through the heart of the vaunted home rearguard, nimble footwork, jiggling hips and the odd dip of the shoulder enabling him to elude four malicious lunges before Tommy Lawrence thundered off his line like a startled hippo. 'Kenneth Wolstenholme, who I'm proud to say comes on my weekend golf breaks at Meon Park, said in his commentary that I reminded him of "the great David Jack". When I saw it on TV I thought, Jesus Christ, yes! Everybody said I didn't have pace, but it was the change of pace, a swivel of the body. It was a new thing. People like Ron Yeats weren't used to you running at them. I had Terry Venables, Bobby Tambling, Bert Murray and Barry Bridges supplying me and George Graham holding the ball up front for me. As soon as I got the ball I'd take off. It was easy for me.'

So easy, in fact, that by the time the Fairs Cup quarter-finals came around, TSV Munich were singling him out as the man to stop. Peter had spent the weekend before the second leg being pumped full of penicillin, Docherty hyping up the extent of the flu symptoms 'to lull the Munich planners'. 'I knew he wasn't feeling very strong but that he was determined to play against Hull on the Thursday. I didn't want to overtax the lad, so I was hoping for a couple of goals' lead by the middle of the second half so I could have pulled him off before he had played himself out.' The visitors' Eiger of a keeper, Radenkovic, scotched that plan and with ten minutes to go the aggregate score was still 2–2 when, closely marked in the Munich goalmouth, Peter stole away from his shadow to meet Hollins' chip from the right, ducking low to direct home a powerful header. Two days later his mere presence was sufficient to undo Hull in an FA Cup sixth-round replay. Claiming possession in the centre circle with Chelsea holding a tenuous 2–1 advantage, he accelerated through the middle. Pushing the ball to Bobby Tambling upon reaching the edge of the box, he moved on, waiting for the return, causing the defence to hesitate long enough for Tambling to spin away and fire in the deciding goal. Flashes of that ilk would earn Peter a berth (alongside five club-mates) in Alf Ramsey's preliminary World Cup 40, a gesture more than a statement of intent but nonetheless encouraging for that.

With his feats regularly relayed by the *Match of the Day* cameras, Peter was televised football's first English teen idol. It would have been unnatural had the physical demands, public glare and abrupt change of lifestyle not told at some time or another. In February, Docherty handed over the keys to a club-owned semi near Twickenham and instructed him to take a week off, reasoning that 'a mental as well as a physical rest' was overdue. Peter was finding the expectations hardest to handle. 'The thing was, every time I played I didn't just score, I scored great goals. I don't think there was one from inside the 18-yard box during that spell. They were always benders or volleys. The standard was set and you had to live up to it. Then the vibes start going round. "He's a good-time Charlie", "He won't last". It hurt.' Not for long. In April, Roma made an approach after Peter had created four goals in a 6–2 whipping of West Ham. There was talk of the Italian authorities lifting their ban on imports but Docherty was in no mood to talk turkey with the Roman club whose archly provocative conduct in a bitter Fairs Cup clash a few months earlier had persuaded him not to risk Peter in the second leg. 'We wouldn't dream of selling Osgood any more than Brazil would sell Pele,' proclaimed the manager, 'not even if they offered us £500,000.' Real Madrid tabled a formal bid of £100,000 and were turned down flat. Docherty was not about to dispense with his golden gosling. Respect, in this case, was a two-way street. 'Tommy was a real mentor. I still call him Boss even now. I love the man, I really do. He taught me to be arrogant. He also taught me that there were times when you had to bow down.' The former lesson was absorbed more easily.

Surging from the stalls as never before, Chelsea streaked away at the outset of 1966–67, carrying an unbeaten League run and a two-point lead into November. By then, though, Peter was a non-runner. In an FA Cup tie against Shrewsbury earlier that year he had demonstrated an ability to look after himself, kicking out after a bad tackle and earning a severe wigging from Wales's leading referee, Leo Callaghan ('If someone hits you, my dad always said, hit 'em back'). In a third-round League Cup tie at Blackpool in October, another intemperate action ensured he would never again be quite the same force. 'Emlyn Hughes had sorted me out early with a bad tackle and when this 50–50 ball came in I went in pretty strong. I was looking for him. The upshot was that we crashed shins and I broke my right leg. It was gone, snap. When you're 19 that's a hard thing to take. You're in the Chelsea first team, you're getting accolades from all round the world, you've played for the Under-23s, you're in the World Cup 40, then all of a sudden you are told you have to sit still for three months. Ask any 19-year-old. You want to be out there enjoying yourself. And I'd gone from bricklayer to Chelsea regular in 18 months, a dream come true. Of course I still wonder what might have happened to my life had I not gone in for that tackle. It remains one of my great regrets, not that I'm short of those.'

Sitting still has never been Peter's forte. Docherty first discovered that he did not have a compliant starlet on his hands when an £80 fine for turning up late to training was greeted with a dismissive laugh. Inactivity provided the cue for further disobedience. In town for treatment, Peter sneaked out of his Kensington Palace hotel room to go up west, earning another eighty quid's worth of slapped wrists. Then there were those ill-advised stabs at golf and ferreting with Tony Hateley, the far from adequate replacement Docherty had shrewdly dispatched to live with the Osgoods until he found a home of his own (as Docherty correctly foresaw, Peter's self-belief allowed his relationship with Hateley to be marked by friendship as opposed to jealousy). When the cast cracked at the knee, a specialist attributed it to the pressure Peter had been exerting on the limb. The outlook was bleak. The fracture was in the lower third of the leg, the chances of professional survival no more than 50–50. 'I had to do something with myself. I can't sit still even now. I'm the world's worst at dinner parties. After an hour I have to go and sit on the sofa, have a drink and let the rest keep talking. I get bored easily. That's probably why I've had three wives.'

At the same time, it was this very restlessness that spurred Peter's recovery. Come the Summer of Love he was screaming blue murder over the board's refusal to send him on the close-season jaunt to Bermuda. By August he was back on the runway *en route* to leading the club scoring charts with 18. More impressive still, he figured in each of Chelsea's 56 first-team engagements in 1967-68. The turn of pace, unsurprisingly, had gone. Ten stone seven wet through prior to his injury, convalescence had seen him put on two stone, reducing stamina. Understandably, a certain hesitancy was evident early on. 'I was looking for people,' he subsequently admitted, 'waiting for them to hit me.' Nevertheless, many – enough – of the old trappings lingered, notably the touch and predatory instincts. Docherty did not. A shadowy affair to this day, his resignation in early October coincided, not insignificantly, with an FA suspension pertaining to undisclosed 'incidents' in Bermuda. There was, too, the not inconsiderable matter of a 13-match run in which his team had conceded 29 goals and won just twice.

Extracting Venables, Murray, Bridges and Graham amongst

others, Docherty had perplexed many, Peter included, by undertaking major root-canal treatment on his team in the latter half of 1966, yet still succeeded in becoming the first man to lead the Blues out for an FA Cup final at Wembley. Had Peter been available to complement Charlie Cooke, a £70,000 capture from Aberdeen, Tottenham might not have prevailed and those unspecified Bermudan transgressions, whatever they were, would presumably have been absolved. As it was, Docherty's own fidgety nature was as much a catalyst as the erraticism and volatility that alienated his players, not to mention a board now denuded by the death the previous year of its longstanding chairman, Joe Mears, who had hitherto kept the Doc in check. In 1968 alone Docherty managed three clubs, one, QPR, for 28 days. 'Stamford Bridge,' according to Ron Harris, 'was a hotbed of unrest' when he left. 'He was a restless man. A player could be "in" for weeks, then out of favour in a flash. He took us to the threshold of greatness but decided he needed a short cut to success.' Peter concurs: 'He's a bit like me. He gets bored. In the end he went against the rules and regulations. he simply didn't care. He was ready to go.'

As opaque as Docherty was transparent, the deep-thinking, undemonstrative Sexton was promoted from coach in his stead, placing greater emphasis on ball work in training. A comparative calm held sway. Whereas Docherty initially insisted that the players referred to him as Tom before graduating to 'Boss', Sexton was always 'Dave'. With Dave Webb stiffening the central defence (and frequently adding weight and flexibility to the attack) and the powerful, hard-running Alan Birchenall signed from Sheffield United to assist Peter up front, progress was immediate. Of the last 31 games, just seven were lost, Chelsea finishing sixth to qualify for the Fairs Cup. Involvement in Europe would be brief, DWS Amsterdam ousting them on the toss of a coin in round two, but a rise to fifth in the League compensated, aided by Sexton's deft market-trading. Fulham did the neighbourly thing by parting with their Irish Republic international stopper, John Dempsey, the final piece in Sexton's defensive jigsaw, permitting Webb to shift to right-back. Hutchinson, a courageous bullock of a striker and a former engineering apprentice, arrived via Burton Albion and Cambridge United for a derisory £2,500, the bargain of the decade. 'I was shaking when I entered the dressing-room that first day,' he recalls. 'Real *Roy of the Rovers* stuff. Me still working in a factory and changing across the way from Peter Osgood. It was Mr Osgood then.'

On 1 February, a slightly built 17-year-old reinforced an injury-riddled midfield at Southampton, a 5–0 hiding all but obscuring the début of Alan Hudson. Even though the Hudson prefab lay in Upcerne Road, barely 400 yards from Stamford Bridge, loyalty to Chelsea had not always been unquestioning. A rugged midfielder who had played in the Southern League for Wimbledon before setting up shop as a painter and decorator, Bill Hudson had stopped supporting the club when they sold Roy Bentley nearly a decade earlier. During Docherty's tenure, furthermore, he had made his disgust abundantly clear when the manager reneged on an assurance that he would sign his elder son, John, as a full-time professional. Word, apparently, had reached Docherty that John drank not wisely but too well. Fulham were similarly dissuaded.

Bill had better luck with his other offspring, coaxing and educating Alan while allaying his fears that a puny frame would prove an insuperable barrier. A council-owned play area popularly referred to as 'the Cage' served as the ideal launchpad. On a gravelled surface strewn with broken bottles, balance and courage were critical assets. 'I was always the youngest player there among all these boys I thought were the bee's knees, but my old man kept pumping into me the same message: "You know you're going to get bigger, you know you're going to get stronger, don't worry about them".' After passing his 11-plus, Alan blew his chances of a place at grammar school by informing the headmaster that his ambitions lay in professional football. How quaint. Fulham did turn him down on sizeist grounds but Chelsea issued an invitation to join the ground staff when he left Kingsley Secondary at 15. Alarmed by a mysterious knee condition, however, a specialist was soon instructing him to desist from so much as kicking a plastic ball. The bone, the medic deduced, was not growing in the right position. At a pinch, he predicted, Alan might just be ready to resume his career by the time he was 21. To their credit, the club kept him on, occupying him with various menial tasks – cleaning boots, sweeping terraces. 'I used to watch my mates in the youth team having kickabouts and cry with the misery of it all.'

Departing as puzzlingly as it had arrived, the problem cleared up after six months. Before long, Alan was captaining the youth team and training with the national youth squad. Shortly before his 17th birthday, Sexton gave him two months to prove himself, which he did. Standing in the Shed, he would glean confidence from what he saw below. 'I could see myself doing everything just as well as the players. Afterwards, we'd go back to the Cage and kick a ball around, and we would do things better than the pros. So I came into the game not caring about the big names.' Peter scored just nine times in 35 League appearances in

1968–69, but then he did spend a good deal of the time in midfield, languidly creative if not quite inspirational. At the outset of the next campaign an extensive casualty list let in Hudson to prime the pump. The advent of a rare find was affirmed during a League Cup third-round replay against Leeds at the Bridge. 'During the first half, Paul Madeley overran me in midfield. I couldn't keep up with him; he kept running by me and getting into the box. I was so busy trying to pick him up I wasn't getting forward, but then Dave put me out wide at the start of the second half and the next thing I knew I was sticking the ball through Terry Cooper's legs and doing one-twos, doing what I was good at. We went on to win 2–0 and Dave must have decided then and there that I wouldn't be picking anyone up anymore, that it was best to let me run.'

The passes were almost exclusively short and direct, conservative rather than flashy. Prompting and probing with surgical exactitude, Alan mapped out moves three passes ahead. 'Long passes are so much easier to defend against because defenders have got time to see them coming. Sometimes Tony Currie's passes were fantastic, but by the time they got there they weren't always as dangerous as the little ones. That's why we would have been so good together. There was a real mutual respect there. He'll probably say I was better than him, but I'd say he was better than me.'

'Huddy was so energetic,' marvels Webb, 'a great athlete. Where his brilliance lay was in recognising where the opposition's weaknesses were, getting the ball and servicing those who could best take advantage. He could tell if the centre-forward was having a good time and he'd keep serving him the ball if he was. Tony Currie was like that. I might just have made some desperate clearance off the line and Huddy would be there, ready to get the ball. He was always, always available. I've never known anyone to be more readily available. And when he got the ball he'd create something, work out how he was going to get the ball back to where we needed it. That was why he was such an exceptional talent – but it wasn't recognised. People just thought, "Here's a young man who runs with the ball".' John Hollins was taken aback by the unshakeable certainty. 'Being so young, you'd think Alan would need to draw confidence from the more experienced players on the team. In fact, it's the other way round – he gives us confidence.'

Though goals were scarce, 70-yard solo dashes against Sheffield Wednesday and Coventry supported the view that the shortfall was as much down to Alan's contentment in servicing others as his relative weakness of shot. 'There is no end to what this boy can achieve,' opined

Ramsey after watching him unpick the QPR defence time and again during a 4–1 win at Loftus Road in the sixth round of the Cup. The first time I detected something out of the ordinary was a goal he conceived for Peter against Burnley in the fourth round. Hemmed in as he moved to collect a throw-in on the right, just inside the visitors' half, he cut inside and clipped the ball over the head of an advancing defender. Now bouncing it gently on his right thigh, he proceeded to send over an exquisite, curling, outswinging pass, on the volley, perfectly weighted, to the far post. Peter nodded it in from the best part of a foot. 'When I went past the defender I looked out of the corner of my eye and saw Ossie moving towards the far post. It wasn't even a glance. It was instantaneous. I knew he was going to be there because we'd worked the same move in training. I bet he got a dozen goals that season through that little manoeuvre. When everyone else was running in, he would pull back, or, as in that Burnley instance, pull wide. We did it against Bruges in the Cup-Winners' Cup the following season. I went to the left byeline and, as all the defenders ran back, Ossie pulled back to the six-yard line and I cut it straight back into his path. Time in, time out, no one ever sussed it.'

In Peter's estimation, Alan was 'one of the greatest players I ever played with or even saw. Even at 17. Incredible skills, great brain, great stamina. The only thing he couldn't do was score goals'.

Alan is more specific about what set Peter apart. 'Ossie's greatest asset was his supreme confidence, his arrogance. He would take the field knowing he was going to score and he didn't give a monkey's who he was playing against. Sometimes he'd score and not get the least bit excited. It could be boring for him. He once beat Shilton and Banks from the edge of the box in the same week. It all became a little bit of a joke for him, it was so easy. He was born for the penalty area: he was too tall to have been a great midfield player. In terms of talent and ability Charlie [Cooke] was the best we had then, no doubt about it, but Charlie had a mental problem. He had to feel right on the day, whereas Ossie could just turn it on. He was a complete showman. He thought the crowd had just come to see him, and half of them probably did. When he came out he looked up at them as if to say, "I'm going to show you something else today".'

That season, the showman was indomitable. When Birchenall went lame, Hutchinson filled in and stayed put: the pair shared more than 50 goals, Peter heading the national lists with 31, including one in each round of the FA Cup. Not that he entirely forsook midfield. The 4–2–4 formation adopted by Sexton was a flexible friend, converting easily into 4–4–2. Sometimes both wingers, Cooke and Houseman, would drop back, sometimes Peter. Deriving due encouragement from that League Cup win over Leeds, Chelsea took the moral honours in a riveting home draw with Everton, Alan and Hollins matching the accomplished Mersey midfield trio of Ball, Kendall and Harvey jab for jab. Beaten but once in November and December, the Sixties closed with three successive wins and 11 goals. The swagger was infectious, filling the young mind with all manner of fanciful dreams. Indeed, the title might have been a more feasible proposition but for Bonetti's enforced absence against Leeds in January. The untried, flu-ridden Tommy Hughes endured a wretched time as deputy, a suddenly insecure defence caving in after the break as a 2–1 interval lead evaporated into a 5–2 thrashing, the only home loss of the season. Leeds and Everton were still within range come Easter, whereupon the unfortunate Hughes was pressed into service again, this time at Goodison: another five clattered past him. A final haul of fifty-five First Division points, nevertheless, comprised just one fewer than the club record set in 1965. Even if we leave aside the 150,000-odd who attended the FA Cup final, the number of spectators who watched Chelsea's other 52 fixtures still totted up to nearly two million.

Peter, meanwhile, had found a compartment on the gravy train. 'Buy your car from Peter Osgood – phone him today', enticed a Ford ad. A member of League football's élite £10,000-a-year bracket (Pele, it seems pertinent to point out, was raking in ten times as much from Santos), he supplemented his income with occasional stints as an area sales manager for a Ford dealership in Slough. There were contracts with Bukta for equipment. His agent-cum-partner, Gregory Tesser, was peddling a profitable line in posters (eight shillings a time, sixpence to Peter). 'Tesser was a whiz kid. He was brilliant. He got me TV, posters, you name it, but in the end things fell apart. That was what happened to everybody in those days. Most agents never had any foresight. They just thought, hey, we can make a quick buck out of this guy, instead of realising that careers last ten to 15 years.'

One of Peter's less inspired stabs at self-marketing came in the shape of an autobiography published a few months before the Mexico World Cup, wherein he took the none-too tactful step of predicting that Ramsey would never place any trust in a player with his individualistic tendencies. 'I recognised in 1966 that if he could drop someone like Jimmy Greaves, what chance did Peter Osgood have? I'd been around for five years without a look-in apart from the odd Under-23 game. What was I supposed to think?' The call to full colours came nonetheless, sparked by an FA Cup hat-trick at Loftus Road. Five days after his 23rd birthday, Peter made his England début in Belgium, manufacturing a goal for Alan Ball and impressing hugely with his balance and control on a snowbound pitch. 'After the game, Alf said to me: "Son, that was absolutely brilliant." Bobby Moore said I was in a different class. Coming from the England captain, that was wonderful. A few weeks later I had to pull out of the squad to play Wales because of the Cup final replay when I'm sure I would have played given the makeup of the 16 chosen. I know Bobby Charlton had to come back but I'd fitted in to the side as if I'd been there all my life. I didn't play again before the World Cup squad was chosen, but at least I was in that.' Alan Hudson came close to joining him. The day it was announced that Peter would get his chance to sprout in Brussels, he himself had been named in the Under-23 team to play Scotland at Roker Park. Posing for the paparazzi, he cuddled his black poodle, Ossie. Ramsey included Alan in his initial 40 but, as in Peter's case four years earlier, he lacked the courage, let alone the imagination, to go the whole hog.

If Chelsea's passage to Wembley was not exactly littered with awkward obstacles – Burnley, bound for 14th in the League, were their strongest opponents on paper – 21 goals for and seven against in six games represented the most imperious advance on the Twin Towers since 1961–62, when Tottenham managed 21 for and nine against from the same number of matches. Come the appointed hour, however, Alan's season was over. At the Hawthorns on 30 March he rose to kill a loose ball, misjudged the bounce and fell awkwardly, breaking his left ankle. 'It was never the same after that. I was still struggling with it a couple of years later when Bestie trod on the other ankle and smashed that up. After that I had problems kicking the ball so I stuck to hitting passes I knew were going to get to their destination. I was physically unable to hit accurate 40-yard balls.' Baldwin stood in, a billy club replacing a foil.

Leeds's schedule had been relentless in its demands. Defeat against an arguably inferior Celtic side in the European Cup semi-final was one direct consequence, a collapse in the League another. Revie willingly risked official censure (and what turned out to be a £5,000 fine) by fielding what was tantamount to a reserve team at the Baseball Ground, having taken his cue from a ruse first knowingly practised nine years earlier by Burnley. All the same, there had been sufficient strength of character to see off Manchester United in a mini-series masquerading as an FA Cup semi-final, Bremner dashing the hopes of the connoisseur by scoring the only goal amid five hours of bitter attrition. Indeed, such was the awe in which Leeds were held, every Blues fan of my acquaintance approached the final with apprehension. True, our recent record against them had been as good as any. There had been that win at Villa Park in the 1967 FA Cup semi-final, and another in the League Cup that very term. To this 12-year-old, however, Alan's absence seemed insuperable. *Cup Final Grandstand*, I consoled myself, was a treat in itself. The only day of the domestic season when live footie was on the box. Victory was not imperative.

Nor did it seem in the vaguest bit likely when Eddie Gray's first sleight of foot left Webb floundering on the churned-up turf. David Broome and his horsey friends had just completed a brief residency, the destructive legacy of which was quick to manifest itself. Midway through the first half, a corner swung over. Brushing aside Bonetti's challenge, Jack Charlton headed gently towards a Chelsea goal-line manned by Harris and McCreadie. Both swung a boot at where they anticipated the ball would bounce, only for it to squat on the dead surface and creep between them. Houseman levelled just before the break, Sprake, similarly unsettled by the bounce, diving over a speculative shot from outside the area, but Gray persisted in making Webb look as if he had swapped his boots for a pair of webbed feet. Somehow, Chelsea clung on, kept afloat by Bonetti's agile reactions and the boundless energy of Hollins, not to mention tackling that veered between the gung-ho and the cynical. Hutchinson knew the score. 'You knew that if you didn't compete with Leeds you were going to get kicked off the park. So you geed yourself up before you went out. It was out-and-out war.' Peter nonetheless noted the off-field cameraderie: 'At the same time, 'you could go out for a drink with them afterwards, and that's what the game's all about.'

There were moments of optimism, notably when Peter and Hutchinson each came within an ace of scoring during one chaotic scrimmage in the Leeds box. Pulsating fare though it was, however, the outcome looked inevitable, all the more so six minutes from time when Allan Clarke struck a post for Mick Jones to thread in the rebound after Dempsey had clearly been obstructed. I thought I had picked my venue carefully, wheedling an invite from a close friend's uncle who just happened to own a 24-inch Ferguson colour TV. Yet as soon as the ball crossed the line, car keys were being jangled as the other guests headed for the door. We were due at my mate's grandparents' house for tea. 'Hang on a minute,' I implored my host, 'you never know.' How could they be so disloyal? Surely it was our duty to sit through every last millisecond. My reward came inside two minutes, Hollins floating a free-kick to the near post for Hutchinson to fling himself among the studs and head past Sprake. 'If Jack [Charlton] had gone for the ball instead of my head,' the scorer now alleges, 'he would have won it. Normally, Hunter used to pick me up and Jack looked after Ossie, so I can only assume I must have upset Jack earlier in the match or else during one of our League encounters. Thinking he was in it, Ossie once wound him up about his little black book after a testimonial match at Brighton. Jack had talked about it on TV and it was supposed to contain the name of a player he intended to sort out, so to speak. "It's not for you," Jack told Ossie, "it's for that twat next to you." I was that twat.'

Extra-time brought a few close scrapes but the impasse remained. For the first time, a Wembley Cup final required a replay. Getting that far seemed heroic enough to me. When hostilities resumed 18 days later, Leeds having lost to Celtic at Hampden Park in the interim, Sexton switched Harris to right-back. 'I think you're very wise,' congratulated Webb. I watched the rematch alone on the family black-and-white portable, shuddering when Jones clattered into Bonetti shortly after the kick-off, reducing the Cat to a hobble for the duration. Worse still, a sumptuous run from Clarke was soon setting up the assailant for a chilling goal, putting Chelsea behind for a third time. On we went deep into the second half, the confrontational, often vengeful tackling evoking an ugly, shameful mood, the referee an indulgent, impotent bystander.

Something was sorely needed to cleanse the soul, and Peter duly obliged. Taking possession ten yards inside the Leeds half, he moved a stride or two towards the right-hand touchline whereupon Hutchinson, stooping as he cut inside from the opposite direction, took over, switching the direction of play. Now the ball came inside for Cooke to glide into the frame at a slight angle from right to left. A couple of paces and in came a delicately weighted chip with the inside of that erudite right foot, floating in a flattish, inviting arc towards the penalty spot. Peter RSVPed in style, launching himself horizontally to send a flying header beyond Sprake's deputy, David Harvey. A move to kill for, a finish to match. Peter took special pride in the interchange with Hutchinson. 'That was something we worked on a lot, the takeover. We lost the defenders with that little switch. It gave us two or three extra yards and that's all we needed. Having said that, Charlton did his bit by losing his head and chasing after Hutch, leaving me unmarked.' The biter bit, again. And again in extra-time as Webb thrust those Wembley woozies behind him. Hutchinson's sturdy arms windmilled one last time, hurling a throw-in to the far side of the Leeds six-yard area. Charlton could only deflect it behind him, allowing Webb to bundle the ball in with what looked suspiciously like a right ear lobe. 'Whenever we come home from an evening out with friends,' Peter shamelessly confesses, 'I get myself a glass of port, turn on the video and play that replay again. I can't help it.'

For Alan it was a decidedly less joyous occasion. 'It was a strange feeling watching at Wembley, very difficult. In the lead-up to the final I kept going to Harley Street to consult different specialists, which got me into a lot of trouble with the club. I even went to see a faith healer. You name it, I saw one. To get so much in your first season and then have it all snatched away at the climax was a bit cruel. I can't really remember much about either game. I felt so helpless sitting there at Wembley, especially since I knew that, if I had been fit, Leeds wouldn't have been all over us. I guess I thought I had the measure of Giles and Bremner. One Sunday paper asked all of us who we wanted to play in the final and I was the only one who chose Leeds instead of Man United. I relished the prospect. They were the best team in the country. At the end of the first game Dave put his arm around my shoulders as we walked across the pitch, telling me how he was going to get me back to hospital and get me fit because that was the only way we were going to win the replay, but there was nothing the doctors could do. In the end, I didn't even go to the replay. I do remember sitting in a pub on the King's Road the day after, watching the lads go by on the bus, parading the Cup. I didn't have it in me to join them. My family felt as mixed up about it all as I did, so we had our own party.'

The World Cup was not a good one for the Chelsea-inclined xenophobe. Bonetti was made the scapegoat for defeat against West Germany, although I've never been quite sure why. Maybe his positioning was at fault for Beckenbauer's opener, but Seeler's back-header was freakish and Muller's winner the result of weariness and slack marking. Besides, Ramsey's premature removal of Bobby Charlton in order to preserve him for the semi-final was the real own-goal. Peter, meanwhile, barely got a look-in. Having replaced Francis Lee midway through the second half of a far from illustrious opening win over Romania, he was given every reason to believe he would play against Brazil. 'I'd worked my butt off in training. I'd been taking all the salt tablets, hadn't had a drink for three or four weeks, did everything by the book. I always played in the A side during practice games. One day we beat the B team, as it were, 3–1, and I put two of them past Banks, one of them after sticking the ball through Nobby Stiles's legs. I was flying.

Mooro [Bobby Moore] told me he was positive I would play so I thought, right, that's good enough for me.

'Then Alf read out the team. "The side that finished against Romania," he said, "will play against Brazil".'

'Ossie's face lit up,' Moore, a frequent room-mate, would recount. 'I remember his expression of delight, and how it crumbled.' Ramsey had not quite finished. 'I'm sorry,' he had continued. 'I meant to say the team that *started* against the Romanians will play Brazil.'

Peter was mortified. 'Unbelievable. It was as bad as breaking my leg. I wouldn't have minded so much if Alf hadn't brought Jeff Astle on as sub. Absolutely ridiculous. Alf said he was looking to beat them in the air but all they did was close us down and stop the crosses. Jeff was a lovely fella. We roomed together out there. A great club player, probably a better one than I ever was because of the weight of goals he scored, but he wasn't international class. Then he blazed over with only the keeper to beat. I'd never have missed that, never.' Compounding the insult, Astle, a more-than-useful practitioner in the air but otherwise limited in scope, started against the Czechs before giving way to his room-mate: neither got a look-in when Hurst returned against the Germans.

Local heroism had to suffice. Losing Hutchinson with a broken leg early on in 1970–71, Chelsea gained the energetic, cultured Keith Weller and quickstepped through Europe. A Cup-Winners' Cup romp against Aris Salonika was succeeded by a brace of 1–0 squeezes against an accomplished CSKA Sofia. The first leg of the quarter-final in Bruges produced a 2–0 reversal but Peter returned from an eight-week suspension to reignite the flame. 'That suspension was for three bookings, that's all. Bestie had been up in front of the Disciplinary Committee the week before and they promised to clamp down on the next player to come before them. Brian Mears decided to fight the case and the suspension went up from six weeks to eight. Incredible. It was mainly a case of protecting myself. I used to stick my foot in and let people know I was around but I never broke anybody's leg. While I was out of commission I used to run on the Downs every day, but I was shattered by the end of that Bruges game. We'd just sold our house, the buyers were moving in that morning and and we had to go to the new place in Epsom to shift our furniture.'

Levelling the aggregate scores with two minutes left, Peter then broke the deadlock in extra-time courtesy of Alan's cut-back from the byeline. Alan quelled all doubts by laying on the fourth, ensuring a place in the last four, where the holders, Manchester City, were eased aside

1–0 in each leg. Real Madrid awaited in Athens, the 1971 model a Morris Oxford by comparison with the Di Stefano-driven Bentley that had cruised round Hampden Park 11 years previously. Chelsea were the more inventive side but despite another opportune strike by Peter, Zoco forced a replay. Forty-eight hours later, the issue was settled in the first half, two long-range missiles in quick succession from Peter and, of all people, Dempsey. Fleitas halved the deficit to heighten the butterfly activity but Real had nothing left. Two trophies in two seasons: the unusual had become the usual. Who would have thought that an obligation could give more pleasure than pain? Excuse me while I slip into something more comfortable, Ursula dear.

I Don't Wanna Go to Chelsea

'We were a horrible, ugly, noisy, scruffy, arrogant, intimidating, inconsiderate bunch of arseholes. I think we were successful because that's what the audience were like, too.'

Pete Townshend on The Who

The Jewish guilt complex is a terrible thing. Mere association with the guilty can be enough to trigger it off. Thus it was that, for all the untold if not quite untrammelled joys of Old Trafford and Athens, shame began to gnaw away at my devotion to Chelsea. A letter to *The News Chronicle* in 1950 captured the wry, fatalistic nature of the average *aficionado*. 'I have been a regular paying visitor to Stamford Bridge for many moons,' wrote someone calling himself 'Shorty', 'but owing to my stature (only 5ft 3in) I never see much of the match. Why do I go? It is because that, no matter how much of the game is blocked from my view, there is the satisfaction in feeling that I have not missed much.' As late as 1966, John Moynihan could talk about accompanying Chelsea fans on excursion trains returning home from a defeat, when the reaction had been merely 'a tense silence, a grim lethargy in which sad chins remain sunk in the pink classified editions of Northern newspapers, trying to dissect disaster'. Fast forward three decades and a handful of trophies, a couple of days after Matt Busby's death. Clive White of *The Observer* begins dictating his report of Chelsea's draw with Aston Villa at Stamford Bridge. 'A match that began with a few Chelsea yobs choosing the minute's silence in honour of the late Sir Matt Busby to abuse their former captain, Andy Townsend, was never likely to end as a fitting tribute to the memory of the great man, but then the Bridge has never exactly been one of the last bastions of sporting decency.' Things change.

Millwall and Cardiff have both demonstrated that the degree of skulduggery off the field does not necessarily have to be commensurate to a club's strength on it, but it certainly helps. By the end of the Sixties, Chelsea were the foremost attraction in the capital and the Sta-Pressed urchins in the Shed had repulsed the challenge of their Stretford End counterparts to stake an indisputable claim as the hooligan's hooligans. Tense silences on excursion trains were now the preserve of their fellow passengers. 'Chopper' Harris, a player not exactly noted for his gentility, refused to acknowledge their cheers. In September 1968, after Chelsea had walloped QPR 4–0 at Loftus Road in the West Londoners' inaugural League meeting, two hundred or so of the guests' sizeable entourage laid waste to the local market, kicking bottoms and much else besides. 'That,' Harris pondered with apt incredulity, 'was in the flush of victory.' During his youth team days, Alan remembers being unnerved by a Chelsea–Leeds encounter. 'I thought I'd never go into the Shed again. The Leeds fans started it so the Chelsea fans obviously had to defend themselves. I hated it. Another time we were playing at Old Trafford and I got off the train in Manchester on a Friday night: all their fans were spitting at us.'

By the middle of the decade, the attitude was universally damning. 'One thing that gets me,' Alan told *Titbits*, 'is that my son, who is taken to every match to watch me, will never be able to stand on the terraces when he's older. I would never let a son of mine go near them. How any mother could let her young children go alone beats me. You see them every Saturday at every ground. Kids of ten and under with flick knives and bottles.' The very same hordes who chanted his name, moreover, were among the chief culprits. When Harry J and his All Stars entered the Top Twenty in November 1969, reggae found a wider English audience, the Shed the most apposite of theme songs: 'The Liquidator.'

My parents' ignorance of all things football permitted me to join the congregation in 1971. While most of my Jewish friends went to Tottenham or Arsenal, the majority of my classmates subscribed to Watford; to almost every teenager I knew who did share my affliction, Stamford Bridge was off-limits *sans* chaperone. In my case, northward jaunts were out of bounds. Uncle Sonny's son David had a season ticket and helped out when possible, but that meant driving, parking and sitting. Too remote. Given that the human load transported to and from Fulham Broadway went to the opposite extreme, habitually conspiring against efficient breathing, I would generally arrive late and leave early whenever I was fortunate enough to find someone of my own generation to go with. The ground itself had an unpretentious, tatty charm, a once eligible-bachelor fallen on hard times. A sort of downmarket Wembley. Far from worrying about the way the greyhound track was supposed to reduce the intimacy, I relished the distance between me and my heroes. Like a movie screen, the track was a line dividing the immortal from the mundane. Indeed, a packed Stamford Bridge was not unlike the Marble Arch Odeon on Boxing Day. The chanting and the crush of flesh, furthermore, generated something extra: solidarity. The unannounced surges, conversely, bred sheer terror. When the combined weight of 5,000 heaving bodies is pinning you against a horizontal iron bar, crash barriers tend to lose their credibility as safety devices. The vituperation sprayed in the direction of the visiting supporters was similarly disconcerting.

First-hand evidence of assault and yobbery came in November 1971. Four days after my 14th birthday, a terrific 1–0 scrap with that reviled lot from Tottenham had kept me hanging on to the ref's final peep. Floating along on a low-flying cloud, I was wending my way back to Fulham Broadway station when I suddenly found myself shunted off the pavement as half-a-dozen blokes sporting Spurs rosettes tore past, hotly pursued by a herd in braces, blue-and-white favours knotted to each wrist. Glinting in what remained of the late afternoon sun, a flick-knife spat out. I headed for the District Line sharpish. The next morning it was reported that a Tottenham supporter had been stabbed. Shame festered, hardening the heart. It was like seeing your father hit your mother for the first time.

Unable to transfer my affection elsewhere, I continued to make infrequent pilgrimages until 1985. Tormented by Clive Walker, that erstwhile Shed favourite best known for flashing his wares at unsuspecting females, Chelsea had just conceded a third goal in the second leg of the Milk Cup semi-final against Sunderland, rendering defeat inevitable, when a cluster of far from gruntled supporters began ripping up the metal-framed seats and shot-putting them on to the field, endangering the players. Oblivious to the widespread evacuation towards the far touchline, Walker hared into the Chelsea box once more, only to be put off his stroke by the close attentions of a mounted policeman. Standing high in the press gantry next to Suggs, the lead singer of Madness and another true blue, I noticed that he, too, had gone rigid with anger, incapable of intelligible speech. 'That's it for me,' I informed him once the last horse had trotted off, allowing play to resume. 'Never again.' Suggs concurred: 'Me neither.' Aside from reporting duties, I know I've kept my end of the deal.

The King of Stamford Bridge, though, is not about to badmouth his courtiers. 'I forgave 'em for it,' reasons Peter. 'Obviously we didn't like it but I forgave them because of the way they supported us. They followed us everywhere around the country and sometimes we'd travel with them, have a few beers. There was an element of hooliganism but in all fairness they were a fabulous crowd. When we were at Old Trafford, one down in the final for the third time, they were still chanting. Chel-sea, Chel-sea, Chel-SEA. They still believed we could do it. That gave us a bigger boost than anything. They were lucky because we were a successful side but we were lucky to have such incredible support. And supporters *do* make a team. When we went to Athens for the Cup-Winners' Cup final and had to stay on two days for the replay, they were all there. They slept on the beach on the Thursday while we spent the day drinking, and then came to the ground again on Friday. They took a chance of not getting back.'

With hindsight, that victory over Real Madrid can be regarded as the single worst thing ever to happen to Chelsea. It gave Brian Mears and his board ideas above their station. Ludicrously ambitious plans were drawn up for the redevelopment of Stamford Bridge, beginning with the West Stand. They might have stood a chance had the team kept performing. As it was, injury (Hutchinson in particular) and loss of form (Cooke went into steep decline following the breakup of his marriage) mitigated against that, while an assortment of expensive purchases (Bill Garner, Chris Garland, Steve Kember) created a mood of unease without taking up the slack. More debilitating still, scaffolding supplanted fans and a funereal atmosphere pervaded, robbing the players of a vital source of energy. In addition to the lacklustre display in the League Cup final that handed Stoke their first major trophy, 1971–72 brought two even more numbing reversals, an FA Cup fifth-round humbling at Orient (wherein a two-goal lead was squandered) supplementing an away-goal defeat at the hands of the mediocre Swedes, Atvidaberg, in the second round of the Cup-Winners' Cup. In the previous round, perversely, Chelsea had run in a British record 21 goals without reply against Jeunesse Hautcharage. By this stage, Hutchinson, having re-broken his left leg almost as soon as the initial fracture had healed, had effectively missed two seasons. Reaching the sixth round of the FA Cup and the League Cup semi-finals in 1972–73 counter-balanced a drop of five places in the League to 12th, the worst since 1961–62.

'The plans were far too ambitious,' declares Hutchinson. 'Brian Mears is a lovely fella but he seemed to be out of his depth. There was a mass exodus, just to get the money to pay for this bleeding stand. The kids Dave brought in did terrifically well but they needed a year or two's seasoning, so we went down in 1974–75 and came back up again two years later, then went down again two years after that.'

'The day they decided to take that stand out, the old marble dressing-rooms, the long bar where all the film stars went, they took the heart out of Stamford Bridge,' Alan laments. 'You could see it crumbling. It was a graveyard.'

For his part, the task of coping with a squad of free spirits proved beyond Sexton. Brian Glanville, who observed him at close quarters for three decades or more, regards Sexton, a devout Catholic, as 'a strangely innocent man, very unworldly'. His immersion in his trade was such that he would have an Italian football magazine sent to him every week when he was reserve manager at West Ham. 'Let the sorrow go' and 'A manager needs motivating too' were favoured expressions. Sexton Senior was Archie, a notable middleweight boxer; the family nest was in Islington. Dave's own playing career was ended prematurely by a knee injury, whereupon he took up coaching with marked success. The FA interviewed him for Don Revie's job in 1977 yet he has always been a better coach than man-manager, his work with QPR and the England Under-21 side worthy of special merit. His helplessness amid the days of booze and poses is best conveyed by Peter's almost certainly apocryphal tale about him inviting a friend in for a drink and inquiring whether he wanted gin in his Scotch.

Doubtless exacerbated by the player's own frustrations in the aftermath of the World Cup, Sexton's schism with Peter had entered the public domain at the start of the 1970–71 season. The day before Chelsea's visit to Old Trafford 'some nutter' rang the front office to leave Peter a death threat. A couple of days later, Sexton dropped him for lack of effort. 'I needed something like that to make me get up and go,' he confessed at the time. 'Maybe this was the one way, perhaps the only way, that Dave could get me to play for him.' On reflection, he resents the charge. 'You never go out there and not try, do you? Just because you don't turn it on doesn't mean you're not trying. It was a disgrace for him to say that. On the other hand, I had got older and wiser. Why should I run around like a blue-arsed fly when I can just take the ball and score goals? I don't think the great players ever run around unless they've got the ball.'

Not that Peter could plead complete innocence. Later that season he was banned for eight games following a glut of bookings, most of them for petulant tackles. Ignoring his pleas of provocation, the FA took the unprecedented step of sending the disciplinary report to the

International Committee. A poisonous vein had crept into his game, much to Alan's dismay. After the League Cup semi-final victory over Tottenham, Peter ended up in Alexander's on the King's Road, the team's favourite restaurant. 'The waiters were all poofs but we liked them. Everyone used to go there – Michael Crawford, Jane Seymour, lots of Chelsea fans. We came out at two, two-thirty in the morning and the police just came from everywhere. All we were singing was "We're on our way to Wembley". No swearing, nothing. I asked this copper what was going on and he accused us of being loud and rowdy, then suggested we got in our cars and went home. The next thing I know, this friend of mine, Danny, who I think is now Phil Collins' minder, is banging this copper's head back and forth. "Leave it out, Danny," I shouted over, but then all of a sudden my arm was behind my back and I'd been nicked as well. I was picked on, absolutely. It was just these young coppers trying to make a name for themselves.' Accused of offering to take their disagreement into a quiet alley, Peter was duly cleared of being drunk and disorderly.

'Perhaps I had the bright lights too soon,' he wondered in October 1972. 'I knew I wasn't doing myself justice before this season.' He certainly made amends over the subsequent six months, rising above his largely inert colleagues to win the club's Player of the Year award. He even funnelled back to central defence in the second half of a game at The Hawthorns and expertly blunted Jeff Astle.

'I would say that he has accepted more responsibility,' observed Sexton. 'He particularly went out of his way to help the youngsters. His concentration during a game is better, far better. He is more mature all round.'

That summer Peter claimed that his now notorious comment about being unsuitable for Ramsey's tastes had been 'stupid, something I said to sell the book'. With another World Cup looming, it was time for a bit of brown-nosing, albeit to little avail. Restored to the England squad after three years' absence when Ramsey belatedly began to think in terms of attacking the opposition, Poland had already rewritten the script by the time Peter was recalled to the starting line-up against Italy. If his first Wembley international was to some extent a personal vindication – the Italian manager acclaimed him the most dangerous Englishman on the field by a goodly mile – collective defeat deadened the impact. Thank you and goodnight.

Alan's relationship with Ramsey was even less harmonious. The 1972 home internationals saw him drafted into the full squad for the first time. 'Congratulations, son, you're playing tonight,' Bobby Moore advised him in training prior to the Wembley date with Northern Ireland. Just as Moore's assurances had raised Peter's expectations in Mexico, so the England captain's word was good enough for Alan. 'Even though Sexton had assured me beforehand that I'd get a game, when Bobby said that I couldn't believe it. I felt on top of the world. Ten minutes later Alf read out the team and didn't mention my name, not even among the substitutes. Bobby and I looked at each other, completely baffled. After all, Alf obviously confided in Bobby, so he must have changed his mind as he was reading down his list. I was shattered. I knew the man was off his head when Bobby pulled out and Alf made Colin Bell captain instead of Alan Ball. You should have seen Ballie's head drop. He hadn't even been picked. I remember walking out of the room and thinking that, if this was what playing for my country was about, I was probably better off without it. So, when I wasn't chosen for the Scotland game either, I walked out.'

A week later, on the eve of the Under-23 tour of Eastern Europe, Ramsey rang Alan to advise him that his services were still required. The feeling was not reciprocated. 'I told him Maureen [his wife] was pregnant, that I was moving into a new house in Wimbledon and that I had to get it straight before the new season, that I had to put my club first. It was half true. Maureen was pregnant and I did need to get the house fixed up but I was damned if I was going to put him before my family if that's the way he was going to treat me. "Well," he said, "your problems are no concern of mine. Be there in the morning. You'll take the consequences if you don't come." "In that case," I replied, "you'd better start now because I won't be there." For that I got a two-year ban from international football, although it was eventually commuted after one, mainly, I think, because of media pressure. Colin Todd said he was too tired to go and got the same treatment, whereas Malcolm Macdonald got away with it because his doctor gave him a sick note about his back even though he couldn't actually detect anything wrong with it.'

The outlook was slow to improve. Opening 1972–73 with a masterly exposition of the creator's art against Leeds at the Bridge, Alan devised three of Chelsea's four goals only to run aground a fortnight later at Old Trafford, where a vindictive challenge from Best broke his right ankle. 'We went to a nightclub after the match and Bestie was there. I asked him what the hell was going on. Why had he done it? "Oh," he said, "I thought you were Ronnie [Harris]." "How can you fucking mistake me for Ronnie?"I asked him, so he explained that he'd gone into a group of us looking for Ronnie but things had happened so fast he got me instead.'

Alan returned to the first team after three months, whereupon Sexton dispatched him to the right side of midfield, the industrious but constricted Steve Kember having taken over in the middle during his convalescence. The sense of pique was acute. 'I felt I'd been stripped of everything – I dreaded every match. It was like knowing I was going to have toothache every Saturday.' A constant companion for some years, drink offered a handy if illusory crutch. Once upon a time he would go to bed after a game and replay it in his head, reliving, correcting, obsessing. Not any more. 'I just wanted to shut everything from my life,' he subsequently admitted to his good friend Terry O'Neill, then a photographer with *The Sunday Times*. 'I had no concentration to play for Chelsea. Then all the disappointment of the England ban came back. All I had to play for was the money and that was nothing compared to the feelings I get from football. In a sense I was dying. I was just a vegetable and I drank more and more to enjoy myself.'

'Birds and boozers not for me' pronounced a not entirely factual headline in *The Daily Mail* in January 1970. 'Given the amount Huddy drank his stamina was unbelievable,' asserts Hutchinson, a room-mate for four years. 'The times I put him to bed were untrue. He'd get up and say, "I think I'll have a vodka day today" and proceed to drink vodka all day. The next day would be a brandy day. He'd drink a bottle and a half of vodka and half-a-dozen pints, go into training the next morning and do the cross-country, even the sprints, as if nothing had happened. He was phenomenal, absolutely phenomenal. Obviously, it caught up with him as he got older. But he and Ossie were both rebels. They knew they could play the game and they wanted to do it their way and that was that. Ossie was unbelievable. Always falling in love with someone. Sexton once went through a phase of telling players not to make love the night before a game. On a Saturday morning Ossie would promise him that he hadn't made love the previous night, omitting to mention the fact that he'd got his leg over with an air hostess that morning. Free love – it was the in thing. And the press weren't always around us as they are now. We went to a party in Sweden after playing Atvidaberg in the Cup-Winners' Cup and our full-back bedded three different birds in one night.'

Sexton, according to Alan, was regarded as an outsider. 'After every Saturday away game we used to congregate in the Markham Arms. We'd have a £10 whip and then spend an hour talking about football. No outsiders, no women. At closing time we'd go to a club and forget the football, but during that hour we would sort the game out, all our problems. If someone was having a bad time we'd try and pull him through, build his confidence. You're not going to do that by going home and sulking, are you. Sexton couldn't handle the fact that we conducted our team talks without him. If it had been Tony Waddington, he'd have been in there drinking with us.'

Coming in the wake of seven wins in the opening 21 League and cup fixtures, Christmas 1973 marked the watershed. On Boxing Day West Ham overturned a two-goal half-time deficit at the Bridge, romping home 4–2; three days later, Liverpool, the champions, won there by the only goal. Sexton's patience was exhausted. 'Dave called me into his office before the Liverpool game and told me I was going to be the new captain,' remembers Peter, still bemused after all these years. 'I said, "I don't think so. Ron Harris is my captain and I look up to him. He's the guv'nor as far as I'm concerned." Dave then said he didn't think Ronnie was a good influence on the side. "You're a leader," he told me, "everyone looks up to you." "Very nice of you, Dave," I said, "but in all fairness I'd rather play under Ron". "Well," he said, "that's my decision," so I said I'd give it a go. On the Saturday Liverpool beat us by the only goal, no shame in that. On the Monday morning he calls me into his office and tells me he's making changes for the trip to Sheffield United the following weekend. Fine, I said, not suspecting a thing, and in the next breath he says he's leaving me out, Huddy as well. "You've got to be joking," I said. "I've gone from being the next captain to not even being in the side." "You didn't put it in for me on Saturday," he said. I told him I couldn't believe that. We'd been beaten 1–0 by the champions, a great side. Anyway, that was it.

'Huddy and I went training with the reserves and the lads beat Sheffield United 2–1, a great result. The next week we go training with the reserves again but this time Dave's assistant, Dario Gradi, calls us over and tells us the boss wants to see us. Dave said he wanted us to train with the first team, so I said: "What's the point? We're not going to play in your team: you won 2–1." If we won't train with them, he replied, we may as well go home. I told him that was fine by me and walked away with Huddy. "That goes for me too," said Huddy, "and, by the way, can I have a transfer?" And I got blamed for that. Next thing you know, of course, I was on the list myself.'

At the time, Alan was unaware of Peter's discussions with Sexton over the captaincy. 'He didn't tell me about that until a year or so ago. I couldn't believe it because it was so ironic. After I'd missed the Cup final, Sexton told me not to worry, that I had a great future at the club and would be captain one day. That was my ambition at the time. It must be every player's ambition. And I think I had more right to it than Ossie. A few weeks before the training incident, Sexton told me he was under pressure to sell players but that the only way I would leave would be over his dead body. I thought I was going to spend the rest of my life there. The trouble with him was that he wanted everyone to be the same. But he didn't make us the players we were: he just came in and tried to change everything. The day he bought Steve Kember he assured me he thought Steve wasn't in my class. Two weeks later Steve was playing in my position, in the middle, and I was on the right. I was dumbfounded by that. I'd rather he'd have been honest. In the end I was relieved to get away. We were making Dave's life a misery and he was making our lives a misery. Something had to give. One day he and Ossie nearly went behind the stands for a bit of fisticuffs. A manager must be in a right state when he considers solving his problems that way. Playing there was coming to represent everything I didn't like about the game. We beat Ipswich in the FA Cup with me wide on the right. We were useless. Brian Mears walked into the dressing-room and said how wonderful we were. I asked him if he had been watching the same game. It was crap. So, I thought, nothing matters so long as you win. That was the beginning of the end.

'After we'd lost to West Ham in what turned out to be my last home game, Dave called me into one of the portakabins and told me my breath stank of alcohol. I'd been out drinking the previous afternoon with Eddie McCreadie, my best mate at the club, but Eddie was a fixture so Dave wasn't going to have a go at him. Prior to that he'd never said a word to me about drink. I reminded him of that and told him the only reason he was saying anything now was because we were losing, and if he wanted to blame the drinking that was his problem. Ossie stuck up for me. He told him I'd been the best player in the side for months. Drink didn't affect the way I played.'

Alan's wife, Maureen, a striking model, had erected three plaques in the Hudson lounge. 'It's nice to be important, but more important to be nice,' read one rather pointedly. 'There are many reasons for drinking,' theorised another, 'and one has just entered my head: if a fellow can't drink when he's living, how the hell can he drink when he's dead?' Alan was merely Chelsea's least anonymous alcoholic. 'You only have to have two pints a day to be an alcoholic so maybe we did have a few of those. Me, Eddie Mac, Charlie, Tommy Baldwin, Hutch. We never used to drink on a Friday but we'd make up for it on the other days. I wasn't turning to the bottle as an escape: the game is a social one. We were always being invited to parties by the fans. They loved drinking with us. The Liverpool players used to go to the Adidas factory at least once a month and they'd shut the place down, bring out all these cases of beer and vodka and have a day out. That builds team camaraderie. I went to watch Chelsea play at Forest five or six years ago and saw them on the bus afterwards. They were all sitting apart. None of them was in the bar. I couldn't believe it. And it showed on the field.'

'The thing with Huddy,' says Peter, 'is that he lived near the ground for so long, with all his friends around him. Ridiculous. You can't do that. That's why I moved to Epsom. You can't be one of the lads anymore once you start earning the sort of money we were. That's what happened to Gazza at Newcastle. If you can put fifty quid down for a round of drinks they won't take it that way. They won't think of you as the nice guy, they'll think of you as the flash bastard.'

Alan was on his way to Stoke within a fortnight for £240,000. Any thoughts of redemption for Peter looked to have disappeared when he was sent off in training for fighting with Gradi. However, the asking price of £300,000, together with Peter's less-than-unblemished complexion, kept the number of suitors down. In the aftermath of a six-hour board meeting at the beginning of March, one unnamed player was quoted in *The Evening Standard*, saying that the board had decided to sack Sexton and keep Peter. 'Osgood has proved to be greater than the club,' lamented our informant. The next morning Brian Mears claimed that the press had 'misunderstood' the situation and stressed that the board were right behind their manager. At this, Peter asked for his cards and threatened to resign. Eight days later, Southampton took the plunge, paying a British record fee of £275,000. 'Of course it was a wrench to leave. I'd grown up there, made my name there. I was the king of Stamford Bridge. You can't beat that. You look forward to going there and playing every time, but obviously things had started to go wrong. The team wasn't the same and Dave had different ideas. He completely changed everything. We had a nice balance but he was playing people out of position. His whole mind had altered. He was looking for something that wasn't there. If we'd stuck to our guns and kept playing the same system we could have gone on, we could have built on those successes. But for those two 5–2 defeats against Leeds and Everton in 1969–70, who knows? As it is, we weren't quite good enough to win the League, but being in three consecutive finals, you would have thought that all we needed were a couple of extra players.

'Huddy and I both felt we'd had enough of the guy. His moods were always changing. The annoying thing was his attitude to training. Peter Bonetti's goal-kicking was the worst thing you ever saw in your life but Sexton never had him back practising. Chopper Harris couldn't hit a ball from me to you but he never had him back. The people he did have back were the flair players, all the time, for running. I loved his training but Dave thinks that everyone has to train the same way. We used to do four 40-yard sprints, have a minute's rest, then do another, then another, seven on the trot. Dave thought everyone should be able to run like John Hollins. But no one ever came back for passing the ball or sticking it in the back of the net. That hurt me more than anything.'

Since Sexton himself declined my request to put across his side of the story, it seems only fair to elicit the impartial view of Dave Webb, defensive lynchpin of the imaginative QPR side Sexton would pilot to within a hair's breadth of the Championship two seasons later. In all, Webb spent 11 years of his career under Sexton's stewardship, the pair reuniting at Loftus Road after Mears and his comrades had sacked Sexton a month into the 1974–75 season. The previous campaign had been Chelsea's worst since 1961–62, 17th place in the League capping instant dismissals from both knockout tourneys. 'There was no denying Dave's talent to make a team inventive. He allowed the likes of Osgood and Hudson to develop and become the players they were. The trouble was that we were all very immature, and we would do silly things. I suppose we all became a bit like spoilt kids. Let a kid get too spoilt then try to chastise him – that makes you just as guilty. I think I understand it more now than I did then, but perhaps Ossie and Huddy don't. They're very bitter.

'Sexton wasn't as open with us as he could have been but he was under intense pressure because this massive improvement programme was pulling the club down. The planning was done with Dave's say-so but he was the one who had to supply the wealth to pay for it. Keith Weller was the first to go and everything went downhill from there. There is a tendency for a manager to want to change things after he's been in the job a while, otherwise it does become boring. After five years at Brentford I know I felt that way. You've got to inject a bit of colour into it. Dave had been managing Chelsea for six years. Where he went wrong was, instead of nurturing the Osgoods and the Hudsons and the Cookes, he embarked on bringing people in who he thought were needed to win the League. They weren't brought in to help those players but with a view to replacing them. Suspicion crept in. A few went off the rails.'

Alan more than most, so much so that Bill Hudson stopped picking up the tickets his son would leave at the gate before every home match. 'He went way off the rails,' asserts Webb. 'He went off the rails with his own team-mates. He was a lovely kid. Everyone thought the world of him, but it became a standing joke: he would never turn up on Monday morning for training. Headache, flu, everything but having a baby. But if you went to his watering hole in the King's Road at one o'clock he was in there. We all knew but no one would ever grass. Dave must have had an idea of what was going on. If I'd have been him I would have stayed with Huddy for a week and brought him back into the fold. We were all such individuals . . . we all went a bit wayward at the wrong time. I don't think Alan ever grew up. He was a bit petulant. He played the game to enjoy it, all the time. That was probably his trouble.'

Market day, Uttoxeter, April 1994. Despite all circumstantial evidence, Alan is adamant that he has never been happier. The cheeks are certainly puffier, the blue eyes discernibly sunken. He looks a little crumpled, but then living out of a suitcase has its drawbacks. Divorced by Maureen after the best part of 20 years, he spends weeknights at the homes of various sympathetic friends in Stoke, weekends at his girlfriend's flat. Hired to coach Burton Albion a month earlier, internal upheaval at the club had prompted a sharp exit. Not only is he jobless but debts are high, thanks in the main to an abortive venture with Tampa Bay Rowdies. 'Rodney Marsh was managing them at the time, 1991. I had a verbal agreement from the Tampa board to stage a tournament there featuring Celtic, Forest, Man City and Sheffield Wednesday. We were talking about sponsorship with Budweiser. We spoke to the US Soccer Federation. It was a done deal but somebody made sure it didn't happen. I lost my house on that. It skinted me. I'm still paying the debts now. We would have been millionaires. We're still trying to sue Tampa but it's taking so long.'

The candour and good-humoured warmth do not, however, befit a fearful man. 'As Dion said, "They call me the wanderer". I love having no ties, feeling footloose. I can't ever remember feeling happier.' Alan's nephew Billy, 18-year-old son of John, is due to join us after he has finished his training duties with Crewe. Terry Venables had been an enthusiastic advocate of his at Tottenham before Billy upheld family tradition by walking out. 'I can see quite a bit of myself in him,' Alan concedes, 'but Billy is better than I was at his age.' Before Billy arrives, Alan must discuss terms for a charity function at Denstone College, Quentin Crisp's alma mater. There is talk of getting Charlie George along as well. The Denstone sports master, Tom O'Brien, an old friend who was once on Leeds United's books – 'Revie taught me certain things I wouldn't like to teach these boys' – has brought the first XI to town for a fixture against the local school, Alleyne's. As we amble up the high street towards the games field, the shouts ring out from all manner of nooks and crannies. 'How ya doin' Huddy?' . . . 'Good dig about Stoke in the paper last week, mate' . . . 'Don't fancy Arsenal's chances tonight'.

Tony Waddington had passed away a few weeks ago. 'I've cried more during the past week than when my dad died,' Alan had informed *The Independent*. Twenty years earlier, Waddington had emerged from behind a phone box outside the Russell Hotel – 'I thought he was a crank' – to escort Alan into Russell Square. Sitting him down on a bench, the Stoke City manager proceeded to spell out why the best thing the troubled 22-year-old could do for his career at that precise moment was to sign for an unfashionable club that had never won anything of note and were currently mired in the relegation zone. Having failed in his attempt to tempt Peter to the Potteries in a joint £500,000 deal – Peter didn't fancy the area – Waddington pounced while QPR dithered, then installed Alan in Geoff Hurst's bungalow while he was house-hunting. Maureen was delighted. Their marriage had been close to breaking up 'because our home was always full of people and I always seemed to be cooking for them'.

In his first practice match at the Victoria Ground, before he had even been introduced to his new workmates, Alan was handed a green bib. 'Whenever you get the ball,' Waddington instructed the rest of the first team, 'just give it to the green bib.' Waddington had found his fulcrum, Alan living up to expectations immediately with a spellbinding début at home to Liverpool. 'We only managed a draw but it was just the sort of confidence boost the team needed. At the end, Bill Shankly asked Tony if he could come into the dressing-room and talk to me, which was something Tony insisted he had never known another manager to ask. Right there, in front of the rest of the team, Shanks told me it was the finest performance he'd ever seen. He said Peter Doherty was the finest player of all time but that he'd never seen him play the way I had.'

Eight days later, Peter was at the Victoria Ground to provide moral support as Stoke defeated Chelsea. For the next two-and-a-half seasons, Alan was at the zenith of his powers: 24 points from the last 17 games – culminating, appropriately enough, with Alan riding a storm of boos to score the winner at the Bridge – lifted Stoke to fifth and a UEFA Cup berth. (Peter had experienced a similarly hostile reaction upon his return to the old neighbourhood, 'but it was just their way of saying "you shouldn't have left us".') In 1974–75 they came fifth again, Jimmy Greenhoff and Alan (who didn't miss a match) wielding the brushes for the League's pre-eminent stylists. Leading the division as late as 22 February, the eventual four-point margin between themselves and the champions, Derby, might easily have been reversed had it not been for four broken legs. Average home gates rose by more than 25 per cent, the biggest improvement in the division. Nestor Almendros, assuredly, would have referred to it as the Golden Hour of the Potteries.

Alan had been at Waddington's side an hour before he died. A month later, the sense of loss is showing few signs of receding. 'Tony was like a second father to me. He was everything Ramsey and Sexton weren't. He thought there was more to life than football. Alf was eat, drink and sleep football and yet he had some of the biggest drinkers in the world in his side. Nobody drank more than Bobby Moore. That didn't bother Tony. Work hard on the field and play hard off it, that was his motto. He was a mastermind. All he wanted you to do was go out and express yourself.'

The eyes moisten as the memories rush back. 'Easter 1975. I told Tony I couldn't make it for the Liverpool match because the ground was so bumpy. "Prepare for the game," he said, "and we'll go out and get drunk together afterwards." On the day of the match I turned up at one o'clock and the pitch was waterlogged even though we hadn't had a drop of rain – he'd had the fire brigade out the previous night to swamp it. I thought, "This fella doesn't mess around when he wants you to play, does he?" The conditions were perfect for me, we won 2–0 and for 90 minutes I was in heaven. It was one of those days when you know you can do no wrong. Near the end Tommy Smith came flying towards me near the touchline, sliding through the mud, and I just slipped the ball through his legs and kept going. I can't recall ever playing better than I did that day.'

While the drinking persisted, a greater seriousness of intent manifested itself. Within two years Alan had reduced his fighting weight (13 stone 10 pounds in 1973) by nearly three stone. Potatoes, bread and lunch were out, tea the beginning and end of breakfast. The urge for comfort eating had passed. With Ramsey gone, an international recall was back on the agenda. Oddly enough, sleep proved difficult when he was playing well. 'Night matches were the worst. I couldn't get the game out my head. A couple of sleeping pills on the night before a match would only knock me out, so the process would start all over again. Lying in bed, looking at your watch, cursing, then going downstairs to make a cup of tea. By Sunday I'd be shattered, so I learned to take a nap in the afternoon. I even fell asleep watching TV before my first game for England and had to be woken up to catch the coach to Wembley.'

Alan slept for all of ten minutes that night. Making one of the most widely acclaimed débuts in an England shirt, he had toyed with a West German side numbering four of their World Cup-winning team, Beckenbauer included. Prior to the kick-off, Don Revie had prefaced his third game as national manager by taking Ball and Alan aside for one of his more inspired pep talks. 'I'm sick and tired of seeing continentals come here and take the mickey out of us with their skills. Go and take the mickey out of the Germans. Be cocky, be confident. Show me you're the greatest.'

'It was music to my ears,' Alan told the press. 'Alf Ramsey used to drop people for being too cheeky.' In the seventh minute, Alan brought off a one-two with Ball, sending Mick Channon clean through only for the Southampton striker to be brought down. From then on the new kid ran the block, directing a 2–0 victory. The notices were rhapsodic. 'The memories of Raich Carter and Wilf Mannion stirred again,' reported David Miller in *The Daily Express*. 'At the heart of the Germans' destruction stood the languid, hip-shrugging Hudson, commanding the Wembley stage with classic skills and razor perception. All the years of unfulfilled potential rolled away as Hudson at last, at the first asking, assumed his proper place in football – at the top.'

'I just wish Netzer had been playing,' Alan reflects. 'I remember walking through the tunnel, looking across at Beckenbauer and thinking, 'You've arrived'. Playing against him, playing against the world champions, meant more to me than playing for England. And I'd been the best player on the field. As soon as I came off, I rang my dad and told him that was for him.' When Fleet Street descended on them the next morning, Alan and his family were still rolling out the barrel. Keeping an ankle injury to himself, Alan was retained for England's next date, a 5–0 European Championship waltz against Cyprus wherein Macdonald became the first man to net five goals in a senior fixture at Wembley. The contrast between the two occasions could scarcely have been more marked. 'It was like a Sunday morning match. The fella that marked me was a waiter from Fulham. Our full-backs kept racing upfield and bombing in crosses: everyone was queuing up to score. Horrible. Afterwards, Ballie had a go at me for not getting involved, so I asked him how I was supposed to do that. When those full-backs were playing against the Germans, I told him, they couldn't wait to get rid of the ball. Against sides like Cyprus everyone wants to be a star. That's why I always say I only played once for England. Mind you, I played better in that one game than most guys with a hundred caps have ever played.'

The ankle continued to play up, ruling Alan out of the home internationals. Consolation of sorts came when the Football Writers Association voted him runner-up to Alan Mullery as their player of the season, endorsing the decision of his peers in the PFA to elect him to their official Division One XI. Revie then chose him as an over-age player for the Under-23 trip to Hungary, a thinly-veiled insult. 'On the way over, Revie told us to get the business done and we'd have a few drinks on the flight home. In the event we were beaten and weren't allowed a drink, but Jimmy Greenhoff and I got stuck into our duty-free Canadian Club anyway. Who was he to tell us we couldn't have a drink? I was training with the full squad a month or so later when Revie took a number of players aside individually, myself included. I can't remember who else was involved but I'm sure Frank Worthington was one and Tony Currie might have been another. Revie told me he knew we'd been out drinking the previous night and that we weren't the sort of players he wanted. I've always said that Revie put me in against the Germans hoping I would fail. He didn't like me but, more than that, he didn't like Chelsea because of the rivalry with Leeds. He still saw me as part of that. You know something, despite all the compliments I received, he never said a word to me after the German game.'

The flak descended thick and fast in September when Alan told *The News of the World* he couldn't give two hoots whether Revie picked him again. Soon afterwards he received a letter from George Best which he treasures to this day. 'I know you're the best around,' it began. 'I know you ought to walk into that England team, but if they don't want you, you go out and ram it down their throats on the pitch. Go out and show them they can't do without you.' Much as this galvanised Alan for a while, he had clearly become dispirited. 'I try to subdue all my instincts about the game,' he confessed to one Sunday paper. 'I get out there and run around and tackle like a lunatic and when I come in I'm told, "Great Alan. That was much better." Then I get home and go to bed and think, "Bloody hell, I didn't enjoy that." If that's the way they want it played they can get someone else . . . If Cruyff came over here we'd try and teach him how to tackle. We'd make him just another player.'

'You'll play for a World XI before you play regularly for England,' Waddington had once predicted. To him, the brevity of Alan's international career constituted 'a condemnation of managers rather than him'.

I DON'T WANNA GO TO CHELSEA

A turbulent 1975–76 season ended prematurely when Alan broke his leg against Derby, ironically in the same match Charlie George paid so heavily for his reckless tackle on Dennis Smith. A £5,000 bill for tax arrears had been preoccupying the mind and sapping the confidence. He continued to struggle on his return and was accused of skiving by an unsympathetic doctor. Waddington packed him off to see a psychiatrist. It was difficult to dispute the psychosomatic theory. Enter the *deus ex machina*: the roof of the Butler Stand blew off. 'Arsenal were interested in me and the board were interested in their two hundred grand to help pay for a new roof. I went to Tony and told him I couldn't pay the tax bill and that if he could pay it I'd extend my contract. He said he couldn't do it because the club had no money, so I told him I was going to have to sign for Arsenal. A couple of days later Tony went to the bank and tried to raise the money but it was too late because I'd signed the night before. Maureen saw him outside the club offices and he was crying. It was hard to leave him, but the directors were giving him a hard time. If they can't look after him, I thought, where does that leave me? At 25, I was still a baby. I had a lot of football left in me.'

Not in England. Much as Alan's zest had been renewed by the thought of forming a midfield triad with Ball and Brady, that particular scenario vanished when it became clear that Terry Neill had signed him to *replace* Ball. Three months and a string of hotels and friends' abodes later Alan was diagnosed as suffering from severe depression. Neill gave him a dressing-down when he complained to the press about the club's negligence in finding him a permanent residence, whereupon a mooted return to Stoke was quashed by Waddington's resignation. When Alan fell heavily following a clash with Norwich's Colin Suggett, one scathing Highbury regular was quick to pounce: 'A light ale bottle must have fallen out of his shorts and hit him on the ankle.'

Alan nonetheless stayed put at Highbury until the following summer, his form during Arsenal's run towards the FA Cup final so impressing Revie's successor, Ron Greenwood, that he received a late summons to play against Brazil in April 1978. Pride dictated refusal. 'That was probably one of the great regrets of my life. I thought I should have been in the original squad. Then someone dropped out and a call came through from Greenwood while I was in the Wellington pub in Sloane Square. "With all due respect, Mr Greenwood," I said, "I thought I should have been in the side anyway. I don't want to get picked just because you've got injuries." You get so many knocks along the way, people picking you when it suits them rather than on merit. It was like Frank Sinatra being asked to fill in for Cliff Richard at the Albert Hall.

Frank would have told them where to go.'

If Alan was more monochrome than off-colour in the Cup final, the same could be said of just about every other Arsenal player who participated in that undistinguished 1–0 loss to Ipswich. On an ill-starred close-season jaunt to Australia, Alan and Malcolm Macdonald were found drinking after hours in Melbourne, sent home and placed on the transfer list. Macdonald was ultimately forgiven but Alan was soon upping sticks and heading for the States, vowing never to return. As a member of the Southampton side that day, Jimmy Gabriel had predicted a bountiful future for Alan following his Chelsea début nearly a decade earlier. As manager of the Seattle Sounders, it was Gabriel who met him on the King's Road to discuss terms. 'I know you like a drink,' Alan was told. 'I know you're serious about your football. I know you keep in shape. All I want is your ability out on the field.' Inside two years Alan's finances were vibrant enough for him to own three homes, including one in the Gulf of Mexico. Contentment at last, apparently.

Peter's career, meanwhile, had come full circle. But the man who swapped Philadelphia for Stamford Bridge shortly before Christmas 1978 had more in common with the Tin Man than the Wizard of Os. Unlike Alan, Peter struggled to replicate his Chelsea form after leaving SW6. Commuting from Tadworth until he found a home for his family, Rose, Anthony and Mark, near Windsor Safari Park, it took him ten games to score his first goal for a stolid Southampton side that duly dropped back into the Second Division at the end of the 1973–74 season. The Dell warmed to him, gradually.

'Lawrie McMenemy fancied me as a player. If he'd been England manager I reckon I would have won 60 or 70 caps. At the same time, he made a mistake at first by playing me upfront so people could build off me. I simply didn't have the pace or stamina to do it. It took him a year to realise that. Then he bought Ted MacDougall and we were a much better side because Ted was a target man, which was what I was used to playing off. I was also frozen out at first. Mick Channon was the kingpin and he used to get all the passes. He didn't pass much either. "I'm in so many good positions, why don't you pass to me?" I asked him at one point. "Ossie," he said, "when I see the whites of those posts, nobody's got any chance, not even you." Hughie Fisher was the worst culprit. If there was a choice of a five-yard ball to me or a 40-yard ball to Mickey, he'd go for Mickey. On the other hand he was the guy they'd all grown up with and they respected him. Hold on, they were saying, this new bloke has to earn his stripes.'

Less than a year after his arrival the new bloke was up for sale and off the road, banned for 12 months for a drink-driving offence. MacDougall supplied the jump leads, and the following May Peter had his final fling under the big top, helping Southampton collect the FA Cup at the expense of Tommy Docherty's listless Manchester United. The glow soon dimmed. After the celebrations were over, he and Peter Rodrigues found themselves drunk in possession of football's most ancient prize. Locking it in the boot of Peter's car for safekeeping, they were hauled over the coals by McMenemy the next morning. Forgiven though he was for that escapade, Peter was no longer automatically selected come the autumn and went on loan to Norwich. Hitherto in two minds whether to jack it all in, three outings in the First Division proved sufficient to reawaken the desire.

Nevertheless, for all that cocksure, laddish veneer, Peter was obviously grappling with self-doubt. Reclining in a London hotel lounge one Saturday in November, kick-off a couple of hours distant, he opened up to Peter Batt of *The Evening News*. 'The punters never see this side of it. They see big, flash Ossie having half a shandy on a Friday and they shout, "Oh, he's drunk again." They don't see me sitting here wondering how the bloody hell I'm going to get through the next two or three years. Look, I'm not the player I was and I know that better than anyone. I've turned into a mug, a carthorse. I've been a bricklayer's labourer instead of a bricklayer. Tell me I'm great and I love it. Tell me I'm a mug and I'm sick to my stomach. Maybe I did go to Southampton thinking I was the best in the business, but I'm paying the price now. Mick [Channon] is one of my best mates but the two of us in the same team just didn't work. I started thinking about turning it all in when my mum and my sisters decided to go and watch Southampton play at Chelsea while I was with the reserves at Birmingham. When your biggest fans desert you, you are really in trouble.' When Peter was called back to the Dell in December he was contrition personified. 'I admit I've let a lot of people down in the past. Most of all, perhaps, I've let myself down.'

Twelve months later Peter was released by Southampton, joining the transatlantic exodus before the spark refused to go on flickering. A transparent ploy to drum up activity at the turnstiles, his Chelsea comeback failed to stimulate much bar regret. Unable to inspire by example, he made ten appearances for a relegation-bound side then had an almighty row with the manager, Geoff Hurst, whom he accused of easing out his predecessor, Danny Blanchflower. At 32, Peter had had his fill. 'I just got bored with life and bored with football. I wasn't married at the time, I had no responsibilities and I had a bit of money in the bank so I sat back for a year or so, deciding what to do.'

When the cash-strapped Seattle Sounders board terminated his contract as player-coach in the summer of 1983, Alan, who had fallen out with the club's new general manager, not only went back on his word by re-embracing English football but followed Peter's lead by returning to native terrain. At the press conference called to welcome him back to the Bridge, the air of self-justification was inescapable. 'In a way, my reputation was justified, but I've been to a few clubs where players have behaved a lot worse than me and got away with it. I feel I was unfairly treated because so much was expected of me. George Best experienced the same sort of treatment. He was built up as something special and then people were only too keen to knock him down again.' In the event, Alan was continually at loggerheads with Ken Bates and did not appear in the first team. Waddington rang to say that Stoke could do with a hand and a month's loan was agreed in February 1984. In his first League match for six years he starred in a 1–0 win at home to Arsenal, Stoke's first win in six games, whereupon Alan rejoined the staff and was instrumental in keeping the club in the First Division. Mick Mills, the new manager, appointed him captain for 1984–85 but a knee injury restricted his involvement and there was little he could do this time to steer the club clear of the trapdoor. In November 1985 he took out joint ownership of a £280,000 Stoke nightclub ('another of my madcap business schemes') and retired. 'In the end,' he explained, 'you can sense that people are wondering if you are cheating. That's never been my style and I'd rather quit now than struggle on in that atmosphere.'

When Peter finally stirred himself, he bought a pub in Windsor in consort with Ian Hutchinson. Neither saw eye-to-eye with the other's domestic partner, however, and the venture ended after four years. Then came a painting and decorating business. Keeping his hand in with a series of coaching assignments ranging from Butlin's to the Far East and Gambia, Peter had recently stepped down the aisle for a third time, with Lynn, when his old mucker Alan Ball, now managing Portsmouth, invited him to coach the youth team. He held down the post for two years, nurturing Darren Anderton among others, before Jim Gregory dispensed with his services upon becoming chairman in June 1988. 'There was an uproar when Portsmouth took me on. People were saying things like, "How can you ask a drunk and a womaniser to look after kids?". People like me and Huddy, Stan, Marshy, Currie and Worthy, we all had a bad name. It was a great thing for Bally and his chairman, John Deacon, to have done. They gave me a chance not many others would have granted. They're frightened of you, you see. Frightened of your ability.'

Caspers Restaurant, Hanover Square. The week before Cup final week. An odd venue for lunch. Chicago-style bar, multinational fare, TV screens dotted around, a phone on every table. Ours keeps ringing but then goes dead whenever I pick up the receiver. Some gimmick. On an adjacent table less than two feet away sit four women in – at a guess – their early 20s, hunched together in conspiratorial titters. I still haven't caught on by the time the ringing resumes. Reaching over for the receiver once more, I spot one of our neighbours trying to disguise the fact that she is giving the mouthpiece of her phone the kiss of life. Now she knows that I know, she speaks into it and asks whether we are in a meeting. Peter nods. Are we golfers, she wonders. I tell Peter it must be his sweater, a Pringle number chockful of cream and green diamonds, Turnberry to a turn. His eyes twinkle, lapping up the attention. A besuited Alan joins him for a photo session with a snapper from *The People*. The oversized coin Alan dangles in front of the camera turns out to be his Cup final *losers'* medal. The readers will never be able to tell the difference. 'Look at that,' he chuckles, flipping it over to read the inscription: 'Unlucky'. Alan may have missed the 1970 final but Chelsea had obtained a winners' gong for him all the same. 'My mum'd die before letting that out of her sight. I reckon that's why my dad died. She kept prodding him all those years in bed, telling him to make sure it was still there.'

Alan had just spent the weekend at the Osgood abode near Winchester. With Chelsea in the Cup final for the first time since their own haymaking heyday, the spotlight beaming in their direction once more, all seems set fair for a reunion of the Class of '70. All that remained was for every member to be tracked down and a price to be agreed. Together they run through the list with Alan's friend and partner, Paul McCormack, pausing only to pay their respects to 'Nobby' Houseman, victim of a fatal car crash in 1977. Brian Madley from *The People*, trusted ally and matey intermediary, points out that only Ron Harris had 'really made anything' of himself, snapping up some land in the West Country with his testimonial kitty, turning it into a golf course then selling off the whole enchilada at some unseemly profit. Chopper is now running a hotel in Wiltshire. 'You guys must've thought you had it made,' teases Madley. Still homeless, still unemployed and still never happier, Alan shrugs and smirks; Peter, whose numerous pies include golf weekends, sports promotion and after-dinner rapping, seems a mite offended.

The roll-call begins. Peter Storey's one-time accomplice and fellow jailbird, Tommy Baldwin, still 'ducking and diving' according to

Alan, is a definite starter. Dave Webb manages Brentford. Peter Bonetti swapped the pastoral delights of a postman's job on the Isle of Mull for coaching goalkeepers, most recently at Wolves. John Hollins doubles as players' agent and media pundit. The Jocks went west: Charlie Cooke runs a soccer school in Cincinnati, Eddie McCreadie, the promotion-winning manager Chelsea sacrificed over the price of a company car, has a painting and decorating concern in Memphis. John Dempsey is a sports instructor at a North London centre for the mentally and physically handicapped. Marvin Hinton, substitute at Wembley and Old Trafford and arguably the most skilful English defender of modern times never to win a full cap, ran a removals business until a car accident left him partially disabled, compelling early retirement. Although he is expected to join us (but doesn't) there is grave concern about Ian Hutchinson, landlord-turned-unemployed chef and now beset by liver problems. 'I love Hutch,' Peter whispers plaintively, 'but I can't take him to my golf club because he knows the bar staff and they'll give him a drink.'

Madley says he has been trying to persuade his editor to offer a £10,000 package for the photo shoot and story. Taking a deep breath, he then warns that budget constraints at the Mirror Group might render the whole project impracticable. Strangely, this news does not appear to perturb either Peter or Alan. Having spent the past three decades zooming up ladders and slithering down snakes, middle age has instilled a degree of phlegmatism. By the same token, neither passions nor egos have diminished. Fiercely protective of their accomplishments, dismissive towards those whom they regard as having sought to crush their spirit and individuality, both plead innocent to the charge of wilful under-achievement. The time for remorse has long passed.

Alan will not be attending the final. For one thing, he is being sued by Ken Bates for some typically forthright indiscretions in Madley's organ. Peter is employed in a PR capacity for Chelsea's home fixtures, yet he, too, is not entirely at one with the club chairman, the man responsible for proposing that the hooligans could be defeated by the simple expedient of electrified fences. Evidently not a sentimental character (how many sentimental self-made millionaires do you know?), Bates certainly makes intriguing company. Bluff, gruff and rarely short of a crass joke – invariably boyish blue ones – he craves attention while harbouring a deep sensitivity, which might go some way towards explaining why he bangs off writs with almost as much vigour as he thumps out polemical programme notes. One of Peter's party pieces revolves around a conversation with Bates in which the chairman asks him how he imagines the 1970 Chelsea would get on against the fitter, faster present-day aggregation. 'We'd win 1–0,' forecasts Peter, drawing a quizzical look from Bates. 'Then again, we are all nearing fifty.'

Alan tells Madley that since Tommy Docherty was responsible for 'building Chelsea's name', Bates should have sent him an invitation. A few weeks earlier, Hutchinson had offered an explanation for this apparent oversight. 'Bates has been very jealous of the success we had – we even had a Chelsea Seventies side that used to play every Sunday for charity – because he hasn't really had any. He resents us. I drove up to the Bridge one day, past the old gateman, who I knew well, and went to ask Sheila [Marston, the club secretary] for a couple of complimentary tickets. Bates came out and said: "I pay for my tickets, you'll pay for yours." I went on about how I'd played for the club for ten years and how I had been in the Cup final side but he told me to get out. Called security and everything. Then he sacked the gateman, who'd been there for 27 years.' Hutchinson swore he would never return. 'But I have,' he admits, helplessly – 'twice.'

When Peter spins a yarn he enjoys it so much that he avails us of an immediate encore. One of the runners in the 4.10 at Chester is My Lovely Lady, owned by Alan until financial difficulties struck him amidships. 'Is she a stayer?' Peter demands to know. 'What,' quips Alan, 'like your first two wives?' If this sounds suspiciously like a well-rehearsed routine, the boyishness of the banter infers otherwise. Alan makes no bones about the fact that earning a packet in one's mid-20s is a hoot. 'Stoke were at White Hart Lane and I go to collect the ball for a throw-in when all of a sudden this woman from the stands starts shouting at me, calling me a cunt. So I look up and spot a bloke sitting next to her. "'Ere, missus," I yell up to her, "how much does your old man make a week?" The ref comes over and tells me to get on with it but we just carried on shouting at each other.'

Firm friends though they are, there is a vague tension between Peter and Alan. Whereas the former exudes a genial aloofness, legacy of all those years on a pedestal, the latter is more self-effacing. Ken Furphy, who once managed him on an England Under-23 trip to France, remembers Alan giving him his commemorative medal when he discovered that they were only being distributed among the players. Now less inclined towards forelock-tugging, Alan makes no secret of his contempt for the ungentlemanly lengths Peter was once prepared to go to assert himself in the face of flying studs. 'Huddy was always a wimp,' laughs Peter. Alan's respect for his talent, conversely, remains profound. 'West Ham, Boxing Day 1973, our last game at the Bridge together.

We're 2–0 up at half-time and Sexton says to me, pointing in Ossie's direction: "You're not doing us any good passing to him all the time." So I said, "I don't know, my dad always taught me to pass to the best player in the side."' Not that Alan has ever been one for self-deprecation. 'I used to take Ossie down the King's Road to kit him out when I was still a teenager. I reckon I knew every boutique owner in the street. "You're the Wizard of Os, mate," I told him. "If I'm going to make you look good, you ought to look the part." '

As coffee punctuates the endless stream of Chardonnay, the circle expands to incorporate a rather sheepish Bobby Stokes, whose 15 minutes began and ended with the goal that ensured Peter's second FA Cup winners' medal. Alan cracks a joke about John Barnes's penis and Kenny Dalglish's penis envy. The boys are still being boys. It is generally agreed that the nearest approximation to a star in the present Chelsea firmament is Gavin Peacock, whose goals had twice beaten United in the Premiership. Son of that Gillingham perennial, Keith Peacock, Gavin is a devout Christian whose faith was cruelly repaid when his own son was born with his right arm truncated at the elbow. Able though he is deemed to be, the consensus of the table is that Gavin does not come remotely close to recapturing the spirit of 1970. Nor, for that matter, does anyone else. Naming all 11 likely starters is beyond us all. Alan doesn't even want Chelsea to win. Glenn Hoddle or no Glenn Hoddle, he denounces them as a collection of 'scufflers', attracting a slightly disapproving glance from Peter. Not only do I echo these sentiments, I blurt out my desire for a 5–0 United win, for complete justice. After the way they have enriched our lives over the past nine months, Alan concurs, Giggs, Kanchelskis and Cantona deserve no less.

Eleven days later, I almost get my wish, although Cantona's two penalties do remove some of the gloss. After catching fleeting glimpses of the second half in The Oval press box, I get home and forget to tune in to *Match of the Day*. The thought of trying to obtain a ticket had never crossed my mind. Obligations be damned.

Queen's Park Arrangers

'If you've got it, flaunt it baby, flaunt it.'

Max Bialystock, *The Producers*

In terms of contrasting images, 10 is far and away the most evocative of numbers. Downing Street and Tory misrule, Barry John and Welsh omnipotence. A film buff would probably swallow hard and nominate Bo Derek and Dudley Moore. Most football purists would opt for Pele, Cruyff and Maradona. Those whose allegiances lie with Queen's Park Rangers, however, would doubtless cite another trio united by the number on their backs. Between 1966 and 1983, that fetching blue-and-white hooped No. 10 shirt was handed down from Rodney Marsh to Tony Currie via Stan Bowles. It is hard to conceive of any other club blessed with such an illustrious line of succession.

As the Chelsea razzle lost its dazzle, so QPR picked up the wand. From 1974 to 1977, the Shepherd's Bushwackers were the cock of the metropolis, never mind the west side. Neither was this just any old irony. Not only did John Hollins and Dave Webb have a hand in this coming-of-age, but so too Dave Sexton, evidently more content as he was amid a less pressurised environment.

Prior to Sexton's appointment in October 1974, those soul-destroying ructions with Osgood and Hudson had coincided with QPR's best League season thus far, eighth place pushing them above the Stamford Bridge brigands for the very first time, a feat they would repeat on eight occasions over the ensuing ten seasons. The recipe was conventional enough for an ambitious club with a modicum of cash to flash: homegrown youth produce (Gerry Francis, Dave Clement, Ian Gillard), mature local bargains (McLintock, Webb, Hollins) and pricier imports (Bowles, Don Masson, Dave Thomas). Together they marched to a jaunty beat, interpassing at pace, invention and cheek to the fore. Although he had left for Crystal Palace by the time Sexton came aboard, Terry Venables was the major catalyst, his free-kicks a monument to ingenuity, his main legacy the confidence he imbued in the younger players. It is difficult to recall anyone taking the piss out of a Liverpool defence quite as thoroughly as did Francis in the opening minutes of the 1975–76 season – sauntering through the middle, laying off one-twos, scoring with aplomb. These, assuredly, were bullish times at the Bush.

The onset of insurrection can be traced back to the mid-Sixties. During that decade, seven clubs entered Division One for the first time – Ipswich, Leyton Orient, Northampton Town, Southampton, Coventry, QPR and Crystal Palace. Luton, conversely, were the lone successful wannabees of the Fifties. Unsurprisingly, the common denominator among the three clubs that put down the strongest roots – Coventry, Ipswich and QPR – was a well-heeled chairman. Derrick Robins, John Cobbold and Jim Gregory were each infused with an entrepreneurial vision, none more so than Gregory, a wide boy in every possible sense. Graduating from the North End Road market to second-hand cars, Gregory had widened his portfolio to encompass property. He had time for rough diamonds like Rodney Marsh and, especially, Stan Bowles, because he was one himself. Indeed, some would maintain that his edges were even more jagged.

QPR's early mode of existence had served as an object lesson for any budding nomad. From the amalgamation of St Jude's Institute and Christchurch Rangers in 1882 to the club's graduation as founder members of the Third Division in 1920, home encompassed no fewer than 11 venues, the westward shift whisking them from Kensal Rise to Shepherd's Bush via Brondesbury, Kensal Green, Kilburn, Notting Hill, Park Royal and Wormwood Scrubs. Between 1917 and 1963, they flitted between Loftus Road and White City before settling at the former site. Midway down the Third Division at the time, they were still there when Gregory joined the board in November 1964 after spurning a similar offer from Fulham. Elected chairman the following spring, his impact was immediate on a club hitherto unable to compete in English football's most congested marketplace. Accustomed as they were to churning out mediocrity on a shoestring, so stretched were Rangers' resources that Alec Stock had bought just one player in the whole of 1964–65. During the close season, however, Gregory's chequebook lassooed Les Allen, Ian Watson, Keith Sanderson and Jim Langley. Stock's shrewdest purchase, though, was undoubtedly that of Rodney Marsh in March 1966. Without Gregory, it is possible that Rodney might still have taken that short hop from Craven Cottage. Without Rodney, it is inconceivable that Queen's Park Rangers would ever have been known for much else besides being the first English football club to be referred to by their initials. If Gregory made Rodney, Rodney made QPR.

(i) The Jean Genie

Erotic preferences aside, David Bowie's bawdy bisexual is not all that far removed from the genie who materialised from Stock and Gregory's magic lamp. Both have a predilection for denim, both like to outrage, both love to be loved. Neither, furthermore, needs any encouragement to let himself go. Before Rodney Marsh breezed into the picture, QPR were Third Division in every respect, with average gates hovering around 8,000. Two seasons later the mean was 18,447, a rise of 115 per cent. One devotee pounded ceaselessly on a bass drum, raising the tempo according to the degree of assistance he felt the side needed. Others painted their homes blue and white. Or their gardens. Consecutive promotion campaigns played their part, of course, but it was Rodney's braggadocio that did most to provoke the stampede. His colleagues were mere co-stars, the club but a soundtrack. When the crowd chanted 'Rod-nee, Rod-nee', it was not intended as a tribute to their idol's inhibitions.

Watching Rodney stroll into Langan's Brasserie in an open-necked white shirt and faded blue jeans, wispy shoulder-length hair now a distinguished silvery grey, reminded me that Mick Jagger was not the only Peter Pan due to turn 50 in 1994. Until a week ago Rodney had been employed by Tampa Bay Rowdies, for whom he had served as manager and player for 17 years all told. The health of domestic soccer in the pre-World Cup USA had been far from rude. In Rodney's words, the club's owner, Cornelia Corbett, heiress to the Standard Oil trillions and a close friend, had 'lost energy' and ceased operations. 'I'm officially out of work for the first time in my life,' he announces. 'It feels great.' Not that he has any pressing need for employment. There's the Greek villa and condo in Tampa, the Wimbledon flat, a yacht anchored in the Gulf of Mexico. For the past couple of years he had been talking about buying Manchester City, assembling proposals, outlining a blueprint for the future, but Francis Lee had beaten him to it. The only Maverick still hitched to his original spouse, his children, Jonathan and Joanna, are both in their 20s. This erstwhile Astaire-in-liniment is sorely in need of a fresh challenge, preferably within the profession he has always seemed so keen to convert into a Broadway show.

George Best has sent apologies for his absence. Rough night. He is forgiven. He always will be. To listen to Rodney, the Greatest Living Irishman has apparently stacked up enough credit to last two lifetimes. 'George gave us the link between football and the world. There were so many players that had character and desire but we didn't have a champion. George was the champion. We came on to the scene at the same time but he was the catalyst. He made it possible to play with freedom. He also brought the game to a new level. When I was growing up 30 years ago, the back page of the paper was football and inside all the other sports were covered. Now there are seven pages of football. If George had played in the World Cup he would have been the greatest player of all time. The only reason people think Pele was the best is because he did it four times.

'That's not to disparage Pele, mind. He paid me the biggest compliment of my life. He was playing for New York Cosmos against us, Tampa, and during the pre-game talk he got up and said: "This could be a difficult game. They only have one player, number 10. His name is Marsh. He's English but he plays like a Brazilian".' For proof, try the most sublime hat-trick in the history of the known universe. QPR v Birmingham, October 1970. Taming a steeply bouncing ball with the outside of his left foot, controlling it with the heel, Rodney volleyed No. 1 from 30 yards. Rising a good foot above his marker as a corner swung across, he flick-headed No. 2 from 12 yards with a snap of the neck muscles. Then the *pièce de résistance*: back to goal, 15 yards out, four defenders immediately to the rear? Child's play. A deft pirouette then a feint with the sole, first to the left, then to the right. Removing one obstacle and leaving the other three wobbling, he created a foot of space to slot home a measured shot that would not have looked out of place on the 18th green at The Belfry.

Rodney, understandably, did not attract universal admiration among his peers. If there is one thing the mediocre envy even more than excellence, after all, it is excellence without sweat. Some considered Rodney the idlest English footballer of his generation, some merely the vainest. 'The trouble with Marshy,' mused Frank McLintock, 'was that he'd rather put the ball through someone's legs one more time.' In truth, Rodney's intelligence distanced him as much as that perceived

Jack the Laddishness. 'Unlike most of the blokes I played with, I think I could have done something else with my life, something just as exciting. I could have been a painter, for instance. The only memories I have of my League career revolve around the camaraderie, not the game, but at the same time, the only player I've ever felt *simpatico* with is Bestie. We can sit in a room and somebody will say something and we'll say exactly the same thing at exactly the same time. It's amazing. I didn't feel that way with Stan Bowles or Bobby Moore or Francis Lee or Colin Bell. I first met George in Manchester at Slack Alice's. I didn't feel a bond straight away, but when we played for Fulham we roomed together a couple of times and struck up a relationship there. We think so similarly about the game and about life that it was probably always there. It just needed time to come out. About three years ago he called me in America and asked if I wanted to do a series of speaking engagements and it worked really well, so we carried on. There is a script, but we basically do it off the cuff. Most of the stories are basically true, we just embellish them a bit, have a bit of fun. It's nostalgia, and I'm very flattered that people want to hear what I have to say.'

The azure eyes twinkle impishly. 'If I could write my own epitaph, it would be: "You can do whatever you want in this life provided you are prepared to take the consequences." I basically didn't give a fuck what anyone said. Everybody should be a non-conformist, because if you listen to all these pricks telling you how to eat your breakfast or how to park your car, you end up with Big Brother. I played for the crowd. I wanted them to enjoy it as much as I did. I played the way I wanted to play and I didn't listen to anybody unless I believed in them. Malcolm Allison was probably the only coach I've ever played for who made any sense so I ignored all the others. I tried to ignore Alf Ramsey but at that level you can't do that. Ask Stan Bowles. It's ridiculous that he only played five times for England when you get people like Carlton Palmer, who sometimes cannot pass the ball accurately from 25 yards, winning more. Alan Hudson playing twice for England is an indictment of the game. Having said that, this is a very exciting time for English football. We've got players like Le Tissier, Sutton and Cole, Terry Venables is manager of England, Manchester United are playing great football. The next four years could be very, very exciting.'

With the exception of his father Bill, an East End docker bent on steering his only son down the career path he would have preferred for himself, the most profound influence on the young Rodney was Ferenc Puskas. After that most magical of Magyars had enchanted Wembley in 1953, Bill began to ape the Hungarian's party tricks in the cramped back yard of the family home in Stoke Newington. While Bill juggled matchboxes and coins, Rodney, never happier than when bucking convention, practised his trickery on Bakewell tarts. Horrified at the prospect of scrumming down with the rugger buggers, he turned down a place at Hackney Downs Grammar after passing his 11-plus and went instead to the Joseph Priestley Technical College and thence, at 14, to Brooke House Technical College, where he excelled at English and art. 'I was a painter and still am. I started out trying to paint like Matisse, Gauguin, Manet, Monet, Renoir, and realised that I didn't have a gift for that and went on to try and copy Salvador Dalí. I've got three originals of his.' An avid accumulator of general knowledge and statistical ephemera, and a show-off to boot, he was 16 when he wrote to *Pear's Cyclopaedia* pointing out an error in an entry about Apollo. 'Dear Mr Marsh,' ran the gist of the reply, putting the clever young dick in his place with due delicacy, 'you were referring to the Greek god Apollo, we are referring to the Roman god Apollo.' Not that this infused greater humility. 'I realise this sounds very arrogant, but I always thought I knew better than anyone else.'

Nightly five-a-sides at the Alexander Boys Club sharpened the competitive instincts before regular appearances for the Hackney District side brought Rodney into contact with Ron Harris, then an inside-left of all things. Rodney himself started out in the side as left-back but switched to the left wing after scoring an opportunistic hat-trick when the first choice flanker left his boots at home. Spotted by West Ham at 16, he was training at Upton Park twice a week and playing for the juniors until Sir Stanley Rous, then the FA secretary, wrote to the club reminding them that schoolboys were not allowed to represent professional clubs. By the time Rodney was eligible, Fulham were quicker off the mark, offering him £8 a week as an apprentice.

It did not take long for the hazards of his chosen field to make an imprint. Deputising for the injured Johnny Haynes, Rodney scored on his League début against Aston Villa in March 1963. Six months later he contested a cross with the rugged Leicester right-back, John Sjoberg, headed the winner and sustained a broken jaw. Permanent deafness in the left ear was compounded by a narrowing of his field of vision as well as a loss of balance. Jogging along the track at Craven Cottage, he would suddenly find himself veering away towards the pitch, convinced he was 'running downhill with a steep camber dropping away to the left'. He considered giving it all up but after four months his balance and vision were restored. He was back in the first team by April and annexed a regular spot the following season, scoring 17 goals in 41 League games.

The Craven Cottage of the early Sixties certainly suited the extrovert. 'Every week, some superstar would be there. Tom Courtney, Oliver Reed, Michael Crawford, Honor Blackman. For that moment in time Fulham were so special. We had all the great characters – Johnny Haynes, Jimmy Hill, Tony Macedo, Jim Langley, Alan Mullery. Win or lose, the fans would still be there. But then it all got too serious, too mechanical, right at the time when people like Osgood and Venables were coming through at Chelsea. So Chelsea became the showbiz team and all the superstars defected.'

Rodney, too, although in his case the club were quite happy for him to go. Haynes, it was said, did not approve of the youngster's stylistic excesses. The Fulham manager, Vic Buckingham, duly insisted he cut out the dribbling and when Rodney declined he was offloaded to QPR for £15,000. Alec Stock was exceedingly grateful. 'Whatever Fulham gave away I grabbed. It started with Roy Bentley and Jim Langley, then Rodney, then Bobby Keetch and later Malcolm Macdonald. The lovely thing about these players was that they had all been brought up to pass the ball. That was the club style, the Haynes influence. When I started managing them a few years later, I asked Tommy Trinder why the hell he let me have someone like Marshy. "Johnny didn't think he could play very well," he answered.'

The dapper, amiable Stock knew otherwise. 'Marshy was 22, six-foot one and 13 stone. A big bastard. But if you whacked him, he didn't take umbrage, he just came back at you with the ball, pushed it between your legs or over you or under you or through you. Marshy would do amazing things. At Fulham he did them occasionally but with them he was quietly entertaining. With Rangers he was not only entertaining but made sure we got results, a complete professional. We taught him application. He scored some fabulous goals from free-kicks, not that we practised them. He would run at fellas, looking at them and chatting to them while dribbling the ball between his heels. I used to tell his father he could charm the birds off the trees. After that first season he wasn't always consistent, but then, as Danny Blanchflower said, only mediocrity is consistent.'

Stock was the Mr Fixit of the underclass. 'By trade,' he states proudly, 'I turned clubs professional.' Although clearly not meant in the strictest sense, the claim is justified. He guided Yeovil to the fifth round of the FA Cup in 1948–49 – Sunderland the prize scalp – then spent nine years managing Leyton Orient, whom he led back to the Second Division in 1956 after an absence of nearly three decades. Although he left two years later, he could still bask in reflected glory when promotion to the First was attained in 1962. In 1970 his Luton charges gained promotion to the Second Division; in 1975 he was manning the bridge when Fulham reached their first FA Cup final. As much as anything else, players respected him for his honesty. When Steve Earle and Paul Went missed Fulham's opening game of the 1972–73 season through injury, Stock immediately held his hand up, admitting he had been working them too hard. Small wonder he was never hired by any member of the ruling class.

At Loftus Road, as was his wont, Stock built from the bottom up. 'We started up a junior side in the Harrow and District League until they won everything and no one wanted to play us. So we stuck them in the South-East Counties League and still they kept winning. We had a great array of juniors, people like Ian and Roger Morgan, Tony Hazell, Ron Hunt and Mick Leach. One day I thought, "Let's be bold," so we put six 18-year-olds into the first team. We couldn't stop them winning. That's when Rodney and Les [Allen] came, thanks to Jim Gregory's money. Jim had time for the spivvy types like Rodney, and later Stan [Bowles] of course. He thought you could do something with them. So, on top of all these fit and extremely virile young people we now had really talented ones as well.'

Fruition was swift. Rodney had scored eight times in 16 games as a Ranger before the 1966–67 season catapulted him into the wider sphere. QPR rampaged through the Third Division, taking the title by 12 points, with Rodney responsible for 30 of their 103 goals. More noteworthy still were the ten strikes that powered the club to the first League Cup final staged at Wembley. Two down at half-time to First Division West Bromwich Albion, both of whose goals had emanated from the former Rangers winger, Clive Clark, the outsiders sprang back with three of their own. The equaliser was pure, unadulterated Rodney. 'The field was lush, magnificent, and I was playing on Cloud Nine. We'd got it back to 2–1 when Mike Keen hit a 40-yard pass to me. I had my back to goal and as this orange ball arrived everything felt as if it was in slow-motion. The ball just stuck to my foot. As soon as I controlled it I knew I was going to score. I wandered around with the ball until I found an opening. I didn't know I'd beaten four players on the way. Then I shot from 25 yards, hit the inside of the post. It's all destiny, isn't it? Then I ran towards the QPR fans. The smell of the field, the colours, everything was heightened. The surge of adrenalin was so strong, I could have done anything at that moment – climbed a mountain, stopped a car in its tracks. It's like when you feel the blood pumping through your neck when you're having sex. Scoring a goal like that was an incredible high, almost surrealistic. Your head explodes.' How did he celebrate? 'With Alec Stock's daughter.'

Three days later, Rodney was still floating when he took the roadshow back to Loftus Road to face Bournemouth, scoring twice in a 4-0 romp: 'It was the only time in my life I've ever played drunk.' If Stock was aware of his condition, it evidently didn't bother him. 'He played so-oo well that night. I sat on the touchline and at one point I asked the referee to keep the game going for another half an hour, just to see what the big fella could do. After the game, the Bournemouth chairman, who also happened to be an FA councillor, comes up to me and says, "That Marsh, he ain't half a lucky player." "That's funny," I said, "but he's just scored his 39th goal of the season and that's more than your lot have scored this season." People can be very bitchy in football. If someone has a good player we are inclined to say "he's not very good but we could do something with him if we had him".'

The momentum carried QPR through 1967–68, which was just as well. Rodney broke his foot in pre-season training and missed the first three months, attracting more than 3,000 to Southend for his reserve-team comeback. Three colleagues suffered breaks of some description (Keith Sanderson twice), five more underwent cartilage operations (Frank Sibley twice) while Ron Hunt had four months out after a kidney operation. In the final fixture at Villa Park, nevertheless, an own goal eight minutes from time put QPR up on goal average. Capped twice at Under-23 level that season after tonsilitis had forced him out of the previous summer's junior tour, Rodney cherishes a virtuoso goal at Millwall. Taking a short corner, he nutmegged two defenders on the byeline, stepped inside, switching the ball from left foot to right to improve the angle, then thundered the ball in off the underside of the bar. When the QPR coach stopped in Marlborough *en route* to the West Country, Rodney and Sanderson, a Cambridge graduate, left their team-mates in a tea-shop and adjourned to the local library to settle a factual dispute. 'He bends an ear to progressive jazz,' Geoffrey Green informed readers of *The Times*, 'and extemporises his football much like a jazz soloist.' A jazz club in Manor House was the appropriate setting when Rodney met his future wife, Jean. Seldom one for procrastination, he proposed on the spot.

By August, a new £210,000 stand on the South Africa Road side was finished, and so was Stock, who went off in search of another batch of waifs and strays to groom for stardom. After waiting nigh-on 20 hours for the club's first win in Division One, Bill Dodgin lasted until the end of November. Cue Tommy Docherty for a 28-day tenure that ended when Gregory refused to sanction the signing of Brian Tiler from Rotherham, though Docherty had the last chortle – his new employers, Aston Villa, prevailed when the clubs met in the third round of the FA Cup. QPR's eventual tally of 18 League points, moreover, represented a new divisional low. It is hypothetical to wonder whether the return to more modest climes would have been as prompt had injury not restricted Rodney to 17 appearances. Cynics concluded that his expansive repertoire could not possibly flourish on such a lofty, unforgiving stage, others that the case was unproven. Not that any of this persuaded women to refrain from sending him their undergarments.

In August 1969, Rodney unveiled a less palatable side to his on-field persona during a purported 'friendly' with Glasgow Rangers, incurring a £50 fine after clashing with Kai Johansen and butting Bobby Watson when the latter tried to intervene. For someone whose professed ambitions were to represent his country 'and see the troubles of the world at an end', such actions were regrettable, albeit at least partially excusable. 'I became a very violent player. When I was 20 I played for the love of the game but as I grew older I realised I had to protect myself. I ended up hurting a lot of people, which I regret. Defenders didn't like guys like me prancing around with their long hair. If you're a defender making fifty quid a week and the fella you're marking is on four hundred, plus he's got lovely long hair, women chasing him and an E-type Jag, you go out there to cut him down to size. What happened to people like me and Ossie is that we became the aggressors, getting in first. Ossie was brutal. Manchester City were beating Rochdale 7–0 in a League Cup tie a couple of years later when I went in high on a 19-year-old kid and his leg snapped in two just below the knee. I was only looking to preserve myself but I felt so sick and guilty. I went to see him in Manchester Infirmary and told him how sorry I was. "That's alright, Rodney," he said, "can I have your autograph?".'

Equally distasteful in many eyes was Rodney's aptitude for conning referees into awarding dubious penalties, which he naturally took himself. If there was an element of justice in this as well, the explanation failed signally to placate the sceptics. 'I always keep the ball close when I'm dribbling. Maybe not as close as Charlie Cooke, who is the best ball-player in the world, but never more than a foot away. So if the fellow doesn't get the ball he gets me.' Crowds preferred the sheer sauce of the man. In a League Cup tie against Bristol Rovers in October 1971, the visitors' wall was lined up to block Rodney's right-foot banana shot, so he changed feet and bent the free-kick round the other side to equalise. At Carlisle a few weeks later, during one of his last games for QPR, he raced after a high ball, caught it on his right foot, balanced it for a moment, then flicked it over the advancing full-back, waltzed round him and caught it again. By the end, even the home fans were pleading for him to be put in possession. John Arlott saw the effect in a different if no less complimentary light. 'Rodney Marsh shares a distinction with a few footballers, such men as Matthews, Eusebio, Pele and Greaves, as one of the rare forwards of our time so respected – in truth, feared – that the supporters of opposing teams cheer when they are stopped or dispossessed.'

At international level, Rodney, inexplicably, was the one who was asked to do the stopping – overlapping full-backs, opposite number, you name it. It is a wonder Ramsey ever looked his way. He was 27 when he won his first full cap, in November 1971, coming on as substitute against Switzerland at Wembley for the princely sum of seven minutes. Ramsey also brought him off the bench during that first, calamitous leg of the European Championship quarter-final against West Germany, then started him in each of the next seven internationals. The last of these was a 1–1 home draw with Wales that ultimately did as much to cost England a role in the 1974 World Cup as the subsequent stalemate against Poland. Rodney was not the only casualty. 'Ramsey and I never got on. He was loyal to me but that was only because we were winning.' Unlike his fellow Mavericks, he had had a decent run, yet not once did he come remotely close to the form of which he was capable. The tragedy in his case was that he was prevented from exhibiting the wares that had won him recognition in the first place. The impression was not so much that Ramsey suffocated Rodney, but that he castrated him.

This suspicion was soon confirmed to the press. 'It's easy for people to look at what I didn't do for England and decide that I had a good run and didn't take my chance. But for a player like me it was an absolute feat to stay in the team that long. There was no way I could do the job that was asked of me because I was nothing like Geoff Hurst whom I was replacing. At the time I made a conscious decision to play the way I was told mainly because I had been given an assurance that it was the way to stay in the team. Now I'm slightly ashamed that I didn't do what I'd always done and gamble everything on playing my own game. Those games also robbed me of the most important quality I have – my arrogance. People may not like me for it, but that arrogance is what makes me believe I can do anything with a football. I should have stood or fallen on playing my first game my own way. But like all the England players I settled for doing something I didn't enjoy.'

Even a stunning volleyed goal at Ninian Park produced a bitter aftertaste. 'I knew I couldn't do it Ramsey's way, so in that game I decided to play my natural game no matter what the consequences. We got an early goal, then I scored a second and thought: "This is the chance to show everyone that England can play attacking football." I started holding the ball, taking on players and beating them, doing a bit of mickey-taking. We won 3–0 and the fans loved it. But not Alf. At training the following day I was still feeling well pleased with myself. Then Alf called me to one side and said: "The way you played last night is not the way I expect England players to perform. If you play like that again you're out." I was absolutely gutted. I decided to write and tell Alf that I didn't want to be selected again but I had a talk with Malcolm before posting it. "Stick with it," he said, "and it'll come." But it didn't.'

The fence is occupied by Malcolm Allison, under whose managership at Manchester City Rodney won all but one of his caps. 'Before he sent him on against West Germany, Ramsey said to Rodney, "Run yourself into the ground." He never ran himself into the ground when he was with me. Being the sort of person he is, always looking for faults in people, questioning everything, that was the worst possible thing you could say to Rodney. That's why he didn't enjoy playing for England.'

Exchanging the Epsom stockbroker belt for a more capacious residence overlooking the sixth green of Prestbury Golf Club, Rodney had joined City in March 1972. The two-year contract he signed with QPR in the summer of 1970 contained the proviso that, should the club fail to gain promotion the following season, Gregory would let him go. When that eventuality transpired, Tottenham were the strongest of the early bidders, but Allison ended a lengthy courtship by bringing him to Maine Road for £200,000. 'Rodney Marsh isn't a footballer,' noted *The Sun*'s John Sadler. 'Manchester City know better than that. They've paid £200,000 for a legend, a god. And a human being who became an area of London.' The night before he put pen to dotted line, Rodney drank himself silly. 'I rang Jim Gregory late that night. He loved me like a son. I'd given him my first England cap. I told him I was drunk and that I wasn't sure I was doing the right thing. "It's too late for that, son," he said. Emotionally, he'd already let me go. Having said that, I loved Malcolm.' Allison and Rodney were kindred spirits, intent on living life to its fullest, scornful of the grey and the grim. On a tour of South Africa, they would sit up into the small hours reading Indian poetry and discussing philosophy and mysticism. Not that any of this made Rodney's first few months in Manchester any easier to bear.

Leading the League by four points when he arrived – though Leeds did have two games in hand – City ultimately conceded the title to Derby by one point. Rodney scored four goals in seven games, including a mesmeric solo effort to cement victory over Derby in the last match, yet still bore the brunt of the blame. The antipathy of his team-mates was plain to see. Against West Ham he was all but ignored as he jogged back to the centre circle after scoring. Later in the match he set up a goal with a fine run and cross. Colin Bell embraced Francis Lee, then glanced across at Rodney but thought better of showing any appreciation. 'It was clear Marsh just wanted to do his own thing,' charged Mike Doyle. 'You don't win anything with players like that in your side.'

'We're all big fans of Rodney and we're all great friends but Rodney at that time wasn't the right player for us,' Mike Summerbee elaborated recently. 'We got down the line quickly or got through the middle quickly and had shots. Suddenly he started playing and it all stopped. He was making these 50 to 60 yard runs.'

That City were soon sliding back into their neighbours' shadow – and worse, remaining there – has allowed opprobrium of this ilk to harden into fact. To his credit, Rodney does not shirk the role of goat. 'You've got to understand that City had won five titles in six years before I went there and they won it with the same system they used when they lost it with me. They fucked up by signing me. I didn't play badly, I just upset the rhythm of the team. The thing that really offended me was that nobody said anything to my face. It was all behind my back. Frannie Lee was fantastic but Mike Doyle was completely against me. Joe Corrigan was for me until it suited him to be against me. Mike Summerbee was, and is, a chameleon. If Mike Doyle had come to me in the carpark looking for a fight that would have been okay. I always thought northerners called a spade a spade but I was faced with these arseholes who wouldn't front me up.'

There were consolations. A salary of £15,000 was bumped up at least as much again by boot endorsements, deodorant ads and ribbon-cutting. The numberplate of his Lotus Europa, one reporter smugly pointed out, contained the letters E, G and O. 'What made it so difficult was that the headlines were this big every night. It wasn't a question of Malcolm telling me everything was going to be all right. I didn't realise how big the rivalry between City and United was. It's bigger than Arsenal and Spurs. It's everything. It's all they have. Even the papers hated each other. You had one City paper and one United paper. I couldn't do anything there. If you go to a restaurant in London and people recognise you, they don't bother you. Up there they come to your table and interrupt you. That said, it wasn't until I'd been there for three years and my marriage was going through a rocky period that I started to think about leaving.'

Allison's sole regret is not being aware of Rodney's lack of fitness. 'When you buy things you ask yourself whether you got value for money. The first time he played the crowd was 56,000, the second time 54,000, third time 61,000. I thought he would be better alongside Francis than Ian Bowyer, that he would hold the ball up and make us more effective as a team, and be a superstar. What I didn't take into consideration was that he was unfit. He was about ten pounds overweight and hadn't trained for six weeks because of a groin injury. I used to have six groups of five that I would take separately for training and he was always in the bottom group with the injured players. He was sick every session. He'd never trained properly in his life. Mind you, the training in this country was pathetic then and it still is. Manchester United are a fairly good side physically but when people talk about the high standards of our fitness it's rubbish, rubbish.

'I played Rodney twice then told him I wasn't going to play him until the last game of the season. To give him his due, he promised to start training and get fitter, and he got into the second group, so at Old Trafford I brought him on as substitute. We had this great tracksuit with gold all over it so I told him to put it on. He said he felt like Muhammad Ali. On he goes, scores within two minutes and we're 2–1 up. With five minutes to go it's still 2–1, and he's got the ball in front of the dugout and he's just hanging on to it. Then he shouts over, "How long to go?" Real showmanship. When he came to training that first day he was wearing sandals, jeans and a pullover with all the wool hanging down. When he walked into the dressing-room they were all saying to me, "Who's this scruff we've got here?" I told him he'd better go home and get changed and that I'd work with him in the afternoon. He came back in a pinstripe suit, striped shirt, maroon tie, maroon shoes – and no socks. That's him. That's how he is. They play "God Save The Queen" and he sits down.'

Typical, too, was the £100 Rodney wagered on himself to head the League scoring lists in his first full season at Maine Road (in the event, he scored 11 times in City's first 13 games but ran out of steam and finished with 17). The following season he declined to collect his loser's tankard after Wolves had beaten City in the League Cup final. 'I'm a bad loser,' he explained. 'I did what I thought was the only honest thing for me to do in the circumstances.' Not wanting his action to be perceived as a slight on Wolves, he dispatched a telegram of congratulations to the winning manager, Bill McGarry.

Allison had left for Crystal Palace a year previously, the last straw an FA Cup fifth-round defeat at Sunderland. His tough, militaristic successor, Ron Saunders, brought in expressly to alter the club's 'trendy' image, was about to be displaced by Tony Book. Rodney's growing disenchantment revealed itself after an ugly, negative game against Chelsea had prompted Steve Kember to complain that City had been frustrated 'because we didn't let them play'. 'When teams come to play us with two sweepers propping up a back four,' fumed Rodney, 'we might as well all pack it in. If a team can't see further than stopping the other team from playing, well, who is going to cross the road to watch it?' By the end of 1975, Bell was crocked for good and Lee had been cast off before his sell-by date (he duly helped Derby win the League). Book's strategy, furthermore, was strictly safety-first. Club captain Rodney may have been, but that did not make him any better equipped to stomach what he interpreted as a betrayal of his craft.

'Book didn't like playing. He liked whacking the ball and I couldn't play that way. We had a ruck, face-to-face, very physical. On the Saturday I scored the winning goal at Highbury and on the Monday I was on the transfer list. Although Jean and I sorted things out eventually, I was also going through a terrible time with my marriage and it was in all the papers. I couldn't face the exposure. I spent the next two weeks very depressed, drinking a lot of vodka. I didn't shave, didn't train. Then I got a message that Elton John wanted to take me on his private plane on tour to LA, and while I was there I got a call from this bloke Beauclerc Rogers IV, the owner of Tampa Bay Rowdies, offering me a first-class ticket to come and discuss terms. The moment I set foot in the airport I knew I was going to join them rather than Aston Villa or West Brom.' Shortly after his ensconcement in Tampa, Rodney made his comment about leaving behind a grey country, a grey game and a grey people.

He returned briefly in 1976, linking up with Best at Fulham for seven months. 'We had the same agent at the time, Ken Adam, and he brought us back. I think we were making £300 a week plus a bonus based on the size of the crowd, so I was making about £5,000, but the only reason I went back was to play with George. I wanted to enjoy that moment, the *carpe diem*.' Alec Stock was managing Fulham at the time. 'The first time Marshy and George turned out for us we drew 12,000 extra spectators. George scored with a tap-in but if you had asked the most sober-sided spectator to put his hand on his heart the following morning he would have said he picked it up on the halfway line and went by three men just like that, then rounded the keeper and backheeled it in. That's what reputations do. It was wonderful to have them both playing for you, and don't forget I also had Bobby Moore at that time. And yet there was a sadness. One day we went to Southampton and there were 26,000 people there, TV cameras, the lot. Fathers had brought their kids along to say, "Take a look at this". They'd all come to see Marshy and Moore and the first thing Southampton did was try to kick them off the field. What were they trying to achieve?'

Rodney is more upbeat. 'In the end, we did triumph over the hackers, didn't we? You're not interviewing Ron Harris now, are you? You don't see him on telly.'

(ii) The Bookies' Favourite

Music has rarely done football any favours. 'Nice One, Cyril', admittedly, possessed a certain bizarre charm, adapting as it did a Mother's Pride ad into a eulogy to a left-back. That unfairly maligned couplet from hell, 'Ossie's going to Wembley/His knees have gone all trembly', at least had the virtue of innovation. I have long harboured a sneaking suspicion, however, that all those dire club singalongs were/are written by one person under a variety of pseudonyms. The lyrics to 'Good Old Arsenal', for instance, are credited to one J. Hill. 'Blue is the Colour' was co-authored by a certain S. McQueen. Need I go on? Fans prefer to rejig the hits of the day, evincing a wit and turn of phrase far beyond the scope of those paid to supply them with tailor-made anthems.

As a means of redressing the balance, a football concerto, I grant you, sounds like the height of pretentiousness. Uncowed, Michael Nyman, QPR fiend and court composer to that Holy Roman Emperor of art-house clever-dickery, Peter Greenaway, composed just such a beast for Channel 4 in 1992. Entitled 'The Final Score', jaunty synthesised noodlings held sway, ripples of electronic strings swirling around in the manner popularised by Phillip Glass. To these ears it was nothing short of a revelation, the most eloquent homage imaginable. Paradoxically, the subject was Stan Bowles, probably the least pretentious human being ever to kick leather for a living.

The footage concentrated on QPR's final match of 1975–76, the club's sweetest season in the sun; 24 April: Leeds at home, win or die. Liverpool are but one point clear, their final fixture still ten days away owing to European commitments. Stan, as ever, is in the thick of things.

Shimmying and shimmering, shuffling and sure-footed, winking at this, gobsmacked at that, animated at every turn. A skinny, effete-looking scamp seemingly forever on the make, conning referees and stealing penalties by the truckload, non-believers regarded him as Stanley the Unmanly. To anyone in possession of a working soul, conversely, this was Stan the Man at the zenith of his powers. Dave Thomas stirs the pot with a rare headed goal midway through the second half. Now Stan glides on to Dave Clement's curling through ball and swings inside. Arrowed through a gap only the supremely self-assured would have spotted, let alone contemplated aiming for, the delicately curved shot around the covering right-back deceives the unsighted David Harvey in the visiting goal. As the ball squirts through his grasp and over the line, you could swear it was cackling. When a swarm of blue-and-white hornets threaten to suck his face off, Stan's expression is redolent of a boy whose mother has just observed that the bunch of roses he has presented her with bear an uncanny likeness to next door's prize blooms. A triumphant smirk soon takes its place. Molesworth himself never worked a finer scam. For nine days, QPR are champions-elect. On the tenth, Liverpool win 3–1 at Wolves.

'*Without Walls*,' Stan recalls in a characteristic matter-of-fact tone. 'That was the name of the programme it was on. Half-an-hour they gave it. I liked the music, it was quite lively and interesting. Nyman told me he wrote it in 20 minutes. I liked him, very down to earth.' He did realise, of course, that it was a love letter to Stan Bowles. 'Maybe,' comes the mumbled answer, followed closely by a soft, almost imperceptible grin. The most self-effacing of the Mavericks he may be, but Stan never needed any reminding that he was special. What sets him apart is his indifference. To him, football was merely a means of sustaining an abiding passion for gambling, for having a stake in the uncertain, for walking a tightrope.

At one juncture in 'The Final Score', a series of press cuttings litter the screen. Stan with topless bird on the front of *The News of the World*. 'It was good money, three and a half grand I think, even if it did cost me my marriage. My wife went spare when she saw it. What made it worse was that the model was involved in a car crash a couple of days later and she blamed it on all the ensuing fuss in the press.' Stan on how he took barbiturates and why such drugs should be freely available to help professional footballers cope with the stress. 'They offered me two grand so I thought, right I'll have some of that. I don't know where they got the idea from but I certainly never knew anyone who took them. It was the same when I announced my retirement on the Saturday and returned on the Monday. It was a way of getting back at the press, I suppose.'

Impulsive, irresponsible and irreverent – and that's just the i's – Stan has surfed through life apparently oblivious to the height of the waves. With him, it is not so much seize the day as grasp the minute. A diary of his skirmishes with authority between February 1974 and February 1975 encapsulates the general perception. In the first instance he demanded a transfer on the eve of a fifth-round FA Cup tie, then changed his mind the next day. In May he went AWOL during an England squad session, prompting Joe Mercer to insist that he would never play international football again. A few hours later he was spotted at the White City dog track. In July he signed a contract designed to keep him at Loftus Road for a further five years; two months later he returned from suspension and asked for a transfer because his wife, Ann, had moved back to their native Manchester. On 16 September Anne agreed to come home so he withdrew the request. On 21 September, by which time a change of national manager had wiped the slate, he reported late for an England team-talk. Two days later he declined to report for club training and was duly suspended for two weeks. Shortly before Christmas, he swore never to play for QPR again after being dropped, but reneged on the promise inside 72 hours. Upon being substituted against West Ham the following February, he stalked sullenly off the pitch flashing a V-sign at Sexton, then vowed he would never speak to the manager again. Within four days he was back in the fold. At that stage of Stan's life, stability was in short supply.

The scrapes, too, are legion. There was that time when Stan and his QPR partner-in-devilry, Don Shanks, drove to Epsom in an untaxed car with bald tyres, lost on every race and decided to seek succour in a Chinese meal. 'Thanks for dinner,' said Stan when the bill arrived. 'Whaddya mean,' spluttered Shanks, 'I thought you were paying.' Thinking on his feet, Shanks proceeded to the rear of the restaurant, cool as you like, and began fumbling inside his coat. 'Isn't there any security in here?' he suddenly complained, loudly. 'I've had my wallet lifted.' The red-faced manager scurried over, assured him and Stan the meal was on the house and gave them a tenner apiece to keep schtum. Then there was that time the same pair spent the night in a Belgian jail after a sozzled Shanks had alarmed the guests by crawling over the floor as if in the throes of an epileptic fit. On tour in New York with Manchester City, the teenage Stan had endured another night in the cells in the company of another wayward colleague, Tony Coleman. Upon being informed that he was too young to be served in a bar,

Coleman had picked up a ball from the pool table and hurled it through the nearest window.

It will be noted that, in each of these incidents, Stan was never once the instigator. All the same, he always was more at home with ne'er-do-wells. He was reared in a modest prefab in Moston, a short walk from Hume, one of the roughest, poorest, least salubrious areas of Manchester. His father ran a window-cleaning business and supported City avidly: but for his constant prodding Stan would never have countenanced pursuing football beyond the parks and streets. Not for a moment did he ever regard it as a career.

'I used to run around with a lot of half-villains so I think I would have gone that way myself but for football. They were getting money when there was no money about, and certainly a lot more than footballers were getting. I was brought up with these people and I'm still with them whenever I'm in Manchester now. It's more exciting than the normal way of life I suppose. There was always something happening. I started running bets for them when I was about 13, 14. They'd be in the pub and they paid me to run their bets backwards and forwards to these unlicensed bookmakers. It was a means of earning money but I also found it quite thrilling. The horses, the dogs, poker. I had a few dogs when I joined QPR but they didn't turn out to be very good. But it didn't matter. When I started going to the White City there were so many characters there you could have a good laugh even if you were skint. I'm a man's man really.' At 15 Stan risked his own money for the first time, backing a 12–1 shot and winning £24, instantly transforming a dalliance into an addiction. The most he has won in a day is £18,000, the biggest loss £15,000. Everything was fair game. When Carlisle hosted Tottenham in an FA Cup replay he tormented his marker all evening, yet, by the final whistle, he resembled an undertaker who had just been robbed of his last hearse. Having bet a colleague he could nutmeg the Spurs right-back 20 times during the course of the game, he had only managed 16.

Now a journalist with *The Manchester Evening News* and still a fast friend, Paul Hince signed schoolboy forms with Manchester City at the same time as Stan. 'I knew him as a kid in Moston and we played together in the Manchester and District Sunday League and later for the league's representative side, him at outside-right, me at outside-left. He could open a can of beans with that left foot. He was very shy, very placid. He was a piss-taker but there was nothing malicious about him. He was never the establishment type. If he had something on his mind, he would say it. He didn't drink or smoke back then, and he was never a womaniser, but money and him have never been good friends. When he began to make progress he never got carried away with the glamour part because it was all a means to an end, of doing what he really loved. He would bet on anything, when the fly on the wall would take off, anything. A total one-off.'

When he went round to *chez* Bowles to sign Stan, Harry Gregg, the former Manchester United and Eire goalkeeper turned City scout, was somewhat taken aback when Stan's younger brother began ferreting around in his pockets, looking for spare change. By way of completing the formalities, Gregg asked Stan what denomination he was. 'What?' said Stan. 'What religion are you?' Gregg elaborated, whereupon a quizzical Stan asked his mother whether he was Catholic or Protestant. Pondering the question thoughtfully, she suggested they consult his father when he came home.

Stan signed as an apprentice professional when he left New Moston Secondary Modern in 1967. Pitched into the first team at 17, he scored twice on each of his first two appearances, yet the approach fell some way short of devotion. Malcolm Allison readily admits to being at a loss to cope. 'He had brilliant ability but I couldn't control him. I didn't care about the gambling because when TB put an end to my own career as a player I came out of hospital after a year, went to Epsom the following day and became a professional gambler for the next two years. I just worried about him being out drinking late at night. The older players were a handful yet I'm controlling them all, but there's this 17-year-old kid who's breaking every rule in the book. The gambling and the drinking are intermingled. You have a good night gambling so you celebrate.'

Allison gave up when Stan missed a flight to Amsterdam prior to a friendly against Ajax. 'We were due to take off at 7.30 in the morning and we had this Scottish full-back, Arthur Mann, who was frightened to death of flying. By the time he turned up at 8.15 he'd taken some pills and brandy. We had to carry him off the plane when we touched down. But Stan didn't even turn up. When we got back he came into my office and said he was ever so sorry but his bus had broken down coming through Manchester, as a result of which he hadn't arrived at the airport until 9.30. That's funny, I said, because the plane was delayed for four hours and we didn't leave until after 11. I said to Joe Mercer, "Look, I can't control this guy, he's going to cause a problem for me with the other players. You've got to get rid of him".'

Though he saw it coming, Stan couldn't have cared less. 'As I recall, I was in a betting shop with somebody and the club kept trying to contact me at home but I just kept avoiding them. I didn't like flying and they knew that. QPR let me go on the ferry when I joined them. The point was, I'd had enough. I was enjoying myself off the field but I was a little bit reckless. I'm still friends with people like Bell and Lee but nobody took me to one side and tried to advise me. They saw the people I was hanging around with, the local villains, and just distanced themselves from it. They didn't want to know. It didn't please Malcolm either. He called me into his office and said he was sending me on loan to Bury, but I didn't get on with the manager there, and when I got back to City they sacked me, so I got out of football for a while, living at home, doing little errands, putting bets on.'

Hince, meanwhile, had joined Crewe Alexandra on a part-time basis. 'When Stan was sent to Bury he came to see me because I knew the manager, Tommy McAnearney. I told him he was a real tyrant and that I wouldn't advise it, but Stan needed the money. One day he turned up at Gigg Lane in a cab and handed McAnearney the bill, and that got him the sack. Then, after Stan had been out of the game for a while, we met up when I was at Crewe and I said he had to sort his life out. I told the manager, Ernie Tagg, that he wasn't a bad lad but that he had money problems, so Ernie told me to put him on the train to Crewe Station and he would meet Stan there. I had to give him the fare – he still hasn't paid me back. The first thing Ernie said to him was, "I understand you're on your uppers, here's twenty quid." Stan was his now.'

Given that Allison and Mercer had at their disposal the most exhilarating set of forwards in the club's history, Stan had done well to make as many as 15 first-team appearances in his three seasons at Maine Road. Inevitably, his initial impressions of Fourth Division football were dismissive. 'All of a sudden I was playing against inferior players. The standard was really poor. There are better players playing Sunday League football now than were in the first team then. Then I found out what they were earning and I thought, fuck me, there's a living in this.' Messrs Mercer and Clough tend to get the credit but it was the canny, sentient Tagg who originally conceived the Great Stan Bowles One-Liner. 'Yeah, "If Stan Bowles could pass a betting shop the way he passes the ball he'd be a rich man or whatever." Ernie was quite a witty man. We got on all right. He always thought I was better off in midfield because I was quite a good passer, but then I started to get a few goals and he put me upfront. In one of my early games we played Scunthorpe and Kevin Keegan scored an own-goal for us. Kind of him.'

Once the trial period was over, Stan and his wife Anne rented a small house within a short walk of the club. 'Basically what they were trying to say was, "This way we always know where you are". I don't drive so that kept me out of Manchester for quite a while.' Tagg began to take precautions. Every week he handed Stan £10 from his wage packet and gave the remainder of the contents to Tommy Doig, Crewe's septugenarian odd-job man, who in turn passed them on to Anne.

Stan had scored 18 goals in 51 League games for Crewe when Carlisle, then two seasons away from entering the First Division for the first time, came a-knocking in October 1971. 'Ernie called me in and said there were bigger clubs looking at me but that he felt a couple of years there would equip me for better things. I'd calmed down a bit by then so I agreed.' One of the attractions was Carlisle's fluent passing game, channelled as it was through the willowy, elegant Chris Balderstone, the last full-time professional footballer to play cricket for England. 'Chris was the captain there and we hit it off together because he was like a Glenn Hoddle, putting me through all the time. I always knew what he was going to do and vice versa. We lived just outside Carlisle, which was very nice in the summer when you could see the salmon jumping out of the river, but in the winter, forget it. I didn't miss the city really because the people were quite friendly, and there was a racetrack nearby. I used to run errands there as well. This guy called Top Winstanley used to hand me a canister full of money and give me £20 to deliver it. A week's wages at Carlisle was £130. Everyone used to get the same.'

'Ian MacFarlane, the manager, used to scare Stan to death,' Hince chuckles. 'He used to tell Anne to phone in sick for him, but MacFarlane used to come over to his house and drag him out of bed.'

When Gordon Jago put £110,000 on the table in September 1972, MacFarlane was scarcely in a position to refuse, although at no time did he apply any pressure. Tempted as Stan was by the proximity of the White City, there were other enticements. 'QPR were an ambitious club but, even more important, they played nice football. Terry Venables was the instigator. In effect, if not in name, he was the assistant manager. He could only play one way – feet, feet, feet.' Jim Gregory was digging deep at this juncture. Don Givens had been signed during the close-season and, a month after Stan joined, Dave Thomas came from Burnley to man the right flank. Stan roamed down the inside-right channel because he felt more comfortable coming on to his left foot from that side. Needless to say, he thought nothing of pulling on that No. 10 shirt. 'I don't think the fans were as bothered as the players. It also helped that I scored on my début against Nottingham Forest, with a header as well, very rare for me. None of the other players wanted to wear the shirt because they were scared that the fans would expect too much of them. It was taboo. Coming from up north, though, I'd never really heard of Rodney Marsh. To a certain extent he probably did make QPR, but he meant nothing to me. I never had any interest in watching other players.'

While Rodney's departure triggered a drop in the average gate at Loftus Road, promotion soon changed that. Stan went on to share 40 League goals with the wiry Givens as QPR finished 11 points clear of third-place Aston Villa, to go up alongside Burnley. A year later they were the leading team in the capital and primed to fry some bigger fish. At the heart of this resurgence lay the partnership of Stan and the team's bustling dynamo, Gerry Francis. 'When I arrived Gerry took me out and showed me around London during my first couple of weeks, so we were friends from the start. Our relationship on the field was marvellous, even better than the one I had with Balderstone, but it was purely instinctive. Very little was done in training because as soon as I was finished with the official group practice I was off to the races. We'd stay behind if the racing was off, but I used to go at least three times a week so there weren't too many opportunities.'

In common with Ernie Tagg, Gregory realised that the way to Stan's feet and mind was to balance firmness with a *soupçon* of indulgence. 'That was a good time in my life and Jim had a lot to do with it. If I needed money, sometimes he would give it to me, sometimes he wouldn't. I respected him for that. Having him as chairman was probably the best thing that ever happened to me during my career.' The rebellious streak remained nonetheless. 'I suppose I gambled on the field as well as off it. Gordon Jago used to tell me every week how to play but then I'd go out and do my own thing. I thought I knew better. No one could ever tell me what to do. Even if I was wrong I'd never admit it. Dave [Sexton] used to try and get me tracking back, as he used to call it. I tried it a few times and then thought, "This isn't me, I can't do this", so I stopped. Having said that, Dave Webb and Frank McLintock used to keep on at me, and if you didn't do it for them you'd get a bollocking. So, respecting them, I used to do it.'

The rapport with the fans was both instant and close. Unlike Rodney, Stan felt no need to keep his distance. After home games he would walk the 50 yards or so to The Springbok and share a few jars with the audience. One or two, in turn, inscribed his name on their patios. 'They saw me as one of their own kind. I could do no wrong. If I played badly, it was always somebody else's fault. I played up the theatrical side quite a bit and sometimes got booked, but they loved it.

One day Bobby Robson accused me of diving in the penalty area and I think that sparked the referees off, which meant that I wasn't getting the penalties when I deserved them. Having said that, I did use to trip myself up in the box. Rodney told me about that one.' One Saturday ritual was the sight of Stan endeavouring to discover the result of the 3.15 or the 4.10 by asking people in the stands, sometimes discreetly, sometimes not. Indeed, popular myth had it that he would get himself carried off so he could nip back to Corals for the last couple of races of the afternoon. A more feasible explanation was the fearful hammering meted out to that spindly frame. 'He was one of the best pros ever,' Frank McLintock acclaims. 'They'd kick him from pillar to post, and he had a low pain threshold so he was always being carried off, but he rarely lost his temper. He was very resilient.'

Dave Webb was taken by the industry as well as the fearlessness. 'Like Ossie, Stan would get back and tackle and fight to the death. Rodney had a headache coming back over the halfway line. Whatever corner you were in, Bowles was in there with you, and he would get you out of it by doing something unbelievable, giving you a breather in the way Huddy would. He was the best shuffler I've ever seen in my life. Once we were under the cosh against Arsenal and he held on to the ball for what seemed like about three minutes but was probably 10 or 15 seconds. He had all these guys around him, falling over trying to get the ball off him. You just knew he wasn't going to lose it. I must have sensed what he was going to do next because I headed for their box and he put the ball right on my head for me to score the winner. You have to respect these fellas who could ride those tackles. Tackling was a lot freer because you could still tackle from behind, and people like Stan never received the protection they would have expected today.'

Sexton saved Stan's ankles a certain amount of bruising by suggesting he release the ball earlier. Chelsea's relegation in 1974–75, furthermore, spared Stan from having to contend with Ron Harris quite so often. 'Every time we played Chelsea Ron used to get booked for tackles on me. All he could do was mark man-to-man, and anyone can do that. If you thought, right, I'll stay with this geezer and wherever he runs, I'll run with him, there would be nothing I could do about it. So you can imagine what a trained athlete like Harris could do with his mind set. The ball could be two yards away but all he wanted to do was stay with you.'

'Ossie, Rodney and Bowles were always the ones who got the worst of it,' Webb adds, 'because they were dribblers, but as an all-round talent, Bowles was the best of the lot. Rodney and Ossie were the type who needed the ball to be given to them, more so Rodney because Ossie would either be an out-and-out centre-forward or drop back into midfield and create. Ossie had this presence whereby he could make the extraordinary look basic and the basic extraordinary. Bowles could do even more. He was the most marvellous individual talent I ever played with.'

McLintock lauds the control above all. 'There was no such thing as a bumpy pitch as far as Stan was concerned. He always killed the ball stone dead. To him, everyone else was a mug. In a one-against-one situation, like Greaves, you would always fancy Stan. And he would always pass at just the right time. The main difference between him and Rodney was that Stan's main aim was to win.'

Although Stan's habit of strolling in for home fixtures 20 minutes before kick-off taxed Sexton's patience, he got away with it. 'Dave didn't like it but he stood for it. I was making a bit of a name for myself by then so he didn't want to upset me. He was the best manager I ever played for, and I think he would have made a good national manager. He wasn't bothered about the gambling so long as it didn't affect my game. He was pretty good about it, in fact. We only ever had a couple of rows.' Stan acknowledges that he was hardly the most desirable of room-mates. 'Nobody wanted to room with me. I used to drive McLintock mental because he would bed down at about ten and I'd be on the phone until one or two in the morning.' Yet, as Webb affirms, colleagues accepted the rough because the smooth was reserved for the fray. 'It didn't bother me that he'd turn up late. I was so nervous before a game I used to turn up even later' says Webb. 'Besides, I never once saw him unprepared for a match in a physical sense. Mentally he might be unprepared because he'd lost his money or had a row with his wife, but I never saw him worse for wear. He was like Eric Morecambe. You knew that even if you turned up on a bad day you would get something out of him. That was why he was exceptional. And QPR built on that talent, just as they had done with Marshy. The reason I went there rather than Arsenal was because they had people like Venables, Dave Thomas and Bowles. I thought it would be exciting.'

McLintock rates that 1975–76 collective as the most eloquent British practitioners in his experience. 'It was Total Football. Gordon Jago, Sexton's predecessor, favoured good football and Dave copied the Dutch and Germans, lots of short passes. At 22, Gerry Francis had the head of a 30-year-old, and Masson could keep the ball on a string. Gerry and Stan would create these one-twos out of nothing. A lot of people couldn't get on with Sexton because he wanted to talk football all the time, but I loved him. A great coach. Training was very intense at Arsenal but at QPR it was more relaxed. People were always cracking jokes. You sensed the lightness. We also worked with the ball more. At the end of training we would split into threes and chip it around. I was 35, but my passing improved there.'

'Dave [Sexton] hadn't changed,' says Webb, 'but I do think the move from Chelsea refreshed him because a lot of the fellas were new to his ideas. To me it was a bit old hat.'

National recognition had initially come Stan's way when club commitments prompted a rash of withdrawals from England's trip to Lisbon in April 1974, Ramsey naming six new caps for what turned out to be his final game at the wheel. Stan performed well enough in a goalless draw for Mercer to retain him for the home internationals, and, in the first of these at Ninian Park, scored his only goal for his country – a tap-in from barely six inches after John Phillips had obligingly pushed Keith Weller's drive into his path. In the next game against Northern Ireland, Stan's introduction to Wembley ended after 64 minutes. Shades of Charlie George. 'What annoyed me most was that he [Mercer] told Harold Shepherdson at half-time to let me play another ten minutes then bring me off. In that ten minutes I could have scored twice. Why couldn't Mercer have told me himself? That's why I walked out on the England squad. Malcolm Allison rang me up to ask what happened and when I told him, he said he would have done exactly the same thing, which was nice of him.' Mercer made it abundantly clear that, so far as he was concerned, Stan no longer had a future at this level. 'Football,' concluded Frank McGhee in *The Daily Mirror*, 'does not need people like Stan Bowles and George Best.'

So irrepressible was Stan's form the following year, however, even Mercer urged Revie to take heed. 'You can't ignore him,' he told the new England manager. 'He's one of the rare ones.' Revie eventually succumbed, bringing Stan into the squad for a European Championship qualifier in Portugal. Determined not to be caught with its collective trousers down, Fleet Street changed tune and began praising 'Stan the magic man', only for the new saviour to pull out after being carried off against Newcastle with a severe groin strain. Ignored for the next 12 months, incessant media pressure was an undeniable factor in his recall against Italy in Rome for a critical World Cup qualifier. 'The press were pushing for me throughout that period and I think Revie had to play me otherwise he'd have been out of a job. It was day-in, day-out, this man has *got* to play.' One factor in Stan's restoration was a perceived improvement in his onfield behaviour. 'I'm walking away from tackles now,' he told *The Evening Standard*. 'I'm just older and wiser. I used to get involved but all that shouting at referees and players made me hoarse. I thought I was going to lose my voice!' In the event, that wiliest of hatchet men, Claudio Gentile, kept Stan under lock and key, the hosts winning 2–0 and effectively cementing their passage to Argentina. Three months later, Stan was far from being the only home bystander as Cruyff and Neeskens toyed with the English defence in what was arguably the most consummate display witnessed at Wembley since Puskas and Hidegkuti ran amok 24 years earlier. That, nevertheless, was his lot.

'I won five caps under three different managers, so they can't all be wrong, can they? I got on okay with Alf, but I preferred playing under Revie. He was a player's man, always trying to get you a bit of extra money. I do think I deserved a few more caps, but if I'd never played for England it wouldn't have bothered me. It was a bonus. I never enjoyed it. I can't remember any of the games. The first time was nice because you're playing for your country and they play the national anthem so you get a bit carried away, but it soon dies away. I didn't really do myself justice but then I never really got the service. I was always played in the middle, which didn't help. It always seemed to be every man for himself. If there had been a couple more flair players in the side it might have been different, but it's the same old FA syndrome. They never pick the players the public want to see. Bert Millichip gave me an eight-week ban once. I can just imagine him saying, "We don't want that sort".'

Kevin Keegan may have been the League player who began the continental drift in the mid-Seventies, yet Stan had an opportunity to pre-empt him. In the summer of 1976, he was invited to a rendezvous at the Royal Lancaster Hotel with a cluster of Hamburg officials. 'You know what them Germans are like – 9.30 on a bloody Sunday morning. Jim Gregory was meant to be there, too, but he didn't turn up, so I went into the foyer to call him. He said he wasn't coming and that if I wanted I should leave then and there. He also said to come and see him the next morning to talk about a new contract. "Anyway," he added, "I don't like Germans." And I wasn't going to face half-a-dozen angry Germans on my own so I nipped out the back. That afternoon I went to Jim's for lunch and he said he didn't want me to leave, to which I said I didn't either. He offered me a few extra quid and Hamburg went for Keegan instead. I didn't fancy it. I never was bothered about playing abroad.'

While QPR's League form slipped alarmingly in 1976–77, there were distractions, a strong run in the League Cup being matched by another in the UEFA Cup. In the latter competition Stan set a British single-season record of 11 goals, superseding Denis Law and Dennis Viollet. The milestone was reached in the third round against Cologne at Loftus Road. Swerving away from Harald Konopke, one of two Germans assigned to police his every move, Stan realised the angle was too acute and swept inside Roland Gerber, making space for a snaking left-footed shot that curved mockingly past the helpless Harald Schumacher. QPR went through on the away-goals ruling but then lost out on penalties to AEK Athens in the quarter-finals; three days later, Stan's season came to a premature close when he suffered a double fracture of the right leg in a collision with Bristol City's Gary Collier. Eliminated from the League Cup in a semi-final replay against Aston Villa, QPR's flirtation with altitude, for the moment, was over. Maintaining, not unreasonably, that he had taken the club about as far as he could given the budget constraints, Sexton moved on to Old Trafford that summer, to be replaced by Frank Sibley. Thomas, McLintock and Webb were gone by the end of the year, and with Francis absent for much of the season through injury, relegation was averted by just one point. Sibley resigned, Stock filled in until Steve Burtenshaw was appointed, but there was no escape clause in 1978–79. 'Everyone got old,' Stan reasons.

It was against this background of decline that Stan, now nearing 31, moved to Nottingham Forest for £250,000 in late 1979. Much as it was a wrench to leave London, the lure of joining the European Cup holders was not to be sniffed at. Charlie George came for a month's trial soon afterwards, scoring the goal that enabled Forest to win the European Super Cup. The pair lived in the same hotel for a month. 'Charlie and I got on fine because we both like a drink and a good laugh, but I don't think he was ever happy there. During one game, Cloughie told all the players to move forward and Charlie was dropping back into midfield, so at half-time Cloughie said to him, "When I tell you to play centre-forward, laddie, I mean centre-forward." "Bollocks" said Charlie, and that was the end of him.'

Deployed mainly on the left side of midfield, Stan played in the home legs of the European Cup quarter-final against Dynamo Berlin and the semi-final against Ajax, yet his absence from the return games had nothing to do with his fear of flying. 'I got on well with Cloughie at first – although I preferred Peter Taylor because he was a racing man, more streetwise – but then he had this thing about me only performing in home games and said so in the press. I didn't think that was fair, but that's the way he was. He's a very strange man. The only good thing you can say about him is that he is exactly how he appears to be on television.

That's no act.' Resentment was brewing when, a week before the final against Hamburg, Clough omitted Stan from the Forest line-up for John Robertson's testimonial match. All you ever need to know about Stan is that that game meant more to him than the trip to Madrid. 'I really wanted to play because John was such a good friend, so when I was left out in favour of Ian Bowyer, I just thought, "fuck it", and went home. There was no way I was going to Madrid after that. The club suspended me and I've never spoken to Cloughie since. When I went back to pre-season training we communicated by rumour, and then Orient came in for me. By then, all I wanted to do was get back to London.'

Not bothered in the slightest by the sudden descent into the dimly-lit recesses of Division Two, Stan spent a season at Brisbane Road under the cultured managership of the late Jimmy Bloomfield, and enjoyed himself thoroughly. 'It was like a little family club, although my basic wage was more than I'd been getting at Forest because the bonuses there were so good. I was living in Lancaster Gate, Westbourne Park Terrace, next door to Mick Avory of The Kinks. I could get the train right through to the ground. Perfect.' A couple more terms at Brentford and Stan had had his fill. 'Frank McLintock was in charge at Griffin Park by the end and one day I went into his office and told him I'd had enough. I was never that quick but I'd become even slower. I was finding the aches and pains harder to get over but basically, I just got fed up.'

Cheltenham Festival Week, 1994. Inside the Bricklayers' Arms in Brentford, a yellowing photo of a radiant young Elizabeth Windsor sits on the far wall beside a signed poster of George Best. Above the bar hangs one of the house rules: 'Credit is like sex. Some get it, some don't.' Two elderly ladies ask to see the lunch menu. 'Hot chilli to keep that wind at bay,' recommends the woman behind the bar. 'Spaghetti bolognese, pizza . . .' The interruption is brusque. 'Don't want any of that foreign stuff. We're too old for that.' Clad in a pinstripe suit and polo-neck sweater, Stan strides through the door, scrapbook in hand, those steely blue eyes looking a little hazy. 'Bad day yesterday,' sighs the 45-year-old grandfather as he takes a stool. Producing a comb, he attends, needlessly, to those gun-metal tresses that were once as much a trademark as the winks and dinks. 'It was that Oh So Risky that did it,' he explains, referring to the losing favourite in the Champion Hurdle. 'Didn't win a thing. Then my mate puts £15,000 each way on the last race and it comes in at 10–1. Typical.'

Cheltenham Week is a perennial highlight in the calendar of 'Manchester Stan', as he refers to himself, partly as a reminder to those who assume him to be a Londoner. Given that he has lived in the Smoke for 20 years or more, it is a reasonable misconception. The snooker club had gone west *en masse* earlier that morning but for once Stan had had no urge to tag along. Keeping tabs on developments at Coral's was quite sufficient. 'Too busy these days. They also have these troughs there now, sections where you file through as you queue up for a bloody drink. You can't just go up to the bar anymore.' Aside from acceding to my request to see his scrapbook, a collection of press clippings lovingly collated by his daughters, there is another reason for Stan's absence from the track. Married for the third time shortly before Christmas, he, wife Diane and baby Tom are in the process of moving from their two-bedroom council flat to a more spacious council house all of a hundred yards away. Glance up and across the road and you can spy the red-and-white stripes daubed across the back of the main stand at Griffin Park.

While Diane is far too loyal to criticise Stan, the frustration is unmistakable. Two weeks earlier, they had escorted me to Walthamstow Stadium, my first greyhound meeting. Just as we are about to lay our first bet with one of the roving attendants tootling round the restaurant area, Diane announces she has left her purse at home, leaving Stan with nothing to wager. His face sinks but there are no recriminations. Later, Diane's coy smile confirms her forgetfulness to have been intentional. 'Nothing worries him. He's just so quiet and laid-back. You can't argue with him because he'll always agree with you. Betting is his life apart from me and Tom, and so long as he puts us first I don't care. Money isn't easy for us, but he never worries about what he's missed, what he should have had, what he could be doing.' Stan pleads horribly guilty: 'I'd do the same things again, over and over.'

QPR awarded him a testimonial but the proceeds, needless to add, were soon dissipated. 'Marshy came over from America for the game,' remembers Alec Stock. 'He played in midfield with Gerry Francis and Stan against the Brentford first team and none of the Brentford players could get near the ball. It was beautiful. Stan was lovely, so polite. We used to drop him off at White City on the way home from away games. I also used to drive him back from training, and one day he told me, "I shall finish up in jail like all my mates." I dropped him off and the next thing I knew some police had turned up looking for him. I told them he'd been there two minutes earlier but they thought I was lying.'

When he returned to Loftus Road as manager, Gerry Francis offered Stan a job working with the youth team but by now his interest in the game was negligible. 'They still look after me there, the doors always open for me, but I was bored with football.' A proposed market stall in Brentford came to naught. Visitors to Lord's a couple of summers back could spot him among the reprobates sweeping up after stumps were drawn. In contrast to so many of his contemporaries, peddling memories of onfield derring-do holds little appeal. 'I do football evenings now and again but they get on my nerves. People ask you if you remember some goal you scored in 1971 and you have to say yes or they get offended. But how can I remember something I did 20 years ago? I don't even know what I did yesterday.' One thing he cannot forget are all those bar-room debates about whether he was a better player than Rodney. 'I can go into a pub in Shepherd's Bush at any time of the day and know that someone will still bring that up. Of course I was better than him.'

(iii) Dr Heckle and Mr Jive

In *Queen's Park Rangers: A Complete Record*, 135 players are included in the 'A-Z of Rangers Stars'. Tony Currie is not among them. Since he captained the club in the 1982 FA Cup final replay, this seems rather a gross oversight. Then again, the author, Gordon Macy, does proffer the somewhat contentious view that Gary Waddock was 'probably the most popular player to have appeared for Rangers over the last 30 years'.

Mr Macy, one assumes, was too stony-hearted to forgive the man who deflected Glenn Hoddle's drive past Peter Hucker in the initial Wembley encounter, then conceded the decisive penalty the following Thursday. An ankle injury, in fairness, had begun to impair Tony's effectiveness even before Tommy Docherty signed him in August 1979. Indeed, his début was delayed by three months, whereupon a knee ailment slowed him further still. Docherty nevertheless describes as 'magnificent' the two years' service he put in before body finally conquered spirit, restricting him to one full outing during the promotion season of 1982–83. Even on one sound leg, he was a cut above.

While Manchester Stan found his métier in London, Tony Currie took the opposite route to self-fulfilment. Born in Edgware General Hospital on the opening day of the Fifties, raised in Alan Coren's beloved Cricklewood, he was spurned by QPR and Chelsea before prospering in Yorkshire, first with Sheffield United, latterly with Leeds. Had he not been impelled to do so in a forlorn attempt to save his marriage, it is exceedingly doubtful whether he would ever have gone back, and, as it transpired, the exile became permanent in 1988. Exactly 20 years to the day he signed on at Bramall Lane, he returned there as projects officer on the local Community Programme in Professional Football scheme, a venture jointly managed by the Football League and the PFA designed to provide a link with schoolchildren and unemployed youths. His office is in the club's main stand, the days of refusing the dole long past. So, too, the drinking binges that had seen him put away a bottle of whisky every other day for the best part of three years.

Tony Currie was not merely the most complete but also the most compelling English midfield co-ordinator of the Seventies. He had strength, vision and awareness, two good feet and a penchant for the spectacular, whether in the guise of a 40-yard crossfield pass or a long-range drive. Flaxen locks streaming behind him, swanky of mode, languid and graceful of movement, so content was he to express himself between the touchlines that, for all those big-money transfers, not once did he ever actually request a wage rise. Little, however, did the crowds to whom he blew kisses suspect the innate shyness that characterised his demeanour off the field, even among his own team-mates. 'TC arrived a few months before I left Loftus Road but he'd never speak in training, never really have a laugh,' recalls Stan Bowles. 'He was a completely different person on the field, a bit of a strange fish. I don't think he realised how good he was.'

Tony begs to differ. 'I was a real Jekyll and Hyde but I was supremely confident on the field. That was my stage. Give me the ball and I could do anything with it, yet I've never been that comfortable around people.'

Flying the flag 17 times in total, he, of all the Mavericks, would appear to have had the least cause for grievance in the international context. The sense of deprivation, nonetheless, remains every bit as acute. When the FA handed Ramsey his P45, Tony, arguably, suffered more than anyone. Having established himself over the course of the previous year, a cartilage injury ruled him out of consideration for all seven of Mercer's matches at the helm, forcing him to start again from scratch. Perceived as something of a dilettante by Revie, he made but one appearance in England's next 40 engagements before Greenwood recalled him against Brazil in April 1978, featuring in nine of the next 14 before that left knee re-entered the equation. He sincerely believes he was worthy of 'at least' 50 more caps.

'Managers always have their favourites and I obviously wasn't Revie's. People in this country always seem to want to find fault when you have talent. They see you play half a season and you're out of this world, but then they worry about the other half. What they fail to consider is that the opposition are always trying to stop you. It was always "stop Currie" or "stop Hudson" and you stop their team playing. You might have two players on you throughout a match trying to kick you to bits, so whenever you get the ball you have no bloody time. But all people think is, "Currie didn't want to play today". That wasn't the case at all. People like me and George and Hudson wanted to play every week. We always wanted to be the best player on the field, to have our names in the headlines. People called me lazy and said I was an individual. I wasn't lazy or an individual. I was a team player who blew kisses to the crowd.'

Tony was four when his father, Bill, a storekeeper with Simms Motor Units, flew the family coop. Still, being crammed into a three-storey house with all manner of uncles, aunts and grandparents had its compensations. 'Not having a father as such must have had some kind of effect on me over the years but I never lacked love and affection. Times were hard but me and my brother Paul were always dressed well and fed well while the others went without. My Uncle Bert, who recently passed away, was the one who really raised us. He used to take me to Stamford Bridge and we'd stand in the Shed watching Greavesie and Tambling and Bridges. I cried the day Greavesie left for Italy.'

Tony was operating in central defence when QPR signed the powerfully built, two-footed 14-year-old on schoolboy forms. Unable to make any further headway there, he began working for a local family building firm when he left Whitefields School a year later. A trial with Chelsea had proved similarly unrewarding when he moved upfront while playing in the Hendon League, and duly came to the notice of Frank Grimes, the youth coach at Watford, then in Division Three. A six-week trial had stretched into six months when Bill Currie took a rare, isolated interest in his son's welfare, insisting on some form of commitment. 'Nobody could take the ball off him,' remembers Ken Furphy, then player-manager at Vicarage Road. 'We had a big carpark with boarding all round so we could play non-stop football, one-twos off the wall. He'd put his foot on the ball and whenever anyone got near him he'd stick his backside out, or his shoulder. He had so much confidence but at the same time he was very shy, very withdrawn. He misbehaved a lot early on, swearing during games. A referee rang me up one day and told me his language was disgraceful so I told Tony he wasn't playing for a month. That cured him because he loved to play.'
One of Tony's duties was to clean Furphy's Humber Sceptre: one

morning he backed the car into a wall while reversing it out of the manager's driveway. 'I'll let you off this time,' Furphy reassured him, 'but promise me you'll send me two complimentary tickets when you play for England.'

Tony's lethargic manner persuaded Furphy that his diet was to blame, the attempted remedy a daily trip to a local café for steak and chips. As time wore on, his anxiety would manifest itself in bouts of compulsive eating. 'He tended to drift out of the game for very long periods at that stage,' recalls Furphy, 'and whenever he played in the first team he didn't seem to have the stamina to keep going for 90 minutes so we would try to fatten him up. We would leave him out of away games because it all seemed a bit much for him, but then he came into his own with a hat-trick, against Peterborough. I first brought him on against Stoke in the League Cup. We were 2–0 down and I would normally have gone upfront under those circumstances, but I was 38 by then and I was so tired that, for the first time, I couldn't manage it, so we sent Tony on at inside-right and he hit the crossbar twice. We still lost, but he played so well I picked the same team the next week. I always thought he was better off upfront, just behind the main striker. Pele played for me at New York Cosmos and Tony was very similar, better in some ways. Pele couldn't keep the ball as long with people snapping at his heels. If a player grumbled to me about him disappearing from the game I would simply tell him to give Tony the ball. The fact that he didn't go chasing around didn't bother me because I knew what he could do when he had the ball.'

Nine goals in 17 appearances in the first half of the 1967–68 season vindicated Furphy's judgment. Even though Tony was left out of the third-round FA Cup tie against Sheffield United, the victorious manager, John Harris, tabled an offer of £27,500 for the 18-year-old. With a new stand to finance, acceptance was unhesitating despite Furphy's forceful objections. For all the difference such knowledge would have made, Tony was blissfully oblivious to the fact that United were sliding into Division Two. 'I just wanted to play, I didn't care who for. Most of us were like that then. The money was a bonus. One advantage of playing in Sheffield was that it was easier to make friends because we lived so close to each other. QPR were the only London club I played for and the only time I saw anyone was at training.'

Prior to the Second World War, neither Sheffield club could claim a clear advantage over the other: United had won four FA Cups to Wednesday's three, Wednesday four Championships to United's one. By the time Tony arrived at Bramall Lane, however, United had long since taken up residence beneath Wednesday's coat-tails, 51 seasons in Division One being succeeded by four demotions between 1934 and 1968. During the early Seventies, though, the balance of power was fleetingly reversed. Fixtures in the top division throughout the Sixties, Wednesday were relegated in 1970. A season later, United went up and, in their first year back, led the League in October before finishing tenth. By now, significantly, Tony had convinced his manager that he could better serve the common good from midfield, and it was in this capacity that he made the first of 13 appearances for the Under-23s against Wales in October 1969, he and Osgood sharing the goals in a 2–0 win.

An ever-present during the 1970–71 promotion campaign, Tony was unquestionably the key to United's resurrection, linking productively with the hard-tackling Trevor Hockey, a converted winger. 'We had all these speed merchants – Alan Woodward, Geoff Salmons, Stewart Scullion, Gil Reece, Bill Dearden. I could put the ball where I wanted, they just had to move.'

Tom Finney, no less, was smitten. 'He is a lad who never knows when he is beaten, contesting every ball and making good use of it with uncanny control. Yet, although he does the bulk of his work in midfield, he can still come through on the break to score, and score well.' Manchester United, furthermore, headed an ever-expanding queue of clubs willing to break the British transfer record to reel him in, but the Bramall Lane board steadfastly resisted the bait. In subsequent years, Tommy Docherty, for one, would contend that Tony erred in remaining a 'big fish in a small pool' for so long. The choice, though, was not entirely his.

Despite all the plaudits, our old chum Percy M. Young was almost contemptuous. 'A kind of feverish brilliance attended the play of the United while so much depended on the wayward talents of Tony Currie – a histrionic player with mannerisms characteristic of what one day will be termed the Best era.' In February 1972, moreover, Tony and goalkeeper John Hope, both married men, were accused by Sheffield residents of a host of crimes ranging from late-night drinking sessions to fraternising with loose women. While Harris denounced the charges as 'idle gossip', Tony took exception when the smears extended to his marital relationship. 'I'm scared to make a mistake on the field because the crowd will believe more rumours,' he revealed in *The Daily Express*. 'I've heard stories that my wife Linda has refused to let me in the house at night and I've slept outside in the car. It just isn't true.' Unwarranted though it was, Tony can at least see where the image stemmed from. 'Because of the way I played people assumed I was a nightclubber, which was never the case. On a Saturday night I used to take the wife out with all the other players and their wives, and at that time most of the squad would go out for a drink on a Monday night if we didn't have a midweek game. It wasn't until I started to have problems with injuries and divorce in the late Seventies and early Eighties that I really started drinking. In those circumstances I think most people turn to drink.'

Tony put such distractions behind him a month later to further his case for wider recognition, two goals capping an effervescent display for the Football League against the Scottish League to earn him inclusion in Ramsey's squad for the home internationals. However, Northern Ireland's first win over England since 1957 marred his senior bow, obliging him to wait a year for his next opportunity. Capitalising on the vacancy created by Alan Ball's sending-off during a World Cup defeat in Chorzow four days earlier, he seized it with a will, playing an influential role in a 2–1 victory in Moscow. Rave notices followed. 'I was in,' he reflects. 'I'd made it.' Comparisons with Gunter Netzer were inevitable. 'Watching him play was like watching myself. He looked like me, he had the same hair as me and he played the same sort of way as me, although he was a bit more direct in that he would play it and go whereas I tended to spray my passes. But I didn't model myself on him any more than he modelled himself on me.'

A rasping shot from the edge of the area crowned a 7–0 thumping of Austria in September, only for the return against Poland three weeks later to bring about a reunion with mortality. 'I'd love to see that match again, all 90 minutes. We annihilated them but we simply couldn't put the ball in the net. They only had one attack, and if Shilton had stuck his foot out instead of trying to block Domarski's shot with his hand he would have stopped it. It was an accumulation of bad finishing, lucky goalkeeping and good goalkeeping – and fate. We all sat in the dressing-room afterwards and not a word was said. Everyone was in shock. I was walking around in a deep depression for months afterwards and I'm sure most of the others would tell you the same. As it panned out, I wouldn't have been able to play in the finals because of my cartilage, but for some of them it was their last chance. We didn't feel we let anybody down. It was just bad luck and you had to accept it. I think we would have caught some flak from the fans had we performed badly but we gave everything that night and they knew it. That was what kept the hounds off our backs. The press were quite good about it because they knew it too. It was like somebody boarding the bloody goal up. Having said that, I don't suppose it helped having Chivers, Channon and Clarke upfront with no wide man. They were all very much the same sort of player, down-the-middle centre-forwards.'

That same year, the omnipresent, paternalistic Harris stepped down as team manager at Sheffield United in favour of Furphy after the second of two stints dating back to 1959, a sequence broken only by two years as general manager. An even more persistent habit was broken in 1973 when Bramall Lane, scene of countless Yorkshire fixtures as well as a Test match in 1902, bade adieu to the flannelled fools. This assertiveness was further borne out in 1974-75 when United finished sixth in the League, their highest placing for 14 seasons, four points behind the champions, Derby, and closer to Europe than the club has ever been, before or since. Had they won at St Andrews in their final fixture instead of drawing 0–0, they would have got there. And all this while Wednesday were plunging into the Third.

In March, Tony outdid himself against West Ham. Hovering ten yards inside his own half, he blocked Bobby Gould's hoof upfield – so much for not doing his bit in defence – then collected the rebound and found Woodward hogging the touchline on the other side of the halfway line. A first-time return freed him to skate on through the inside-right channel until the backpedalling Kevin Lock moved across to bar the way on the edge of the West Ham box. Coming to a virtual standstill, he proceeded to deliver a succession of feints – dragging to the right, flicking to the left, the ball never more than six inches away, shoulders swaying this way and that as if on loan from one of Paul Raymond's classier temptresses. Lock justified some of his 'New Bobby Moore' billing (well, he was blond), staying close, head down, refusing to commit himself. Finally, fatally, he took a pace too far to his left, buying a dummy that would not have looked out of place in an Armani window. With half a yard to play with, Tony darted to his left then ground to a halt once more as three defenders converged on him. Taking almost cursory aim, he sent a low shot through the crease of daylight between them, leaving Mervyn Day rooted at the near post as the ball slid into the opposite corner. Bows are taken, kisses blown. On *Match of the Day*, Barry Davies did his level best not to wet himself, proclaiming it 'a quality goal from a quality player'. He might just as well have congratulated Paul McCartney on his ability to assemble crotchets and quavers in an orderly manner. From first to last, a goal to set before Zeus.

Furphy treasures another soliloquy against Stoke the following month. 'We were fourth, Stoke were fifth and Bramall Lane was full. We're 2-0 up and Tony gets the ball with his back to goal. Mike Pejic comes in from the rear and when Tony puts his foot on the ball he dives in as if he wants to kill him. Everyone in the stand gasps because we can see Pejic coming but Tony knew he was there so he flicks the ball up and Pejic goes straight through and ends up flat on his back. Tony catches the ball as it comes down then stands on it again, blowing kisses at the crowd. Everyone is on their feet but now there's another gasp because Dennis Smith is flying in, mad as a hatter, so Tony just drags the ball back and Smith disappears past him on his backside. Wonderful.' This meretricious air was also in evidence during Leicester City's visit to Bramall Lane the following season, albeit in a vastly different context. When Tony and Alan Birchenall ended up sitting next to each other after a collision, Birchenall. a good friend, opted for a bit of levity, saying, 'Give us a kiss, then,' whereupon Tony puckered up. A *Sunday Mirror* snapper captured the embrace and a German gay magazine, *International Man*, reprinted it, much to the dismay of Birchenall's wife. 'I woke up the next morning expecting my normal Sunday cuppa but when the bedroom door opened my wife threw the paper at me instead. It looked as if we were giving each other deep throat. It's the only thing people remember me for.'

Euphoria, though, was shortlived. Players were sold to help pay for the £1 million stand at Bramall Lane and United were relegated the following season. Furphy, meanwhile, had been disturbed by Tony's drift towards chocoholism. 'He used to get on the coach with a pocket full of chocolate caramels and wolf them down like a compulsive eater, so we were forever trying to keep his weight down. It was all part of that nervous disposition. He also developed this habit during games of going down and not getting back up. One day it cost us a goal against West Ham so I turned to the chairman and told him that if he did it again I'd have to pull him off. The chairman said I would be devaluing him if I did that but I did it anyway and that contributed to me getting the sack.'

Tony was frank enough to confess that hiatuses of this nature emanated from self-disgust. 'I want to be perfection,' he explained in *The Observer*. 'I'm disgusted with myself if I give a bad ball. I feel I've failed. I just stand still and let the play go on past me.'

'He's got fabulous gifts,' stressed Trevor Hockey, 'but if he hit a bad pass he'd go off his game for a quarter of an hour. You had to kid him through a match.'

Although Tony had signed a six-year contract in 1974 in the hope that United would make a concerted bid for domestic honours, he had insisted on being released from it in the event of relegation. At first the club refused to keep its side of the bargain. 'I put in three transfer requests after we were relegated and they were all turned down. I didn't really want to leave because I'm not the type who likes to move around. I don't like different environments. But at the same time I wanted to be with a club that was capable of winning trophies. We'd just got home from a close-season trip to Gibraltar when Jimmy Sirrell, who'd taken over from Furphy as manager, told me to report to John Harris's house the next morning. John drove me up the motorway: I didn't know where we were going because I didn't want to ask him. In the end we arrived at Elland Road and after a half-hour chat with Jimmy Armfield I signed for Leeds.' When he set eyes on that £240,000 cheque, Tony's initial reaction was pure embarrassment. 'That's a lot of money,' he gulped. 'You'll be worth it,' Armfield assured him.

With most of the Revie regulars gone and Leeds in the midst of rebuilding, Tony was saddled with the unenviable task of replacing Johnny Giles. Scepticism was rife. That lackadaisical façade had repelled many a potential suitor, the consensus encapsulated by a comment Bill Shankly had made to Furphy a year or two earlier: 'I'll bet your man lives in a bungalow – he'd no' want to be bothered wi' all that climbing stairs.' Yet by the time Jock Stein succeeded Armfield in 1978, such disparaging sentiments had been consigned to the soundbite archives. Stein entrusted him with the captain's armband and referred glowingly to the man around whom he intended to build the team, noting with some surprise Tony's determination to play with a leg strain. Stein's assistant, Maurice Lindley, emphasised the perceived change in approach. 'I don't know the turning point but his workrate has improved. He's also disciplined himself to be not quite so spectacular. Perhaps it has to do with coming to a club with internationals all around. Brings you down to earth: from being God of one side you become one of the many.'

While Tony agrees that he reached his peak at Elland Road – 'I did have better players around me and that does help' – he bridles at any mention of that indolent veneer. 'No manager ever said anything directly to me about my workrate. Before the international against Switzerland in 1975 we held one of the first press conferences to include players. I'm up there in front of all these reporters and they start asking me about workrate. The only reason they did that was because Revie had mentioned it to them. So, because I was influenced by what people said about me, I went out and ran my balls off – and Revie never picked me again. It affected my game. Whenever a report said 'Currie is a weed' or 'Currie doesn't tackle' I'd go out there and show them and it might affect my game for the next week. I should have ignored it. I knew my workrate was fine. I've always been a perfectionist. I wanted to be the greatest player who ever passed a ball.' Perplexed as he was by Revie's decision to overlook him, Tony was even more aggrieved when he jumped ship. 'The way he quit badly tarnished the image and reputation of our game. He just did not give any consideration to the effect it would have, but that was typical of the man. I found him to be a selfish person. He wanted to be close to the players but never achieved it because he treated us like schoolboys.'

Ron Greenwood proved far more palatable, recalling Tony against Brazil in April 1978 and reserving him a regular berth in the squad thereafter until injuries interposed. Against Wales the following month Tony rifled home a 35-yard drive; at Wembley two weeks later came another fulminating effort from the edge of the Hungarian box. Indeed, Greenwood did the unthinkable, frequently preferring him to his erstwhile Upton Park playmaker, Trevor Brooking. That said, Tony derived next to no enjoyment from the experience. 'I used to come off the pitch thinking, "well, what was that all about?" It was great to be in the side but I always came off wondering what I'd contributed. I couldn't relax because I always felt as if I had to prove myself every time. I played five times in a row under Ramsey and that was my best run. It's not easy playing for England unless you're Butch Wilkins or Kevin Keegan and the other players play around you, and that only comes with familiarity.'

Misfortune at club level persisted, Leeds losing semi-finals in three consecutive seasons, twice in the League Cup, once in the FA Cup. 'After Manchester United beat us in the 1977 FA Cup semi the atmosphere in the dressing-room was just like the aftermath of that Poland game. Don Howe, I think, came in ranting and raving, so someone told him to shut up. The third time we were 2–0 up with 20 minutes to go in the first leg of the League Cup semi against Southampton but they equalised and then beat us 1–0 at the Dell. I was getting used to it.'

Which is more, sadly, than could be said for Linda Currie's feelings towards Leeds. Unable to settle there, depression set in and she went back to London. Concluding that his own return to London was the answer, Tony reluctantly requested a transfer, Leeds doing their bit by slashing the asking price from £600,000 to £400,000. 'Linda suffered from depression when we were in Sheffield, especially when the club weren't doing well and it took its toll on me. She wanted to go back to London then and although things improved for a year or two when we went to Leeds they got progressively worse after that. I went to London to fetch her back a couple of times and in the end I said I would ask

Jimmy Adamson for a transfer. Poor sod. When I told him he poured himself a whisky and said, "They'll lynch me". I was very popular there. Within a year of moving back we were divorced. She probably felt her depression was down to me.'

Bent on regaining their seat at the top table at the first time of asking, QPR headed the queue. 'I think they were desperate. I suffered a bad ankle injury playing against PSV Eindhoven in my final game for Leeds and when I went to Loftus Road I was on crutches. How I passed the medical I just don't know.' In a typical show of trust, Tony signed a blank contract: 'Jim Gregory said he'd give me £500 a week and fill in the details later, so I said fair enough.' Notwithstanding the fact that Tony was in no shape to train, Greenwood selected him for his next three England squads then ditched him without the courtesy of a phone call.

In hindsight, Loftus Road was quite the worst destination Tony could possibly have chosen. The unyielding plastic pitch exacerbated the wear and tear on his left knee, limiting him to 78 League outings over the next three seasons. QPR repeatedly missed promotion but there was rich compensation in 1982 when they reached the FA Cup final for the first time. Having vowed only to attend a final as a participant, Tony's joy was predictably unconfined. 'My favourite moment was when the final whistle blew in the semi-final against West Brom. Glenn Roeder and I more or less beat them on our own. For the next six weeks, you're the bee's knees, the king of the castle, but then the day comes and it's a different matter. Being there was wonderful but the event itself was a disappointment. Good side though they were, we could have beaten Tottenham, who had had a very tough season, but Mike Flanagan and Simon Stainrod had stinkers in both games. Simon thought he could beat them on his own but nine times out of ten he would run at the defence and lose the ball.'

When Roeder was ruled out of the replay by suspension, Tony assumed the captaincy. 'I felt reasonably confident, but then I gave away a penalty after six minutes. Graham Roberts picked the ball up in midfield and ran at our defence. At one point he overran the ball and Bob Hazell had a chance to move in and take it off him but for some reason he sat back. I'd been tracking Graham all the way and when he got into the box I dived in with a sliding tackle just as he pulled his foot back. I caught his foot so it was a penalty, yes, but I was going for the ball. If I'd have done it today they would have given me the bloody guillotine. You only have to breathe on someone now and it's a penalty.'

As last hurrahs go, this one was positively cheerless. Plagued by that accursed knee, Tony made two League appearances in 1982–83 –

one of them as substitute – and was summarily released when QPR were promoted. 'Terry Venables was managing us at the time and he came to me one day and said my contract was up and that Gregory didn't want to keep me on. I didn't realise that they should at least have offered me another year. Then Sheffield United more or less agreed wages but I got the impression that the manager there, Ian Porterfield, might have regarded me as a threat, so I saved him any problems and decided not to go. Then Ken Bates called me up and said he wanted me to work with the reserves at Chelsea. I can't remember whether he said he would contact me or vice versa, but neither of us did. I wasn't bothered, which wasn't like me at all. I must have been in a bad way.'

The descent was swift and painful. On Venables' recommendation Tony joined Toronto Nationals in the newly formed Canadian soccer league, and ended up losing the best part of £10,000 in unpaid wages when club and league collapsed inside a month. The PFA financed a series of knee operations, enabling him to turn out on a non-contract basis for Torquay, Southend and Chesham, but by now the mind was making promises that the body was unable to keep. With a £400 monthly pension largely eaten up by maintenance payments for his ex-wife and three children, he drove a cab for a spell, then worked in a video store. When the jobs dried up, pride prevented him from drawing the dole. 'I'm an impatient person and I hate queues, but I also never thought of it as my entitlement.'

Returning to his mother's council house to live with his younger brother Peter and a brace of uncles, Tony poured his heart out to *The Sun* in 1986. 'I should have made a fortune out of football but I have always been naive and immature where money is concerned. When I was at the height of my career I saw how contemporaries like Kevin Keegan got themselves agents and worked hard at making money. I never bothered with all that. I was stupid enough to believe that I did not have to provide for the future because I thought I could play the game I love forever. Now I'm paying the price for being so gullible.' What he didn't say then was that alcohol had become a prop. 'From 1983 to 1986 I went over the top. One day I'd drink a bottle of whisky and smoke a packet of fags, then the next morning I'd feel so bad I wouldn't go near a bottle or a fag all day, but then I'd start again the next day. I'd go through four bottles a week. Classic signs, classic reasons, but it helped me through the day, helped me forget. At the same time I didn't get hooked. I could always give up whenever I wanted. I haven't had a drink for the past year, and I haven't smoked a fag for two years.'

Deliverance, happily, was nigh. Sheffield United awarded him a testimonial in 1986, he married again a year later, and then the community post came up. He applied for managerial positions at Sheffield United and Chesterfield but failed to glean so much as an interview. He suspects, not without good reason, that his reputation as a drinker preceded him, but then the idea of being responsible for the way others play has never held much of an allure. Content as he is with his lot, however, he cannot suppress the feeling of having been cheated. 'The big high for me was playing every week. I couldn't wait to get out there and show people what I could do. I loved it. But it's when you look back that it hurts, more so now than ever. Why didn't I do this, why didn't I do that? Why didn't the England managers pick me more often? Why didn't they pick Worthington, Hudson, Bowles and Currie in the same team? Why didn't someone say, "Right, I'm going to pick them all for three games and see how it goes"? I'd love to have seen somebody brave enough to do that.'

It's Now or Never

You know it never has been easy
Whether you do or you do not resign
Whether you travel the breadth of extremities
Or stick to some straighter line

Joni Mitchell, 'Hejira'

Boys' night out at Hove Town Hall. The Gary O'Reilly Testimonial
Football Evening has just kicked off and all the early signs point to
copious helpings of taste-free fun. 'That your idea of a round?' growls
the portly MC in the Technicolor tie as a latecomer slides in carrying a
sheepish pint of bitter. 'You're Jewish, aren't you? You on the list?'
Boom, and furthermore, boom. After the rabbit punch, the uppercut.
'What's the similarity between Stephen Milligan and Robert Maxwell?
Both found in fishnets.' From Schindler to swindler via Recently
Deceased Sexually Deviant MP. Still, at least we know this bloke
updates his material now and again.

Extending a hand into the wings, our would-be Bernard Manning
ushers on a svelte figure to tumultuous applause. The clothes *are* the
man. Black shirt, black trousers and black suede buckled boots topped
by an emerald jacket, a rose-pink hanky blooming in the breast pocket.
The hair, slicked back and lapping a good inch over the collar, is as long
and as slender as its owner, the sideboards Mr Spock to a t. Three parts
mannequin to one part spiv. The MC's introduction is as poignantly apt
as his opening remarks were knowingly repugnant. 'As many clubs as
Nicklaus, a man with a left foot who, if he'd been around ten years later,
would've bought this place as his summer house. They'd've loved him
in Italy.'

Proceeding to centre stage, Frank Worthington drinks in the

acclaim from a gathering dominated by supporters of Brighton and Hove Albion, one of his 11 League employers. The voice is husky, the accent pure Pennine, the eyes a bleary shade of hale. The ensuing 20-minute autobiographical monologue, nonetheless, is delivered with all the precision timing of the natural stand-up. Not that this is exactly a surprise. Is this not the man who turned the Q&A into a quixotic *tour de force*, declaring his ex-wife to be his 'most difficult opponent' and attesting his 'trade before turning pro' to be that of a 'part-time river widener'. Tested and lubricated by four gigs a week, the one-liners crackle and pop. 'Kiev, a cemetery with lights . . . Thank God Lindy Field only told *The News of the World* about Botham . . . Keith Weller wore black tights on *Match of the Day* because the missus found them in his car on the Friday . . . Terry Butcher was known as the Douglas Bader of the First Division – tremendous in the air, crap on the deck.' Joe Mercer, we discover, used to refer to Johan Cruyff and Michel Platini as 'Johann Strauss' and 'Michel Houdini'. The professed philosophy reinforces the popular image of the footloose fancy dan who actually married a Page-3 model. 'People say I've squandered a fortune on birds and booze,' Frank deadpans, 'but, as my old mate Stan Bowles said, it's better than wasting it.' Small wonder Ian Greaves, his manager at Huddersfield and Bolton, once dubbed him 'the working man's George Best'.

Johnny Giles – surprise, surprise – regards Frank as someone 'who didn't achieve much'. Well, Frank did once characterise Leeds as 'assassins'. At club level, it must be admitted, the facts do bear out Giles's one-dimensional analysis. After all, the summit of Frank's achievements in the collective sphere were the goals that secured Second Division titles for Huddersfield and Bolton. However, even leaving aside those eight England caps and nigh-on 300 goals, his CV also includes 882 senior outings spanning 22 years, a record for an English striker. The hostile environment in which this walking Duracell flourished rendered such longevity all the more astonishing, even if he did have to settle for a succession of off-Broadway stages. 'There was only one way to play against Frank,' vouchsafed Paddy Crerand in tones of wry affection. 'Kick him as soon as you can.'

As it happens, he was remarkably fortunate with injury, though not in other respects. Had Mercer been employed as England manager for four years instead of four weeks, that collection of tassled caps would surely have been closer to a stack than a rack. Had Bill Shankly, moreover, not pulled out of signing him for Liverpool after terms had been agreed, all manner of trinkets would have flooded forth. The deal collapsed because the medical revealed Frank's blood pressure to be inordinately high, a direct consequence of what he calls – with due understatement – 'living a little bit too much in the fast lane'. This notoriety, he strongly suspects, also lay behind the absence of a London club on that CV, persuading those who might otherwise have courted him that he would be unable to resist the myriad temptations of the metropolis. Yet that same determination to travel the breadth of extremities endeared him to a generation. Over and above the boundless skill and exhibitionist leanings, he communicated enthusiasm. Has anyone ever derived so palpable an enjoyment from being a professional sportsman?

Frank was once found guilty of the most grievous felony a player in a team game can perpetrate. 'The way I play is more important to me than the team winning,' he brazenly confessed in *The Daily Mail*. 'I need a good personal performance to be happy about any game.' Nowadays he tries not to sound quite so blatantly self-centred. 'Football is a team game but I have always felt that I should have played an individual sport. That way you know it's down to you whether you fail or succeed, and I always felt I would have succeeded in that situation. When you are part of a team you are one cog in the machine and sometimes I found that a little bit frustrating. If you are playing a certain way and the midfield player is not tuned into the way you want the ball played to you, then that, quite obviously, can have its frustrations. Luckily, I was always told that whenever I received the ball I should try and do something special.'

And never was that bidding done more dutifully than at Burnden Park in April 1979. Alan Gowling flicked on a Bolton throw from the Ipswich right, Frank, back to goal, intercepted the ball with his head and proceeded to juggle it on his left foot as Terry Butcher's nostril emissions showered his neck. Suddenly, out of the corner of his eye, he noticed that the rest of the back four were moving out. A rare opportunity to practise a favourite training routine had presented itself. Looping the ball back over Butcher's head, he spun round, catching the ball as it descended, then lashed home an unanswerable left-footed volley. Frank's 24 goals headed the First Division charts that season, yet none better typified man or muse. What else can one expect from someone who rarely lets a week go by without re-running his video of Brazil's World Cup exploits? 'A perfect goal,' exults Mick Mills, a member of that duped Ipswich defence. 'Frank had tremendous touch, a lovely left foot. Like left-handed tennis players, left-footed footballers seem better to look at. Frank not only was good, he looked good.' Gary Lineker, a junior at Leicester City during Frank's heyday at Filbert

Street, was 'totally in awe of the man', happily retrieving his soiled jockstraps but scared to communicate further.

In some quarters, respect was tinged with exasperation. Mike Summerbee relates how, while on holiday with his wife, he once espied 'this vagrant' walking down the harbour front at Torquay. It was Frank. Running battles over maintenance payments with his first wife, Brigitta, had left him with a pot to piss in and not much else. 'He looked like he didn't have a penny to buy a cup of tea so I took him into a café and gave him my usual rollicking about how he should have played 80 or 90 times for England, that he was the finest player I'd ever seen in his position. I told him he was the only player you could have taken from the League to Italy who would not have looked out of place. He never took a bit of notice.' In a more reflective mood, Frank admits he wishes he had 'gallivanted' a little less, yet conviction is lacking. The title of an Elvis Presley hit springs to mind: 'Got a Lot of Living To Do'.

While Frank himself prefers the more direct message of 'It's Now or Never', the link with Colonel Parker's puppet is nonetheless relevant for that. The Bolton squad were driving across Germany one summer when nine hours of non-stop Elvis tapes proved too much for Ian Greaves, who stomped over to the cassette player at the front of the coach and flung the source of his displeasure out on to the autobahn. Frank refused to speak to him for a week. Set in motion when, at 15, he first heard King Creole at 'an afternoon hop', this, assuredly, was no ordinary obsession. The trademarks were all present and correct: the deep quiff, the jangling medallions, shirt forever open at the chest. Asked for his autograph after a Wembley international, Frank peered down at the small boy concerned: 'What do you want me to sign, Frank Worthington or Elvis Presley?' Much as he cites netting the winning goal for England in Sofia as the apex of his career, or assures you that, at 45, he still gets an almost childlike pleasure out of playing for Halifax Town reserves, the tale of how the King of Rock 'n' Roll sealed his transfer to Philadelphia Fury is recounted with even greater relish.

'One of the people involved in the negotiations to get me over there was Peter Rudge, who was then the manager of The Rolling Stones and a personal friend of Elvis's people in Memphis. Knowing I was a massive Elvis fan, he phoned Elvis's father, Vernon, to obtain his permission to get me one of those necklaces Elvis used to give to his friends, one with his logo, TCB, Taking Care of Business, with the lightning flash underneath, which is the inscription on his gravestone. Peter gave it to me when I arrived in Philly. How could I say no after that? I visited Elvis in a dream once. We were talking as if we were lifelong friends. It might sound daft and stupid but I was there with him just as we are sat here talking now.' All the same, was there not a degree of disillusionment about the man who finished his career as a bloated, drugged-up Las Vegas crooner and met his death over a toilet bowl? The horrified expression and categorical riposte transform the mere suggestion of clay feet into a personal insult. 'None whatsoever, no. The greatest thing about Elvis, besides his charisma and his presence and his style, was his voice. He had the most incredible range of any vocalist I have ever heard. A wonderful talent. I went to a lot of fan club conventions. In fact, I received an award from the fan club of Great Britain for keeping his name alive. Me and Freddie Starr and Simon Bates. It was lovely.'

Though scarcely a slave to tradition, Frank at least did the done thing in the Worthington household by taking up football: his father Eric and two elder brothers, Bob and Dave, all earned their corn with their feet. 'My dad was from Manchester originally and although he never quite made the first team at United he played for the reserves many times before signing pro with Halifax when he moved there after meeting my mother. Bob and Dave, who were both defenders, began their careers at the Shay, and they contributed a great deal to my learning process. Because they were bigger and stronger than me when we were kids, I had to use my skills against their strength, so that was the area I concentrated on. No matter how well you are playing at any given time, whether you're 14 or 24 or 34, you should never, ever, be satisfied with your technique.'

Every Wednesday during his early years at Sowerby Bridge Grammar – a mixed emporium, naturally – Frank would forego the delights of English homework to train alongside Bob and Dave at the Shay. Harry Hooper, then the Halifax manager, was impressed by this 'tiny, scruffy little kid' and remembered the name when he left to become Huddersfield's chief scout. Confounding family expectations, Frank needed no second invitation to exchange Fourth Division for Second when, after seeing him score 16 goals in a game for Halifax Red Triangles, Hooper offered the 14-year-old amateur terms in 1963. He turned professional two years later, yet soon made it quite clear that he had no time for being seen and not heard, informing all and sundry that there was a future England international in their midst.

Ian Greaves recalls how training would revolve entirely around this 'cocky so-and-so' who would rather stay late and work by himself, sharpening the ball-control, honing the twists and turns: 'The other 27 players had to work round what *Frank* wanted to do, or at least he thought that.' Finally reaching the end of his tether, Greaves hauled Frank back after one unproductive communal session for what was intended to be the biggest ear-bashing in recorded history. 'We stood there looking at each other, eye-to-eye. He was talking to me and his eyes never left mine, but he must have flicked the ball up 47 times. He flicked it up and caught it behind him on his neck, down the back of the neck, hoofed it over his back and caught it on his foot, something I could never do if I played forever. I thought, "How do you give him a telling-off when he's doing that?". That's Frank.'

Having moved forward from midfield in 1969, two in-and-out seasons had yielded nine goals in 50 League outings when Frank emerged as the regular focal point of the Huddersfield attack in 1969–70. Playing in all 42 League fixtures, he scored 18 times to help restore the club to Division One after a 14-year gap. During the Twenties, the Town, lest it be forgotten, had become the first club to achieve a hat-trick of League titles, and Frank was not alone in believing that reinforcements were sorely needed if the revival was to be sustained. When it became apparent that the directors disagreed, Frank, Roy Ellam and Trevor Cherry were deputed by their team-mates to take up the matter with Greaves. 'We felt we needed some sort of lift, a carrot, so we agreed to ask for £1,000 per man as an incentive to keep the club up. Given that it would have cost £45,000 to buy a new player, our argument was that you could generate the same effect for less than half the price. Unfortunately, Greavesie turned it round, saying we were holding a gun to his head. Not only did he drop the three of us, the rest of the players made us out to be scapegoats when the team began to struggle.'

When Huddersfield duly went down after two seasons, Frank had no intention of going with them. Liverpool had offered £170,000 and negotiations were in mid-flow when, in June 1972, Alf Ramsey summoned him as a late replacement on the England Under-23 tour of Eastern Europe. The vacancy had been created by the withdrawals of Hudson and Todd: 'I couldn't understand for the life of me why they adopted the attitude they did. Everything in my life was built around the thought and desire to play for my country.' Cancelling a holiday in Majorca, Frank trained alone at Craven Cottage before swaggering into Heathrow Airport in high-heeled cowboy boots, red silk shirt, black slacks and a lime velvet jacket. When Ramsey let fly with a rare expletive, Harold Shepherdson unruffled the manager's feathers by pooh-poohing the idea that this loud individual could possibly be the man they were waiting for. 'I suppose I've always been a bit of a peacock, but that was just me doing my own thing. I used to get a lot of stick for the way I dressed but that was my identity. It didn't really matter whether people accepted me or not.'

Ramsey bit his lip and Frank acquitted himself well before returning to Anfield for a medical. When a second blood test unearthed some irregularities, Shankly dispatched him to Majorca in the hope that rest would cure the problem. It didn't. 'My father had just died so I was probably suffering from some form of anxiety, but I was also enjoying the fruits of being young, of being a personality, and there were a lot of temptations. I used to go nightclubbing a lot, generally running around a bit more than was probably good for me. Anyway, one day I came off the beach in Majorca – it wasn't even a hot day, cloudy in fact – and went to my room for a lie-down. Suddenly the room started spinning, and when I went to the kitchen to get a drink I was staggering all over the place. I didn't wake up until four or five the following afternoon.' To this day, Frank is still unsure whether this was all symptomatic of a nervous breakdown.

Another unsatisfactory blood test back in Liverpool proved sufficient to deter Shankly. The pity, as Ian Greaves points out, was that 'Frank was best suited to an attacking side', a policy only the successful could pursue for long amid such a fearful climate. As things panned out, this was as near as he would ever come to finding such a platform. Aware that other clubs would be similarly put off, Huddersfield were forced to cut the asking price to £80,000 before Leicester, 12th in Division One in the season just ended, stepped in. Acknowledging his own culpability, Frank concealed his disappointment manfully. 'That was Him, up there, giving me the warning,' he told James Mossop in *The Sunday Express* a couple of years later. 'I did not need telling twice.' Besides, brooding was not his style. 'I never let it affect me during my career, although when I think about it now it hurts and it rankles. It was all down to the amount of money Liverpool were laying out, although it was their doctor's attitude that got to me more than anything else. He wrote me off and told me I shouldn't be playing at that level of football. He was cold and callous. I've never forgiven him because he didn't even begin to try and understand. Anyway, that was my bad luck. To have been a part of that Liverpool team would have been something special, but it wasn't to be and I never really dwelt on it afterwards. That's their misfortune, I told myself. I'm the most positive person in the world.'

As it turned out, Frank's fondest footballing memories would revolve around his sojourn at Filbert Street under Jimmy Bloomfield –

and not merely because the manager was prepared to babysit for him and sort out his parking tickets. (Alan Birchenall, his self-styled 'social secretary' at Leicester, remembers the time Frank abandoned his car when it broke down in the middle of the road, triggering an almighty traffic snarl-up. It was the club's responsibility to sort out such trifling concerns, he reasoned, not his.) Bloomfield's training methods centred on ball skills, pace and space. On a Monday the players would sprint and work with weights, but at all other times the ball was the focus of attention. 'My aim is to field a side which is a joy to watch and a joy to play in,' proclaimed Bloomfield, a former England Youth international once hailed by Ron Greenwood, his mentor at West Ham and Arsenal, as 'the ideal inside-forward'. 'Most of all, I recognise that football is an art form and it should be treated as such.'

'Definitely,' concurs Frank, 'without a doubt. Peter Shilton notwithstanding, the one thing we never had right at Leicester was the defensive side. We had the artistic side, the quality and the entertainment. Bloomfield was great, handled me beautifully. Very charismatic, very stylish, smart, always well presented. That's how he wanted his team to be.'

Frank meshed splendidly with the former Charlton winger, Len Glover, so much so that their captain, Keith Weller, once flounced out of a match at half-time claiming that he was being marginalised. 'Len and I had a terrific understanding and we would play to it, and Keith felt a little bit isolated on the right. We used to have these lovely moves. Len was quick, so I would feed him, he'd take the defender on and get to the byeline and then knock it inside for me to score. If the defender sat tight on Len I'd just knock it inside the full-back for him to run on to – he scored a dozen goals from that move alone one season. It all came to a bit of a head one day when Keith blew up because he felt he wasn't getting as much of the ball as he should have. It was understandable in one sense but selfish in another.'

When Mercer filled in between Ramsey and Revie in the spring of 1974, Weller and Frank received their senior England call-ups simultaneously, the former playing throughout the home international tournament, the latter replacing Bowles after an hour of the second match against Northern Ireland then retaining his place at Hampden Park. In a tetchy if vibrant contest with Argentina at Wembley four days later, Frank put England 2–0 up before Mario Kempes laid on a trailer for future splendours to ensure the spoils were shared. While Weller fell from favour, Frank rose in stature on a short, three-match jaunt round Eastern Europe, scoring the only goal in Sofia. 'Clemence kicked the ball downfield, Keegan flicked it on and I took it past the centre-half on the left side of the box then rifled it inside the near post: 4–0 wouldn't have flattered us that night. It was a wonderful team performance, wonderful football.' A night of less-than-sober reflection followed, during the course of which Frank subsequently claimed to have relieved Malcolm Macdonald of £2,000 in a card game.

Mercer's priorities differed from most of his breed. 'He never effing well smiled,' he confided to one reporter who asked him why he had dropped the grim-looking Stoke full-back, Mike Pejic. 'I couldn't have that. He might have made the other players miserable.'

'Joe always had style,' observed Fred Eyre, who played for 'Uncle Joe' and Malcolm Allison at Manchester City. 'Everybody loved him; he had a nice friendly way of beating you, a nice gentle way of getting his own way.'

Allison felt indestructible while Mercer was watching out for him. 'When Joe and I were friends no one in football could live with us. Between us we had it all. I charged into situations like a bull, full of aggressive ambition and a contempt for anyone who might be standing in my way. And Joe came behind me, picking up the pieces, soothing the wounded and the offended with that vast charm.'

Frank, too, was charmed. 'Just after we'd drawn with Yugoslavia in Belgrade, Joe left all the FA people sitting at his dinner table and came over to sit with me and a few of the lads for an hour or so. All these officials want to speak to him and he'd rather discuss the game with us. That was a wonderful gesture. He was so chuffed to be in charge. He was a lovely man with a marvellous philosophy: express yourself, enjoy it, show them how good you are.'

Mercer, sadly, was merely warming the hot seat for Revie, a man capable of keeping enjoyment and self-expression at bay more than adequately. In his first match, a European Championship qualifier against Czechoslovakia, he pulled Frank off after 70 minutes and saw two late goals engineer an illusory 3–0 victory. In the second, again at Wembley, Frank was introduced as substitute but his attempts to pierce a rigorous Portuguese defence proved as ineffectual as those around him. Macdonald and David Johnson alternated in his stead for the remainder of the season, a pair of hoofers preferred to a Fonteyn.

Frank is convinced that footballing considerations had nothing to do with this premature banishment into the wings. 'After that game in Sofia, Harold Shepherdson came up and said, "Look, if you don't do anything silly and you look after yourself, you've got a tremendous future." That meant a lot to me, and at that stage I felt I was carving a niche for myself, but then Revie took it all away. I was never optimistic once he came in. I had these instinctive vibes. When he picked me I was the top scorer in the League at the time and he was under pressure to choose me. He didn't want to. Then one day he pulled me, Huddy and Bowles aside after training and said, "Look, you've got all the skill but there is something I'm not sure about". I knew the writing was on the wall from that moment. He wanted the yes-men. He didn't like the individuals, the characters, the rebels.' Neither does Frank need any reminding that, like so many of his spiritual brethren, he undermined his cause during Revie's very first England get-together, ignoring express orders by sneaking out of the team hotel to join Ball, Currie, Hudson *et al* for an evening's merriment in Manchester. Naughty, naughty boys.

Domestic headaches now compounded the pain of rejection. Indeed, in the immediate aftermath of one of their customary blazing rows, Brigitta Worthington assured the press that her husband's passion for his craft comfortably exceeded his affections for her. She was right, of course. For Frank, playing for Leicester came to represent a means of escape. For four seasons, City held their own, rarely threatening but seldom an easy touch, taking Liverpool to an FA Cup semi-final replay in 1974 and finishing seventh in the League in 1975–76, their highest placing for ten seasons. In 1974, Greenwood considered them the closest approximation to a blend of 'English fitness and continental technique'. Frank grew increasingly disenchanted, however, when Bloomfield pushed him out to the left in order to accommodate the powerful but comparatively limited Bob Lee. After a chaotic 2–2 draw with QPR in September 1976, Frank bit back, aesthetic sensibilities seemingly more offended than pride. 'A few more matches like this will kill football. We don't seem able to string anything together. People are always saying there is a lot of skill in our side. You tell me where it is. There are one or two skilful players but that's all. The others are workers.' Bloomfield fined and dropped him forthwith, and although Frank scored seven times in his next eight games, briefly raising Leicester to the head of the table, he still spent a hefty chunk of the season hopping on and off the transfer list. A truce seemed to have been reached when Lee went to Sunderland, allowing Frank to resume his favoured central role, but while the 1976–77 season ended with Leicester in mid-table, one win in the opening seven games raised the general temperature when term recommenced.

Frank outlasted Bloomfield, albeit only just. Matters were far from eased by the gradual erosion of his marriage, inevitable as it was.

'It was a holiday romance that developed when Brigitta got pregnant and came over from Sweden. We gave it our best shot and we had two smashing kids, but we used to argue too much. She was more of a private person than me and found it difficult to accept that wherever we went people knew me and wanted to come up and talk. In the end it just fizzled out.' When the divorce came through, Frank was hard pushed to support a family let alone a devoutly hedonistic lifestyle, encompassing as it did regular shopping sprees on the King's Road and a rapid turnover of sports cars. A summer contract to tout his wares in South Africa promised to replenish a bank account running decidedly low on sustenance, so when the club directors blocked his path two days before he was due to fly out, he concluded it was time to move on. 'It would have given me a bit of a breather to go there and sort myself out but when they changed their minds I told them they could go to hell. They'd gone back on their word and I thought that was rotten, so I took my daughter up north and went to stay with my mother. Frank McLintock took over from Jimmy not long after and when he phoned up I told him I didn't want to play for the club any longer.'

Only one manager was willing to countenance Leicester's valuation and take a punt on a 28-year-old generally decreed to be an insubordinate iconoclast: Ian Greaves, now manning the bridge at Bolton and happy to bury rusty hatchets. So was Frank. 'Greavesie was a different man, his whole philosophy had turned round. At Huddersfield he was a fitness fanatic, a straight, courageous man with a lot of iron beneath a calm exterior. Back then, football took a back seat, but now all he wanted to talk about was skill. I couldn't believe the transformation. By the same token, he was very strong on discipline and taught me how to adapt, to adjust to the system, to the way the modern game was going. Whether I liked it or not, the game was changing. The timing of the deal was perfect, because it turned out to be a turning point in terms of sorting out my head and my marriage problems. I had five tremendously happy years at Leicester, and the fans were magnificent, but there comes a time when you need change.' With Frank happy to trade a season scrabbling against relegation for the adrenaline surge of a promotion race, a month's loan evolved into a more permanent arrangement when Bolton forked out £90,000, then a club record. Flanked by a pair of evergreen wingers in Willie Morgan and Peter Thompson, he marked his début with a goal against Stoke, one of five in his first six games; six months later, his winner at Ewood Park confirmed Bolton as Second Division champions.

Frank was nearing 31 when he won the Golden Shoe in 1978–79, yet if the Seventies witnessed his prime, the Eighties brought a graceful maturation, even if he did tend to switch vineyards rather a lot. After two years at Burnden Park, he embarked on a breathless stint of club-hopping spanning nine different clubs in as many seasons, a rock 'n' roller harvesting new adherents on an endless farewell tour. It would have been ten had Birmingham – who retained Frank's registration throughout his six-month residence at Tampa Bay Rowdies – not resisted São Paulo's advances. Frank in Brazil? Now that *would* have been a celestial alliance. Since the early venues were of West End stock – Leeds, Sunderland, Southampton, Birmingham – he remained a First Division staple until the mid-Eighties, helping Birmingham win promotion in 1980 and Southampton finish second in the League four years later, whereupon a free transfer spirited him off to Brighton. 'I don't care how you train just so long as you perform for me on a Saturday,' Lawrie McMenemy had reassured him after his first workout at the Dell. 'All I'm trying to do is extend your career.'

As usual, McMenemy did an exemplary job in that direction. Frank had a season and a half as player-manager at Tranmere until a new board moved in and began pruning the budget. A month later, in March 1987, Aldershot sold out of programmes and pasties when their best crowd of the season, 3,649, turned out to see Frank sit on the Preston bench. After the game, noted Roy Collins in *Today*, 'another question that didn't need asking was who the good-looking blonde in the carpark was waiting for.' It was probably the second Mrs Worthington, Carole Dwyer, retired Page-3 girl and daughter of Noel, the erstwhile Fulham and West Ham goalkeeper. Frank's début at Deepdale, meanwhile, swelled the gate from 8,000 to 12,000. 'Sure it's a bit harder at my age,' he admitted, 'and it's more physical in this [Fourth] division than in the First. The players don't give you the same respect for a start. But I want to keep playing as long as I can.' Upping sticks for the final time the following autumn, his presence in the Stockport line-up at Bolton over Christmas drew Burnden Park's thickest gathering of the season to date. The curtain descended for good on 22 April 1988, seven months and a day before Frank's 40th birthday: a 1–1 draw with Crewe on a Friday night before an audience of 2,000. He deserved something grander.

So thank you, Mrs Worthington, for putting your son on the stage. The abiding memory is not a goal, but a booking. Leading the line for Birmingham at St James' Park, Frank stretches every sinew to keep a ball in play. The linesman, fully 50 yards away and clearly swayed by the home crowd, hoists his flag. Incredulous, Frank drops to his knees in mock supplication to the referee, the upshot a caution for dissent. If those prayers were for the soul of English football, he was right to despair. 'Frank always laughed at the game a little bit,' said Ian Greaves. Someone had to.

Bibliography

Malcolm Allison with James Lawton, *Colours Of My Life* (Everest Books, 1975)

Alan Ball, *It's All About a Ball* (WH Allen, 1978)

Derek Dougan and Percy M Young, *On The Spot: Football as a Profession* (Stanley Paul, 1975)

Eric Dunning, Patrick Murphy and John Williams, *The Roots of Football Hooliganism* (Routledge & Kegan Paul, 1988)

Charlie Gillett and Simon Frith (eds), *Rock File 1-5* (Panther Books)

Peter and Leni Gillman, *Alias David Bowie* (Hodder & Stoughton, 1986)

Brian Glanville, *The History of the World Cup* (Faber & Faber, 1982)

Alan Gowling, *Football Inside Out* (Souvenir Press, 1977)

Jimmy Greaves with Norman Giller, *Don't Shoot the Manager* (Boxtree, 1993)

Willis Hall, *My Sporting Life* (Readers Union, 1975 reprint)

Arthur Hopcraft, *The Football Man* (Collins, 1968)

Gordon Macey, *Queen's Park Rangers: A Complete Record* (Breedon Books, 1993)

Max Marquis, *Sir Alf Ramsey – Anatomy of a Football Manager* (Arthur Barker, 1970)

Rodney Marsh, *Shooting to the Top* (Stanley Paul, 1968)

John Motson and John Rowlinson, *The European Cup* (Queen Anne Press, 1980)

John Moynihan, *The Soccer Syndrome* (McGibbon & Kee, 1966)

News of the World Football Annual 1964–90

Andrew Nickolds and Stan Hey (eds), *The FOUL Book of Football No.1* (Foul Publications, 1976)

John Osborne, *Damn You, England* (Faber & Faber, 1994)

Rothmans Football Yearbook 1971–80

Phil Shaw, *Whose Game is it Anyway?* (Argus Books, 1989)

Gordon Smailes, *Football League Records* (Breedon Books, 1992)

Mike Ticher (ed), *FOUL: Best of Football's Alternative Paper, 1972–1976* (Simon & Schuster, 1987)

Stephen Wagg, *The Football World: A Contemporary Social History* (The Harvester Press, 1984)

Percy M Young, *Football In Sheffield* (Dark Peak, 1981 reprint)

Plus: *Shoot!*, *Goal*, *Football Digest*, and assorted newspapers and periodicals.